Trauma-Sensitive Mindfulness

A Norton Professional Book

TRAUMA-SENSITIVE MINDFULNESS

Practices for Safe and Transformative Healing

DAVID A. TRELEAVEN

Foreword by Willoughby Britton

W.W. NORTON & COMPANY

Independent Publishers Since 1923

New York • London

Note to Readers: Standards of clinical practice and protocol change over time, and no technique or recommendation is guaranteed to be safe or effective in all circumstances. This volume is intended as a general information resource for professionals practicing in the field of psychotherapy and mental health; it is not a substitute for appropriate training, peer review, and/or clinical supervision. Neither the publisher nor the author(s) can guarantee the complete accuracy, efficacy, or appropriateness of any particular recommendation in every respect.

For information about permission to reproduce selections from this book, write to Permissions, W. W. Norton & Company, Inc., 500 Fifth Avenue, New York, NY 10110

For information about special discounts for bulk purchases, please contact W. W. Norton Special Sales at specialsales@wwnorton.com or 800-233-4830

Manufacturing by Lake Book Manufacturing, Inc.
Production manager: Christine Critelli

Library of Congress Cataloging-in-Publication Data

Names: Treleaven, David A., author.
Title: Trauma-sensitive mindfulness : practices for safe and transformative healing / David A. Treleaven ; foreword by Willoughby Britton.
Description: First edition. | New York : W. W Norton & Company, [2018] | "A Norton professional book." | Includes bibliographical references and index.
Identifiers: LCCN 2017026048 | ISBN 9780393709780 (hardcover)
Subjects: | MESH: Anxiety Disorders—therapy | Anxiety—complications | Mindfulness
Classification: LCC RC531 | NLM WM 172 | DDC 616.85/22306—dc23
LC record available at https://lccn.loc.gov/2017026048
ISBN: 978-0-393-70978-0

W. W. Norton & Company, Inc., 500 Fifth Avenue, New York, N.Y. 10110
www.wwnorton.com

W. W. Norton & Company Ltd., 15 Carlisle Street, London W1D 3BS

8 9 0

This book proposes that trauma-sensitive practice involves resourcing social justice movements challenging systemic conditions that create and perpetuate trauma.

————

In this spirit, 60% of the author's proceeds from this book will be shared equally between three organizations:

generative somatics

A national nonprofit organization based in Oakland, California, that combines social analysis with trauma healing (generativesomatics.org).

The Healing Justice Program of Black Lives Matter

The Black Lives Matter Global Network is a chapter-based organization working to end state-sanctioned violence and win immediate improvements in the lives of Black people (blacklivesmatter.com).

The Sogorea Te' Land Trust

An urban, Indigenous women-led community organization that facilitates the return of Chochenyo and Karkin Ohlone lands in the San Francisco Bay Area to Indigenous stewardship (sogoreate-landtrust.com).

CONTENTS

FOREWORD

By Willoughby Britton

In 2012, I found myself sitting across from His Holiness the Dalai Lama at the Mayo Clinic in Rochester, Minnesota. I was at the 24th Mind & Life dialogue—an integration of science and contemplative practice—and was presenting my research on mindfulness and meditation.[1] As a clinical neuroscientist, I was used to speaking in front of discerning audiences, but that day discovered that the customary butterflies in my stomach felt more like pterodactyls. Looking at the Dalai Lama's curious face, I was worried how he might respond to my work.

I study the potentially adverse effects of meditation. While the majority of my research over the last 20 years has focused on the clinical benefits of meditative practices, I've expanded my work over the last decade to investigating some of the more challenging aspects of contemplative practice. In 2007, I started a research study called "The Varieties of Contemplative Experience" based in my lab at Brown University.[2] The project involved interviewing more than 100 meditators and meditation teachers about what, if any, difficulties arose in their practice. Trauma emerged as a major theme, from the graduate student who developed paralyzing flashbacks on a 10-day retreat to the seasoned meditation teacher who, it turned out, had been experiencing trauma-related dissociation in practice for years.[3]

Through this research, the particular relationship between meditation and trauma became a thorn in my side. When people who'd experienced meditation-related difficulties associated with trauma approached me for help, I couldn't do much more than reassure them that they weren't alone, and that what they were experiencing wasn't their fault. During this time, I'd always wanted to provide them with something more—a comprehensive explanation of why this was happening to them, and what to do about it.

Then, a month after my presentation at Mind & Life, I came across a grainy video online of a Ph.D. dissertation defense on mindfulness meditation and trauma. I had never heard of David Treleaven, but sat mesmerized as he articulately provided the answers I had been seeking. For years, I'd been looking for a clear framework that I could offer to the struggling meditators who came to me—including those who were teaching them, and researchers who were interested in meditation and mindfulness. Suddenly, I'd found it. The puzzle pieces clicked into place one after another.

I ended up referring many people to David, and they'd often report back to me that their work together and the framework he provided were lifechanging. Their stories were so compelling—and their progress so palpable—that I decided to embark on a multi year trauma training myself. I thought I had sufficient training as a psychologist and neuroscientist, but through David's insights I realized that I needed to learn more about trauma to competently address the issues I was encountering in my practice and research.

I stayed in touch with David, and when I read the first draft of the book you're holding, it felt like a gift. Based on my conversations with meditation teachers, researchers, and mindfulness practitioners, I believe this book will be a long-awaited resource for many people. With painstaking rigor, compassion, and insight, it addresses some of the most common—but also most neglected—issues that meditators who've experienced trauma can face.

As readers of this book will know, mindfulness has exploded in popularity. From schools and clinics to prisons and businesses, mindfulness and meditation are now practiced in a variety of settings—with research backing up their benefits. Yet the notion that mindfulness and meditation can be a cure-all for countless conditions and problems, including trauma, has had some unintended consequences. We have all heard of the benefits of meditation, and for many people who practice regularly those benefits become a reality. But I have learned that people who do not have that experience, and who do not share this narrative and trajectory, often feel deeply ashamed—particularly those who have experienced trauma. They often feel that they failed meditation, did something wrong, or are profoundly and irrevocably broken.

David's book tackles the issue of shame head-on. It challenges the notion that those who experience these difficulties are simply flawed or not good meditators. Many of the meditators who contact me—often teachers themselves—express humiliation around the inability to manage their symptoms with meditation. David shows us the perils for trauma survivors practicing mindfulness, explains why they exist, and introduces grounded practices that support a safe and transformative trauma-sensitive practice. His work is evidence based, rooted in clinical research, and receptive to modifications as further research becomes available. As such, the book serves as a foundation for a larger conversation.

This book also offers us a systemic view of trauma. Paralleling David's own journey, it extends mindfulness from the suffering of isolated meditators—and their individual nervous systems—into the social, cultural, and political domains that also play a role in creating and perpetuating trauma. While the idea of interdependence—that we are all deeply interconnected and influencing each other—is not new to the mindfulness community, it is often presented as a kind of metaphysical salve of unity that inspires prosocial behavior but does not require deep personal confrontation. Through his work with social justice movements, David challenges us to question the water around us, to "critically examine the frameworks we have been offered, and be increasingly informed about our role."

Trauma-Sensitive Mindfulness comes at a time when a more nuanced conversation around mindfulness and meditation is desperately needed. I've spent the majority of my academic career advocating for such dialogue, whether in my classroom, at my lab, at academic conferences or

Mindfulness-Based Interventions teacher trainings, or with journalists searching for a catchy taglines about the merits of mindfulness.[4] Sometimes I've felt like a lone voice in this pursuit, arguing that we need to be careful about the use of contemplative practices and increase our awareness of the potential difficulties people face.[5] But recently, more and more of my colleagues are joining in. This year, 15 mindfulness researchers came together to write a consensus statement called "Mind the Hype" that advocates for a more careful and nuanced presentation of mindfulness that includes both its benefits and limits.[6] These approaches aren't meant to discourage people from meditating; on the contrary, their purpose is to make the practices more powerful and applicable to a contemporary audience.

With this book, I'm happy to say we're taking a further step together in this new direction. David has created a rigorous, accessible, empirically grounded resource for those of us looking to teach and practice mindfulness in a trauma-sensitive way. It's a timely gift, and one that I hope helps you as much as it helped me.

Willoughby Britton, Ph.D.

Brown University

NOTES

1. Britton Lab; Dalai Lama Presentation. See https://vimeo.com/69253042.

2. A summary of the Varieties of Contemplative Experience research project can be found on the Clinical and Affective Neuroscience Laboratory website: https://www.brown.edu/research/labs/britton/research/varieties-contemplative-experience

   For an overview paper detailing the study methods and results, see Lindahl, J., Fisher, N., Cooper, D., Rosen, R., and Britton, W. (2017). The Varieties of Contemplative Experience: A Mixed-Methods Study of Meditation-Related Challenges in Western Buddhists. PLOS ONE 12(5): e0176239.

   The full text of this paper is available at: http://journals.plos.org/plosone/article?id=10.1371/journal.pone.0176239.

3. Lindahl, J. R. (2017). "Somatic Energies and Emotional Traumas: A Qualitative Study of Practice-Related Challenges Reported by Vajrayāna Buddhists." *Religions* 8(8): 153, doi: 10.3390/rel8080153.

   The full text of this paper is available at: www.mdpi.com/2077-1444/8/8/153/pdf.

4. Britton, W. B. (2016). Scientific Literacy as a Foundational Competency for Teachers of Mindfulness-Based Interventions. In McCown, D., Reibel, D., and Micozzi, M. S. (eds). *Resources for Teaching Mindfulness: An International Handbook.* New York: Springer. Also see Britton, W. B. (2016). "Self-Inquiry: Investigating Confirmation Bias." In McCown, D., Reibel, D., and Micozzi, M. S. (eds). *Resources for Teaching Mindfulness: An International Handbook.* New York: Springer.

5. As an example, see The Meditation Safety Toolbox, created by Dr. Britton by aggregating meditation safety resources from different mindfulness centers and programs, including informed consent documents, screening and monitoring tools, and management strategies.

   https://www.brown.edu/research/labs/britton/resources/meditation-safety-toolbox.

6. Van Dam, N. T, van Vugt, M. K., Vago, D. R., Schmalzl, L., Saron, C., Olendzki, A., Meissner, T., Lazar, S. W., Kerr, C., Gorchov, J., Field, B. A., Britton, W. B., Brefczynski-Lewis, J. A., and Meyer, D. E. (2017). "Mind the Hype: A Critical Evaluation and Prescriptive Agenda for Mindfulness and Meditation Research." *Perspectives in Psychological Science.* In press.

Why Trauma-Sensitive Mindfulness?

Part of me wished I hadn't seen the e-mail. It was well past midnight, and I'd impulsively checked my inbox one last time before bed. "Please Help . . ." the subject line read, "Crisis with Meditation." I leaned back in my chair, reading on. It was the third such e-mail I'd received that month.

The message was from Nicholas, a high school teacher in Vermont who'd come across an article I'd written on adverse responses to mindfulness.[1] He'd started practicing mindfulness meditation to help manage his anxiety, and the benefits of his practice had been immediately clear: enhanced clarity, sharper recall, and a more persistent sense of ease. But more recently, Nicholas had also begun to experience an unnerving symptom: when his timer signaled the end of his brief meditation, he'd struggle to reach for the alarm on his phone—his body seemingly paralyzed by fear. It felt to him as if he were being restrained.

The more Nicholas practiced, the more intense and unsettling these experiences became. The moment he closed his eyes, images began flooding his vision—shattered glass, an open sky, smoke. His sleep had become fraught with nightmares, routine tasks produced panic, and the chatter in his mind was becoming untenable. The tranquility he'd sought in meditation was being met by its opposite—an underlying terror and dread that haunted him throughout the day and night.

Nicholas and I met a week later on a video call, and I could immediately see the concern and confusion in his eyes. When I asked whether the images he'd encountered in meditation held any significance for him, he nodded. A few years earlier, he'd been in a serious car accident—

helplessly pinned down in his car for an hour until he was rescued. But it wasn't the accident that perplexed him. It was his bewilderment about mindfulness meditation. How could a practice that had been so constructive and positive now leave him feeling panicked and unhinged?

I was no stranger to this question. As a psychotherapist and researcher, I'd been wrestling for years to develop a deeper understanding of the complex relationship between mindfulness and trauma—an extreme form of stress that can overwhelm our ability to cope. Placed beside one another, mindfulness and trauma can seem like natural, even inevitable, allies. Both are concerned with the nature of suffering. Both are grounded in sensory experience. And while trauma creates stress, mindfulness has been shown to reduce it. Theoretically, it seems that anyone who has experienced trauma could benefit from practicing mindfulness meditation. What could go wrong?

Plenty, it turns out. For people who've experienced trauma, mindfulness meditation can exacerbate symptoms of traumatic stress. This can include flashbacks, heightened emotional arousal, and dissociation—meaning a disconnect between one's thoughts, emotions, and physical sensations. While meditation might appear to be a safe and innocuous practice, it can thrust trauma survivors* directly into the heart of wounds that require more than mindful awareness to heal. By raking their attention over injuries that are often internal and unseen, trauma survivors can end up much like Nicholas was when I met him: disoriented, distressed, and humiliated for somehow making things worse.

At the same time, mindfulness can also be an invaluable resource for trauma survivors. Research has shown that it can strengthen body awareness, boost attention, and increase our ability to regulate

---

* I use the term "survivor" and "trauma survivor" throughout the book as a shorthand for "students and clients that are experiencing symptoms of posttraumatic stress." As I'll detail, not every survivor of a trauma will necessarily experience posttraumatic stress or have challenges with mindfulness and meditation.

emotions—all vital skills in trauma recovery. Mindfulness can also support well-established trauma-treatment methods, helping people find stability when faced with traumatic symptoms.

Consider, then, the urgency of the current moment. Over the past decade, mindfulness meditation has skyrocketed in popularity. It's being offered in a wide variety of settings—including Buddhist communities, secular programs, and psychotherapy—and is often promoted as a benign stress-reduction practice. At the same time, prevalence rates of trauma are high. An estimated 90% of the population has been exposed to a traumatic event, and 8–20% of these people will develop posttraumatic stress disorder, or PTSD.[2] This means that in any setting where mindfulness is being taught, there's a high probability that someone in the room has a history of trauma.

The question thus becomes: how can we minimize the potential dangers of mindfulness to trauma survivors while leveraging its potential benefits at the same time?

This book addresses this issue. I want to demonstrate that basic mindfulness practice is safer and more effective when it's paired with an understanding of trauma. From a meditation teacher leading a long-term silent meditation retreat, to a social worker utilizing mindfulness interventions, to an educator leading a five-minute meditation in their elementary school classroom, I believe that anyone offering mindfulness needs to be informed about the risks it presents to people who are grappling with traumatic stress.

I've been investigating this topic for the past decade. I conducted theoretical academic research, filled walls with cerebral Post-it notes, and informally interviewed mindfulness educators, mental-health professionals, and trauma survivors about the subject. As a psychotherapist, I've also worked closely with survivors who have had adverse experiences with mindfulness meditation. But I ultimately approached this issue as someone who'd had his own challenges with mindfulness and trauma, and wanted to understand what, exactly, had happened to me along the way.

A PERSONAL PATH

I began practicing mindfulness meditation while working as a psycho-therapist with male sex offenders in Vancouver, Canada. I'd come to the work with an interest in sexuality and restorative justice, and a year in found myself burnt out, emotionally volatile, and absent any tools to help me cope. When a colleague suggested I come to her local mindfulness meditation group, I was game: mindfulness had an increasingly positive reputation in psychology, and I loved the idea of developing a more skill-ful relationship with my mind. Sitting and paying attention to my breath, I thought—how hard could that be?

It was impossible, of course. I spent my first meditation period com-pletely lost in thought, only to realize it once the bell to end the session had sounded. Yet I came to love the practice, discovering that it helped me in a number of ways. I was more aware of my body, less identified with tur-bulent thoughts, and found myself happier and more content then I'd ever been. I was relating to the world in new ways and discovering meaning and resilience outside of my forensic work—pausing to listen to the wind through the arbutus trees outside my kitchen window, for instance, or feel-ing my feet on the ground as I walked to work. When I was in emotional pain, mindfulness also provided me with some perspective and space. It helped me relate to myself in compassionate, nonjudgmental ways.

Then, unexpectedly, the lights went out. I was on a silent medita-tion retreat in rural Massachusetts, and I felt something akin to a circuit breaker going off in my body. I'd been struggling to settle into practice, with one particular story of sexual violence from work looping in my mind. When I opened my eyes in the dimly lit room, I saw that every-thing was in its place: fellow meditators poised on their cushions beside me, the statue of Buddha at the front of the room, and the slice of moon between the trees out the window. Nothing stirred, and nothing external had changed.

But then I also saw myself. I was looking down at the tops of my shoul-ders from a perch in the rafters. Panic shot through me, yet I remained as still as the statue I was now focused on. I trusted that like every other experience I'd had in meditation, this too would pass—if not by the end of the session, then surely by the following morning.

It didn't. At least, not entirely. For the next week on retreat, the world became a murky, subterranean place. I found myself floating between two spheres—neither of which felt to be on solid ground. I was physically present, but only on the surface. My senses were muted and muffled, my appetite vanished, and I had a bleak, pervasive feeling that something was wrong. It was as if some essential part of myself had simply gotten up, walked away, and had no intention of coming back.

Every other day, I met with one of the meditation teachers on the retreat—often welling up with tears the moment I sat down. Each interview, I'd also leave with a similar set of instructions: be mindful. Note the detachment. Don't give up. Trust the process. And for the time remaining on retreat, that's exactly what I did.

DISCOVERING TRAUMA

When I returned home that summer, my friends and family members' faces revealed what I already knew: the retreat had left me worse for wear. I was disoriented, numb, and having difficulty returning to my everyday life. Speaking with my friends and colleagues about the experience, I was surprised to hear them use the word trauma—a term I'd studied but never associated with my life. In my mind, trauma was confined to acts of tremendous violence and violation. Assault survivors carried trauma. Combat veterans experienced trauma. People who faced cruel and unjust treatment at the hands of oppressive systems—racism, or ableism, for instance—endured trauma. I'd led a relatively sheltered life, and labeling my personal experiences as "traumatic" seemed to trivialize the enormity of the pain survivors faced.

But trauma, I've since learned, is less about the content of an event than about the impact—sudden, and then ongoing—that it has on our physiology. As veteran trauma specialist Pat Ogden wrote, "any experience that is stressful enough to leave us feeling helpless, frightened, overwhelmed, or profoundly unsafe is considered a trauma" (2015, p. 66). From witnessing or experiencing violence, to losing a loved one, to being targeted by oppression,* people can experience trauma in a variety of ways. And, contrary to what I once believed, addressing different forms of personal trauma doesn't minimize the importance of someone else's more severe injury. In fact, it can open a conversation about the social conditions that so often perpetuate trauma in the first place.[3]

At the encouragement of a few friends, I began seeing a trauma therapist. It had been six weeks since my meditation retreat, and I was still struggling beneath the weight of the experience. I was dissociating frequently, having recurrent nightmares, and for the first time in my life had developed insomnia. A few sessions in, the therapist raised the idea that I was experiencing vicarious, or secondary, trauma from my work with sex offenders. I'd been continually exposed to stories of violence that had eventually become traumatizing. Within this frame, the symptoms I'd been experiencing—intrusive thoughts, emotional detachment, dissociation—began to make sense.

These sessions turned out to be life changing. I'd been privileged to experience different kinds of talk therapy—Jungian, cognitive behavioral, psychodynamic—but had never found that the insights I'd gleaned created lasting transformation. Trauma work proved different, helping me change in ways previous therapy and meditation hadn't. But I could also feel that my mindfulness training was helping me in sessions, allowing me to detect and stay present with the intense emotions and physical sensations that were surfacing. Compelled by the benefits of trauma therapy, I enrolled in a multiyear training program called Somatic Experiencing— a contemporary therapeutic approach created by a biophysicist named Peter Levine.[4] The course taught me about the way the body responds to trauma, including safe and practical ways to work with survivors. It's a powerful methodology that shaped my thinking.

---

* "Oppression," political educator and somatic practitioner Sumitra Rajkumar wrote, "is the social condition in which the violent power dynamics of historical forces such as capitalism, white supremacy, and patriarchy impose undue suffering and limits on life and agency" (personal communication, June 12th, 2016).

But I also felt something was missing in this work. While the teachers spoke about the biological roots of trauma, they never discussed its *social* roots—including systems of oppression that correlate with trauma. I was being trained to think about trauma solely as an individual experience disconnected from the larger world. And while this framework was familiar to me as a student of Western psychology, it felt especially problematic in the context of trauma. I'd been involved in political activism, and was in search of an approach to healing that created a bridge between personal and social change.

A year later, I found it. A friend introduced me to Staci Haines, a teacher, clinician, and social activist who offered a systemic understanding of trauma in her work.[5] Along with Spenta Kandawalla, a social justice organizer and acupuncturist, Staci founded *generative somatics*—a national, nonprofit organization based in Oakland, California, that combines social analysis with trauma healing. Weaving together findings from modern neuroscience, political theory, and principles of transformative justice,[6] the organization offers a holistic approach to healing trauma. Trainings center the experiences of people most targeted by trauma and oppression,[7] and their vision of personal and collective transformation moved me to my core. Through this life-changing work, trauma increasingly became a lens through which I saw and understood the world.

TRAUMA AND MINDFULNESS

During this time, mindfulness continued to have a powerful draw for me. I was still wary from my retreat experience, but I was excited to see research studies confirming what I'd also experienced: that mindfulness could create real, positive, quantifiable change.[8] Still, I found myself wondering: how many people were out there struggling the same way I had? Was my experience an anomaly, or reflective of a larger trend? I began reviewing relevant literature and found that few people had addressed the relationship between mindfulness and trauma head on. Bolstered, I enrolled in a doctoral psychology program, completed a dissertation on the topic, and eventually began speaking and writing about the challenges I had experienced.

I quickly learned that I wasn't alone. After a video of a lecture I gave on the topic began circulating online,[9] I started hearing from people like Nicholas who'd had experiences similar to mine. Not everyone had been on long retreats or had an intensive meditation practice. Often they'd simply tried mindfulness meditation through one of the many channels currently offering it—at a local community center, a stress-reduction program, or instruction they'd found online.

This was alarming. I imagined most mindfulness educators would know what trauma was, but was less convinced that they were equipped to work with it skillfully. Could they recognize trauma, including when a trauma survivor needed help? Did they know when to refer a student to a trauma professional? And had they made connections between trauma and the systemic oppression people faced?

My guiding question thus became: Given the ubiquity of trauma, how could mindfulness practitioners ensure they were offering practices in an effective, informed, trauma-sensitive way?

TRAUMA-SENSITIVE MINDFULNESS

Out of this inquiry, I developed a framework of principles and modifications designed to support trauma-sensitive mindfulness meditation. A kind of "best-practices" approach to the topic, trauma-sensitive mindfulness joins an emerging conversation about what a trauma-informed approach to mindfulness and meditation looks like.[10] It offers practical suggestions in the context of basic mindfulness instruction, and is intended for mindfulness teachers, trauma professionals, and anyone interested in learning more about the topic.

My definition of trauma-sensitive practice comes from the U.S. National Center for Trauma-Informed Care (2016):

A program, organization, or system that is trauma-informed *realizes* the widespread impact of trauma and understands potential paths for recovery; *recognizes* the signs and symptoms of trauma in clients, families, staff, and others involved with the system; *responds* by fully integrating knowledge about trauma into policies, procedures, and practices; and seeks to actively resist *re-traumatization.*

This "four-R's" definition is a practical, common-sense approach to trauma-sensitive practice that serves as a guidepost for this book. In realizing how widespread trauma is, I want you to be able to recognize traumatic symptoms, respond to them effectively, and avoid retraumatization in your clients and students when offering mindfulness. Each chapter and modification I'll offer you has one of these R's in mind.

The framework I'll be presenting contains five core principles designed to support trauma-sensitive mindfulness practice. These principles aren't intended to be a prescriptive approach to trauma recovery—trauma is far too complex for that. Instead, I'll be offering suggestions instead of steps, empowering you to incorporate material in ways that make sense within the context of your mindfulness-based work. I believe it's our responsibility to adapt mindfulness to meet the specific needs of trauma survivors as opposed to expecting them to adapt to us.

How did I arrive at these principles? I started by searching for key trauma concepts that related to mindfulness. I then used each concept as a lens through which to look at mindfulness—a process that revealed the risks and rewards of mindfulness with respect to trauma. For example, many trauma specialists consider working with the body essential to recovery. From one angle, mindfulness meditation can support this, heightening one's awareness of the body by attending to physical sensations. But without the right guidance, mindfulness can be a cerebral and dissociative practice, causing people to bypass sensations that are vying for their attention. Given this, what are the best ways for people experiencing trauma to practice mindfulness with respect to the body?

Throughout this work, I've been guided by three primary goals:

(1) To Minimize Distress for People Practicing Mindfulness

Those of us teaching or utilizing mindfulness in our work have a responsibility to ensure that people are as safe and stable as possible when they're practicing. The goal of any work concerning trauma, Babette Rothschild wrote, must be to "relieve, not intensify, suffering" (2010, p. xi). Taking into account that mindfulness meditation often involves sitting still with one's eyes closed, this can be a deceptively demanding task. How can we know when someone is having a traumatic response to meditation instructions that we're offering?

There are no easy answers to this question. Each person and situation is unique. But as teachers and mental-health professionals, we can do our best to self-educate. We can learn how to recognize trauma, respond to it effectively, provide relevant referrals, and offer tailored modifications within mindfulness practice—all which can help prevent retraumatization. My goal is to offer you practical, common-sense ways to ensure that, at a minimum, people under your care aren't harming themselves in practice.

(2) To Forward a Systemic Understanding of Trauma

This goal is informed by my work with *generative somatics*. I believe that becoming a trauma-sensitive practitioner requires more than adopting traditional therapeutic skills. It asks us to recognize the ways trauma connects to the world around us. If we focus exclusively on individual components of trauma, we can draw attention away from the systems of oppression that so often lie at the root of trauma. Traumatic stress is a physical and psychological experience, but it is also a political one. Knowing this—including our own social context—can build safety and trust, and help us best support the people we're working with.

(3) To Advocate for a Continued Partnership Between Mindfulness Practitioners and Trauma Professionals

Each of these groups has indispensable experience to offer the other. Trauma professionals who understand the biological, psychological, and social dimensions of trauma can help inform mindfulness practitioners about trauma, and play a crucial role in consulting with them. Mindfulness practitioners* have a wealth of understanding about working skillfully with the mind, including difficult mind states. While the relationship between mindfulness and psychology is well established, the burgeoning relationship between mindfulness practitioners and trauma professionals offers rich potential moving forward.

A ROAD MAP

Part I of the book offers a conversation between mindfulness and traumatic stress. I define trauma and mindfulness, examine their unique histories, and explore how modern neuroscience is sculpting our understanding of both. In Part II, I cover the five principles of trauma-sensitive mindfulness, presenting relevant theory and modifications you can apply in your work.

A few caveats. First, I'm sometimes asked whether it's *mindfulness* that's problematic for trauma survivors, or whether it's *mindfulness meditation* that causes issues. As you'll see, I lean toward the latter. It's important to distinguish between mindfulness the mental state and the way that state is pursued. Mindfulness doesn't cause trauma—it's the practice of mindfulness meditation, offered without an understanding of trauma, that can exacerbate and entrench traumatic symptoms. Inside of this, people practice mindfulness in different contexts, including meditating

---

* I use the term "mindfulness practitioners" to refer to both mindfulness teachers and those utilizing mindfulness-based interventions in their professional mental-health work. I use the terms "client" and "student" throughout the book to refer to those practicing mindfulness under the direction of teachers/therapists/healers.

at home, in psychotherapy, or attending long-term retreats. With limited empirical research on the relationship between mindfulness and trauma, our task here is to apply common sense. What's triggering for one survivor—a silent meditation retreat, for instance—can be beneficial for another. Our work is to stay responsive to the unique and ongoing needs of the trauma survivors we work with.

Second, trauma-sensitive mindfulness isn't intended to replace well-established trauma treatment approaches. You won't find me suggesting that mindfulness can "cure" what is a complex, intense, and enduring issue for many. Instead, I'll be focusing on the way that mindfulness can be a resource for trauma survivors, specifically the ways that mindfulness can help regulate arousal and support stability in the midst of traumatic symptoms—a necessary first step of trauma recovery work.

Last, I want to be clear that I'm not saying mindfulness—or the movement in which people teach and practice it—is flawed. On the contrary, I believe it's a profound resource for trauma survivors, and that mindfulness communities are deeply committed to the well-being of their members. At the same time, I believe we can do better. Mindfulness doesn't need to work for everyone, but I'm convinced that certain modifications can help support survivors—at the very least ensuring that they are not retraumatizing themselves in practice. The incorporation of a trauma-informed framework is a natural—and, I believe, necessary—step in the evolution of the contemporary mindfulness movement.

Confronting trauma asks a great deal. As feminist scholar Judith Herman wrote, it brings us face to face "with human vulnerability in the natural world and with the capacity for evil in human nature" (1997, p. 7). Studying trauma also asks us to examine the suffering bound up in larger systems of oppression—systems that leave whole communities more vulnerable to trauma, and others more shielded from it. Mindfulness, thankfully, can support this endeavor. It fortifies our capacity to be present with that which is too much to bear. This, I believe, is a task in trauma-sensitive work: to face suffering in its many forms. As the novelist and social critic James Baldwin wrote, "Not everything that is faced can be changed; but nothing can be changed until it is faced" (1962. p. 38).

PART I

Foundations Of Trauma-Sensitive Mindfulness

CHAPTER 1

The Ubiquity of Trauma:
Visible and Invisible Forms

Things are not getting worse, they are getting uncovered. We must hold each other tight and continue to pull back the veil.
　　　　　　　　　　　　　　　　—Adrienne Maree Brown

Sometimes we encounter experiences that so violate our sense of safety, order, predictability, and right, that we feel utterly overwhelmed—unable to integrate, and simply unable to go on as before. Unable to bear reality. We have come to call these shattering experiences trauma. None of us is immune to them.
　　　　　　　　　　　　　　　　　　　　—Stephen Cope

"My damage was internal, unseen. I carry it with me. You took away my worth, my privacy, my energy, my time, my safety, my intimacy, my confidence, my own voice, until today."

On June 2, 2016, these words were spoken by a 23-year-old woman in a California courtroom.[1] She was addressing Brock Turner, a Stanford University student who was facing sentencing after being found guilty of three counts of sexual assault. The night of the attack, Turner—then nineteen and a member of Stanford's swim team—had been chased down and apprehended by two international graduate students. They'd witnessed Turner accosting a half-naked, unconscious woman outside of a party on campus—the same woman now standing before him in court.

"I stood there examining my body beneath the stream of water," the woman continued, relaying her experience in emergency care, "and decided I don't want my body anymore. I was terrified of it . . . I wanted to take off my body like a jacket and leave it at the hospital with everything else."

Unbeknown to Turner, the statement being read to him would be seen over 14 million times online in the following week.[2] It would also be read, live and uninterrupted for 25 minutes, on CNN. People were shocked and disturbed as the young woman—who remains unidentified to the public—detailed the psychological wreckage she'd endured in the aftermath of the assault: relentless anxiety, overwhelming shame, and chronic nightmares of being assaulted and unable to wake up.

Equally appalling to many was the lenient sentence Turner received: six months in a county jail instead of a potential 14 years in state prison. The judge presiding over the case, himself a Stanford graduate, feared that a longer jail term would have a "severe impact" on Turner and negatively affect his Olympic aspirations—a topic frequently mentioned at trial. In a character-witness letter to the court, Turner's father wrote that Brock was being harshly punished for "20 minutes of action" and "had never been violent to anyone," including the night of the assault.[3]

The day after the verdict, I found myself at a café watching my closest friend read the victim's statement. It was haunting to witness her absorb the words. This was a friend who'd taught me about sexism—who'd raised my awareness about the social norms that objectified her as a woman, and shielded men like Turner in court. It was also someone I loved. Watching her eyes fill with tears, I felt a mix of anger and helplessness. Virtually all the women in my life—my friend included—had been the victim of sexual violence. She viscerally understood the agitation, flashbacks, and isolation that Turner's victim had described.

Later that same morning, we learned that a fourth Baltimore police officer had been acquitted of the second-degree murder of Freddie Gray—

a 25-year-old African American man who had died in police custody one year earlier.[4] It was one of a slew of incidents—Michael Brown in Ferguson, Missouri, Rekia Boyd in Chicago, Illinois, Tamir Rice in Cleveland, Ohio—that involved the violent death of an unarmed Black person at the hands of police. Having followed parts of the trial, my friend and I felt exasperated. Both of us wanted to believe that the cases we'd been reading about that day were anomalies.

But they weren't. In the United States, nearly one in five women will be raped at some point in their lives,[5] and it's estimated that every 28 hours a Black person is murdered by police, security guards, or state-sanctioned vigilantes.[6] That day, we were simply being reminded of this fact, confronted by a kind of traumatic violence that, while familiar to many, is often repressed and kept out of view.[7]

That evening, my friend and I attended a local mindfulness group. Meditation helped me disengage from repetitive thoughts, connect to my body, and build empathy for myself and others. As a White, straight man who'd developed a political analysis, mindfulness helped build my capacity to turn toward—and not reflexively away from—oppressive forms of violence. Finding a few seats in the meditation hall and settling in, I felt my friend reach for my hand, giving it a gentle squeeze as the bell rang to begin the silent half-hour meditation.

Halfway through, my friend began to struggle. She was restless beside me, and when I opened my eyes I saw that her face was tense and her shoulders were quivering. A few minutes later, she quietly stood up and left.

During the break, I found her outside shivering in the cold. She'd become flooded with images from her violent past—memories that had been triggered after reading the victim's statement earlier in the day. Her heart rate had soared during the meditation, and her awareness of her pulse had only intensified her anxiety. Meditation was usually a refuge for my friend, but tonight it had left her feeling trapped and on the verge of a panic attack.

Stepping back into the foyer, a middle-aged woman approached my friend and expressed concern. She'd seen her leave during the meditation and wanted to know if she could help. Comforted by the gesture—and knowing this woman was an experienced meditator—my friend sat down and shared her story of what had happened in meditation. The woman nodded empathically, clearly moved by what she'd heard. In her experience, she said softly, meditation could elicit this kind of pain. It wasn't a practice for the faint of heart. But she also believed that persistence was key. If my friend was determined enough, the grip of the memories would loosen. She was confident—based on her own experience—that mindfulness could heal any pain.

My friend and I thanked her. Silently, however, I wished I could share in her conviction.

TRAUMA-SENSITIVE MINDFULNESS

When people learn that I'm writing about trauma and mindfulness, they often expect to hear exclusively about the ways mindfulness can support trauma recovery. And it can: Mindfulness can enhance present-moment awareness, increase our self-compassion, and enhance our ability to self-regulate.[8, 9] But mindfulness can also generate problems for people struggling with traumatic stress.[10] When we ask someone with trauma to pay close, sustained attention to their internal world, we invite them into contact with traumatic stimuli—thoughts, images, memories, and physical sensations that may relate to a traumatic event. As my friend experienced, this can aggravate and intensify symptoms of traumatic stress, in some cases even lead to retraumatization—a relapse into an intensely traumatized state.

This raises crucial questions for those of us offering mindfulness instruction. What is our responsibility to people experiencing trauma? Is a certain amount of pain to be expected in practice? How can we know when a survivor should or shouldn't be meditating? And how can we grasp our own limitations in understanding other people's experiences of trauma, as a way to best support them?

In sum, how can we offer mindfulness in a trauma-sensitive way?

Trauma-sensitive, or trauma-informed, practice means that we have a basic understanding of trauma in the context of our work. A trauma-informed physician can ask a patient's permission before touching them, for example. Or a trauma-informed school counselor might ask a student whether they want the door open or closed during a session, and inquire about a comfortable sitting distance. With trauma-informed mindfulness, we apply this concept to mindfulness instruction. We commit to recognizing trauma, responding to it skillfully, and taking preemptive steps to ensure that people aren't retraumatizing themselves under our guidance.[11]

The need for trauma-sensitive mindfulness is a reflection of both odds and statistics. Over the past decade, mindfulness has exploded in popularity.[12] It is now being offered in a wide range of secular environments, including elementary and high schools, corporations, and hospitals.[13] Any number of workshops, retreats, conferences, seminars, and institutes offer mindfulness instruction. Books and articles on the subject have flooded the marketplace.[14] At the same time, the prevalence of trauma is extraordinarily high. The majority of us—as I'll detail shortly—will be exposed to at least some type of traumatic event in our lifetime, and some of us will develop debilitating symptoms in its aftermath. If we're targeted by systemic oppression[15]—as someone who is poor or working class, disabled, a person of color, transgender, or a woman— we face a greater likelihood of experiencing interpersonal of trauma over the course of our lives, and live inside of traumatic conditions every day.[16]

What this means is that in any environment where mindfulness is being practiced, there's a high likelihood that someone will be struggling with traumatic stress. From a student who witnessed domestic violence to an elderly person who recently lost their partner in a fall, trauma will often be present. And while not everyone who has experienced trauma will have an adverse response to mindfulness, we need to be prepared for this possibility.

In each chapter, I'm going to present a case study to illuminate the concepts I'm covering. Each case will be a composite of people I've worked with, and all identifying features have been changed. With that said, let's meet RJ—a student who found himself at the intersection of meditation and traumatic stress.

RJ: SUFFERING IN SILENCE

RJ's stomach sank the moment the mindfulness teacher walked in the classroom. It was a Tuesday afternoon, and he'd forgotten this was the period in the week when meditation instruction took place. He began to sweat and looked around to find his classmates looking relaxed and happy—an observation that only accentuated his own misery. He suddenly felt like he was about to vomit.

For the past three weeks, RJ had been learning mindfulness meditation at his high school. He'd initially been open to the idea—appreciating the diversion from his usual studies—but quickly found the practice to be excruciating. During meditation practice, he fought to hear the voice of his teacher over the sound of his pounding heart. He couldn't focus on his breath and found that he left each meditation extremely agitated for the rest of the day. Asking to be excused that afternoon, RJ walked briskly to the bathroom, locked himself in a stall, and took out his phone. He couldn't take being around people and needed to escape to calm down.

Four months earlier, RJ had lost his older sister, Michelle, to a car accident. She'd been jogging in their neighborhood and was hit by a driver who hadn't seen her entering the intersection. He'd come home from evening soccer practice to find a police officer at the table with his parents, both of whom were clearly in shock. He'd learned that Michelle had been wearing his new headphones—likely preventing her from hearing the vehicle. He was pained by a sense of responsibility for her death, and for the rest of that week felt as if his body was in free fall.

The months that followed were harrowing. Teachers often saw RJ sitting alone in the hallway, desolate and lost. Lunches packed by his grieving mother were left uneaten,[17] he dropped out of basketball, and he started skipping school to get high in the local park. He also began having nightmares about the accident and panic attacks whenever he saw runners around his neighborhood. Emotionally absent and numb, he felt caught in some kind of void between his current life and the day he'd lost his sister.

Silence was the hardest for RJ. At night, he'd lie awake in his room in the quiet house, waiting for the sound of his sister to come in the front door. He remembered the particular way she would drop her keys on the table and walk softly to the kitchen to open the refrigerator. He'd wait for the sound of her footsteps to walk past his room, confirming the accident had been some sort of nightmare. But she never arrived.

This made mindfulness meditation feel impossible. When he'd close his eyes, the silence and darkness were overwhelming. He'd try to pay attention to his breath, but all he could see were images of his sister's face. Other times he saw the street corner where she had died. As a whole, the practice kindled a similar set of symptoms that my friend had experienced that night in the meditation hall—a sense of fear and suffocation matched by extreme anxiety. Leaving the classroom that morning—and locking himself alone in the bathroom—had felt like RJ's only way to cope.

STRESS AND TRAUMA

What was happening for RJ? Despite the understandable grief of losing his sister, what was causing these specific symptoms?

Unbeknown to him, RJ was experiencing traumatic stress. His isolation, loss of appetite, heightened anxiety, recklessness, and nightmares were all symptoms of trauma. So were the intrusive images of his sister that arose in meditation. Trauma can be an agonizing, life-shattering experience that leaves us frightened, helpless, and estranged from any sense of ease and joy—and RJ was in the throes of it.

To understand traumatic stress, we can start by defining stress. Our contemporary definition of the term comes from Hans Selye, an Austrian-Hungarian endocrinologist. Selye characterized stress as the nonspecific response of the body to any demand for change.[18] He recognized that stress is neither inherently good nor bad—it's simply anything that requires our effort. Our nervous system doesn't draw a distinction between "positive" and "negative" stress. Bicycling, driving a car, or sexual activity are examples of stressors. Even being told good news—of a welcomed pregnancy, say, or a promotion at work—is a form of stress. Mostly, however, we associate "stress" with hardship and difficulty. Endless work days, financial struggles, interpersonal conflicts, or devaluing messages are all examples of negative stress. There's an entire industry related to stress reduction of which mindfulness is playing a starring role.

Yet while negative stress can impact our quality of life, it remains distinct from *traumatic stress*—the most intense form of stress we can experience. Traumatic stress results from being exposed to a traumatic event or series of events. Many people have multiple experiences of trauma, for instance, in which events are ongoing—and, often, collectively denied. This can include intimate and domestic violence, date rape, or the sexual assault detailed at the beginning of this chapter. Oppression also continues to engender traumatic experiences every time there is another hate crime or police killing. Traumatic stress is not always just a singular, isolated event.

In the current fifth edition of the *Diagnostic and Statistical Manual of Mental Disorders* (5th ed., DSM-5; American Psychiatric Association, 2013), a traumatic event is defined as exposure to actual or threatened death, serious injury, or sexual violation. Such exposure can result from directly experiencing or witnessing a traumatic event, or learning that the event occurred to a family member or close friend. It can also arise through repeated or extreme exposure to the details of trauma, including in the context of one's work—first responders and emergency care physicians, for instance, or anyone who works closely with trauma.

THE SPECTRUM OF TRAUMA

For many, being exposed to a singular traumatic event won't produce long-term consequences. We're impacted, but can metabolize the experience—meaning we can process through the thoughts, memories, and emotions without becoming overwhelmed and stuck.

Sometimes, however, we develop symptoms that extend past a traumatic event. This can include ongoing flashbacks, agonizing physical sensations, or volatile emotional reactions that emerge without warning. Some kind of alarm system inside of us doesn't switch off, and a traumatic experience comes to wreak havoc with our body and mind.

This is known as *posttraumatic stress*—an experience where traumatic symptoms live on past the traumatic event. Because we are unable to integrate the experience, the imprint of trauma follows us into the present, destined to replay itself over and over again. Posttraumatic stress fundamentally challenges the notion that time can heal all wounds.

Sometimes, this is a literal reflection of external traumatic conditions. People who experience oppression often aren't safe, and their fear is well grounded. By virtue of ongoing oppressive conditions, they are often deprived of the opportunity to have closure with a trauma—like trauma that's the result of violence from racism, or living under a military occupation. Other times, a singular traumatic event takes place and we simply don't register that it has ended. Symptoms such as nightmares, dissociation, and alienation continue to define our present experience. As Brock Turner's victim recounted at trial: "I can't sleep alone at night without having a light on, like a five-year-old, because I have nightmares . . . For three months, I went to bed at six o'clock in the morning."

The symptoms of posttraumatic stress often lie beneath the surface of one's skin, and can be difficult to identify or articulate. In RJ's classroom, the mindfulness teacher didn't know he'd lost his sister or that he was having such a challenging experience in meditation. RJ had been struggling in isolation. This makes for a kind of invisible labor that trauma survivors are often forced to perform. Unrecognized by those around them, they may be wrestling with an unseen and unimaginable form of agony. In Chapter 5, I'll provide you with a list of potential signs that someone might be experiencing traumatic symptoms in meditation. For now, I want to emphasize the extensive costs of posttraumatic stress, burdening people—and by extension, their families and communities—with often relentless distress.

As the DSM-5 definition reminds us, posttraumatic stress can also affect those who witness a traumatic event. A year after Freddie Gray's fatal detainment by the Baltimore police, a reporter interviewed Kevin Moore, a bystander who'd filmed the encounter. "I hear the screams every night," Moore said, recounting Gray's last words: "'I can't breathe, I need help, I need medical attention.' This is the shit that plays in my mind over and over again."[19] Traumatic symptoms such as these can also surface by learning that a traumatic event happened to someone close to us, the devastating blow of trauma rippling out from the point of impact. As African American psychologist Monica Williams (2015) writes about race-based trauma, "We are surrounded by constant reminders that race-related danger can occur at any time, anywhere, to anyone. We might see clips on the nightly news featuring unarmed African Americans being killed on the street, in a holding cell, or even in a church. . . . Over the centuries the Black community has developed a cultural knowledge of these sorts of horrific events, which then primes us for traumatization when we hear about yet another act of violence."

For some, posttraumatic stress develops into PTSD, a diagnosis that refers to a specific cluster of symptoms that continue for at least a month after the occurrence of a traumatic event.[20] This includes consistently reexperiencing a traumatic event (or events), avoiding reminders of the trauma, experiencing negative cognitions and mood (anxiety and irritability, for instance), and having problems with arousal (hypervigilance, complications with concentration or sleep). Studies estimate that approximately 8–20% of trauma survivors will develop PTSD,[21] although people can suffer from PTSD symptoms without meeting the criteria for a diagnosis. "PTSD is a whole-body tragedy," social worker Susan Pease Banitt wrote, "an integral human event of enormous proportions with massive repercussions" (2012, p. xix).

In adopting trauma-sensitive mindfulness, it's useful to be aware of these distinctions along the spectrum of trauma—from stress, to traumatic and posttraumatic stress, to PTSD. But for most of us, our job won't be to offer diagnoses. Instead, our primary task will lie in the four R's I described in the introduction: *realizing* the pervasive impact of trauma, *recognizing* symptoms, and then *responding* to them skillfully—all in the service of preventing *retraumatization*. Whether someone's experience fits the DSM-5 definition of PTSD is not our main concern. Trauma-sensitive mindfulness, in this respect, is concerned with the overall psychological impact of traumatic events that include—but aren't limited to—PTSD.[22]

INTEGRATION

You may find yourself asking: What about other forms of intense negative stress? What about emotional abuse, or hate speech? Are these considered traumatic?[23]

These questions bring us to *integration,* a crucial concept for understanding trauma. While many of us will naturally be curious about the content of a traumatic event, we can define trauma more accurately by looking at one's individual response—specifically whether or not they could integrate the experience. As Pat Ogden asserted in her book *Sensorimotor Psychotherapy: Interventions for Trauma and Attachment,* "Trauma refers to any threatening, overwhelming experiences that we cannot integrate. . . . After such experiences, we are often left with a diminished sense of security with others and in the world, and a sense of feeling unsafe inside our own skin" (2015, p. 66).

A pot of soup is a simple example of integration. When we chop up a number of different ingredients—vegetables, chicken, herbs—and add them to a broth, they come together harmoniously into a whole. A more technical definition of integration comes from Dan Siegel, a professor of psychiatry at UCLA who has written about the neuroscience of mindfulness and trauma. Siegel described integration as "the linkage of differentiated elements of a system" (2011, p. 64).[24] Using the metaphor above, the differentiated elements are the different ingredients that become linked in a larger system—in this case, the pot of soup.

Integration happens in a variety of systems. Inside of our bodies, it takes place when our left and right hemispheres of the brain communicate, or parallels are drawn between thoughts and physical sensations. In relationships, integration happens when we engage in a back-and-forth conversation, staying connected to ourselves while attuning to others. In a larger system, such as a medical system, the skills of different health workers and various kinds of technology are integrated together to help provide the best care for a patient. Integration occurs in systems large and small.

Posttraumatic stress, meanwhile, creates *dis*-integration. Thoughts, memories, and emotions become cut off from our experience or continually flood our field of consciousness. We can find ourselves out of balance and unable to trust our senses. Our bodies continue to respond with alarm even though people close to us may try to reassure us otherwise. The connection between mind and body is impacted— even severed.

Think of RJ, for instance. He was unable to integrate the trauma of losing his sister. His thoughts and emotions became unpredictable and chaotic, leaving him removed from himself and others. At any moment, images of Michelle would intrude into consciousness without warning. Brock Turner's victim also described the disintegrating effects of trauma: "I tried to push [the assault] out of my mind," she said in court, "but it was so heavy I didn't talk, I didn't eat, I didn't sleep, I didn't interact with anyone. . . . I became isolated from the ones I loved most." As she continued relaying to Turner: "I became closed off, angry, self-deprecating, tired, irritable, empty. . . . You bought me a ticket to a planet where I lived by myself."

Integration is a powerful frame within trauma-sensitive practice. Rather than try to ascertain whether a student or client is experiencing PTSD, we can ask: Is this person struggling with a traumatic experience they weren't able to integrate? Even more importantly, is mindfulness easing this person's suffering, or exacerbating it? Integration highlights the fact that there's a distinct boundary between events we can metabolize and those we can't.[25]

Integration also opens the door to talking about experiences that lie outside of the DSM-5 definition of trauma. This is especially true with oppression. Facing racism, homophobia, or poverty may not leave someone with symptoms that meet the diagnostic criteria for PTSD, but they can all have a traumatic impact. In her research at the University of Connecticut, Monica Williams found that *microaggressions*—subtle, widespread acts of discrimination—have a compounding effect that can result in traumatic symptoms.[26] While trauma is often associated with war and sexual assault, oppression also holds undeniable relevance for traumatic stress.

I'll return to integration at the end of this chapter, but before we go any further, I want to explore statistics. How often does trauma happen? And to whom? To be trauma-informed means having an answer to these questions.

THE PREVALENCE OF TRAUMA

Several years ago, I participated in Step In/Step Out, an anti-oppression exercise designed to open one's eyes to the ubiquity of trauma and oppression. Standing in a circle of 30 participants, a facilitator read from a list naming particular forms of harm. If one applied to us personally and we felt comfortable revealing it, we stepped into the circle. If it didn't, we stood still, and after a few moments of silence let the others who had "stepped in" step back.

I can remember the sound of the cicadas outside of the open window as we stood in a circle. "Step in if you have borne witness to violence," our facilitator began. A surprising majority of us did. Each of us paused in the middle, taking in each other's faces before we stepped back. "Step in," he continued, "if you or a family member have been emotionally or physically abused . . . if you or someone you know has experienced incest." With each question, our feet shuffled in and out of the circle. We were being asked to feel—not just intellectualize—the statistics we were revealing to one another.

A heavy silence hung in the air at the end of the exercise. All but one of us knew someone who had been raped. Nearly two thirds of us knew someone who'd committed suicide. Faces in the circle revealed a mix of shock, anger, sadness, and shame. We hadn't disclosed any specific details, but had just revealed stories that many of us had hidden and kept out of view. I'd thought of myself as someone who was familiar with trauma, but the exercise had rattled me. I'd known some of these people for years, but clearly didn't know what they'd witnessed and been through. For the rest of the day, I saw people differently, forgetting that trauma so often rests beneath the surface of our lives.

Psychiatrist Mark Epstein spoke to this by referring to trauma as "an ineradicable aspect of life" (2013, p. 3). A glance at statistics underscores the statement: an estimated 90% of the world's population will be exposed to a traumatic event over the course of their lives.[27] In the United States, one in four children will experience physical abuse and one in five will be sexually molested.[28] Bessel van der Kolk (2014), one of the leading experts in the field of trauma, argues that the impact of trauma is one of the most important public health issues we face today. Epstein asserts that it's the bedrock of psychology.

Trauma can confront us with our stark vulnerability in the natural world. Traffic accidents, falls, and drownings account for 45% of injury-related deaths, with traffic accidents being the leading cause of death worldwide among those aged 15–29 years every year.[29] In the United States alone, over 40 million people per year enter an emergency room with serious injuries, and 2 million of these people end up in critical care.[30] From earthquakes to ordinary accidents, we're susceptible to trauma in numerous ways—especially if our material conditions are less than adequate.

Interpersonal violence is another major cause of trauma. Ten million Americans per year are physically abused by an intimate partner,[31] and a sexual assault occurs once every two minutes across the country.[32] On a typical day, over 20,000 phone calls are placed to domestic violence hotlines nationwide,[33] and victims of domestic violence lose a total of eight million paid days of work every year.[34] While discussions of trauma in the media focus primarily on soldiers returning home from war, realizing the scope of this harm is essential to trauma-informed practice.[35]

WHO EXPERIENCES TRAUMA

Let's return for a moment to Freddie Gray, the young African American man whose neck was broken while in custody of the Baltimore police. In the days and weeks following Gray's death, it was impossible not to draw parallels with similar cases. Every month that summer—sometimes every week—a new video appeared that raised awareness about the ways Black people are disproportionately hurt and killed by police in the United States. One example was Eric Garner, a 43-year-old African American man who died following an interaction with the New York City police. In a cell phone video taken by a friend of Garner's, a plainclothes police officer is shown attempting to arrest Garner on account of selling single cigarettes. "Every time you see me," Garner can be heard saying, "you want to mess with me. I'm tired of it . . . every time you see me you want to harass me."[36] After unsuccessfully attempting to place him in hand-cuffs, the officer placed Garner in a choke hold, eventually pushing his face into the sidewalk. "I can't breathe," Garner said multiple times before falling unconscious and dying on his way to the hospital.

Instances such as these remind us that social context plays a key factor in our exposure to stress and violence.[37] The Centers for Disease Control and Prevention reports that Black people are four times as likely as White people to die because of an encounter with law enforcement.[38] While experiencing police violence is one particular example of trauma, it reflects a larger pattern of violence in society that targets particular groups of people. Based on his own words, Garner had been the focus of unwanted and unwarranted police attention before.[39]

Understanding the social context of trauma is a central part of trauma-informed work. It's one thing to quote trauma statistics, but it's another thing to understand how systems of oppression influence people's experience of harm. Some of you will have firsthand knowledge of this based on your own life experience or study. Others—and I include myself here—have been more sheltered from oppression. We'll have been handed unearned privileges that keep us from seeing and validating the impacts of oppression and systemic trauma. We will have been conditioned to think about trauma as an individual tragedy instead of an event that's interconnected to larger systems of domination that shape our world. All of us must educate ourselves on the impacts of oppression, the onus being on those of us with more privilege.

Our experience of natural disasters will also be shaped by our social context. One painful example was the catastrophic flooding of New Orleans after Hurricane Katrina. The racialization of survivors' experiences was undeniable: Black evacuees, some in wheelchairs or with babies, were turned back to the toxic floodwaters by police who fired over their heads to keep them from finding safety in Gretna—a majority White suburb. Even our experiences of weather don't happen in a vacuum. Realizing this isn't a matter of being politically correct; it is a way to build trust, safety, and accountability across our different lived realities. Without this realization, we are living in virtually separate worlds and cannot bridge our realities.

The importance of social context is especially evident with interpersonal trauma.[40] If you're a woman in the United States, for instance, you're four times more likely than a man to be stalked by an intimate partner,[41] and fourteen times more likely to experience an attempted rape.[42] These risks are elevated as a woman if you're poor or a person of color.[43] If you're transgender, you're ten times more likely than a cis-gender man to experience sexual violence.[44] And if you're born with a disability, the odds are 80% that you'll experience sexual violence at least once in your life; 40% of disabled people experience more than 10 incidents of sexual abuse in their lifetimes.[45]

Racism adds another dimension to trauma. Native Americans are twice as likely as any other group to experience rape or sexual assault.[46] Black and Hispanic people have been found to have higher rates of trauma exposure than Whites,[47] with factors such as racism contributing to this disparity.[48] Class and income also impact our exposure to trauma: in a 2014 report, the World Health Organization found that across the globe, "people from poorer economic backgrounds have higher rates of death from injury and non-fatal injuries than wealthier people."[49] Researchers attributed this discrepancy to several factors, including the fact that low-income people are forced into taking unsafe work, have less access to emergency trauma care, and are less able to afford the costs of rehabilitation treatment and lost wages.

What I've tried to convey here is that trauma is both prevalent and political. We live inside of social and economic structures that are designed to respect and create safety and opportunity for some groups, while systematically disregarding others. This is a "power over" model that shapes all of our lives and perspectives, even when we have altruistic intentions. Each of us has to do the internal and external work of becoming conscious of these different systems in order to conduct trauma-sensitive work.

BACK IN THE CLASSROOM

Let's go back to RJ. At the end of his class, RJ returned from the bathroom where he'd been trying to distract himself from the flashbacks of his sister. As students filed out, RJ was approached by Marc, the class's mindfulness teacher. He asked RJ if he had a few minutes to talk.

Feeling he had little to lose, RJ opened up. He talked candidly about the death of his sister, including his experience in meditation. Marc was touched to hear this story and had been unaware RJ was in so much pain. Marc told RJ that he himself had lost his sibling to cancer a few years earlier, and that mindfulness had helped him through that period. It allowed him to be present with his grief rather than push it away.

After sharing his own experience with RJ, Marc asked him if he'd like to try a guided meditation. He could understand why the general meditations had been triggering, and wanted to offer RJ something that might help him manage the pain. RJ nodded, and Marc asked him to close his eyes and report what he noted. RJ said that he could see his sister's face, and that he could also feel a churning in his stomach. "See if you can stay curious about both of those things," Marc said. "Try investigating them with kindness, and just let yourself breathe and relax."

RJ opened his eyes abruptly after a few minutes. He felt scared, he said. "Of course," Marc empathized. "It's great you can notice that. See if you can just allow the fear to be there, without judgment."

RJ closed his eyes, but a minute later reopened them again. When he paid any attention to the fear, it seemed to grow worse and threatened to overtake him. It felt like too much for him to handle.

Looking up at Marc, RJ sank into embarrassment. He couldn't even meditate when someone was helping. He felt helpless and broken, apologizing to Marc as he reached for his bag.

Marc leapt up before RJ could leave. He reassured him that with time it would get easier. He was here to support him, whatever he needed.

RJ kept his eyes downcast and thanked Marc. Mostly, he just wanted to be alone. Outside the classroom, he reached into his backpack and pulled out his headphones. Even though it pained him to see them, he'd held on to them as a way to remember his sister.

OBSTACLES TO INTEGRATION

As a reminder, we can look at the aftermath of trauma in two ways: through the spectrum of diagnostic descriptions or through the lens of integration. For a moment, let's come back to integration. Why is it that some people become stuck in traumatic symptoms, while others are able to integrate a traumatic experience?

This is the million-dollar question with trauma. If we had a clear answer, we'd be much more successful at helping people heal from PTSD. In Chapter 4, I'll describe how trauma affects the brain and body, and the ways neurophysiology offers us important insights about integration. But here are two factors that are immediately relevant to trauma-sensitive mindfulness.

The first is fear. Trauma can make us terrified of our internal experience. Traumatic events persist inside survivors in the form of petrifying sensations and emotions. Understandably, survivors become afraid to feel these again. Van der Kolk described it this way:

> Traumatized people . . . do not feel safe inside—their own bodies have become booby-trapped. As a result, it is not OK to feel what you feel and know what you know, because your body has become the container of dread and horror. The enemy who started on the outside is transformed into an inner torment. (Emerson & Hopper, 2011, p. xix)

This is one of the most haunting, visceral costs of trauma: being forced to continually cope with gut-wrenching—often terrifying—sensations that live on inside.

Consider, then, what it means to ask a survivor to pay mindful attention to their internal experience. In all likelihood, they'll be brought face to face with unintegrated remnants of trauma: feelings of terror and helplessness, or disturbing memories and images. This isn't automatically a damaging experience, but it can quickly become overwhelming. Survivors are scared of their internal experience for a reason. As mindfulness practitioners, our best intentions can't ensure people can successfully navigate the minefield within them.

Take RJ's mindfulness teacher, Marc. Mindfulness had helped him when he'd lost his sibling to cancer, and it's logical that he extended his own experience of loss to RJ. But RJ was experiencing posttraumatic stress. The flashbacks, nausea, and desire to flee provided a clue. As a mindfulness teacher who didn't have an understanding of trauma, Marc couldn't recognize these symptoms, nor did he know how to respond to them effectively. RJ was afraid of what lived inside of him and needed more than what Marc could offer. Simply being mindful—either of his fear or the flashbacks—only intensified his distress.

A second barrier to integrating trauma is shame. Connected to humiliation, demoralization, and remorse, shame is a complex, debilitating emotion that often arrives with traumatic stress. A person who was sexually abused may berate themselves for not having fought back—even though they may know it would have made matters worse. A soldier who freezes under fire during combat is demeaned by others, and comes to feel fundamentally flawed. Someone who is discriminated against can internalize the form of oppression being directed at them and begin to feel defective and unworthy. Shame is a powerful, paralyzing force.

RJ felt shame in two primary ways. First, he blamed himself for his sister's death. He constantly entertained "what-ifs" about Michelle's accident and couldn't forgive himself for lending her his headphones. He felt at fault and disgusted with his perceived irresponsibility. RJ also felt ashamed about meditation practice, humiliated that he couldn't follow Marc's simple instruction. Nothing in his life was working, and he felt weak and hopeless. All of these feelings were barriers to integration.

In light of this shame, RJ needed something more than a guided meditation. He needed relationship. As I'll explore in Chapter 8, trauma survivors often recover and thrive in connection with others. While relationship isn't a panacea, it can—under the right conditions—help rebuild safety and trust. In the container of a safe relationship, we can also work skillfully with shame and forgiveness. Marc's empathy was somewhat constructive, but survivors need a close and consistent guide—someone who is trained in holding trauma. Helping someone be mindful of shame often isn't enough.

It's important for trauma-sensitive practitioners to respect the fear and shame that can endure in survivors. While it can be tempting to think of trauma as simply an intensely negative emotion, trauma is an incapacitating form of stress. It involves survival-based responses that correspond with the deepest aspects of our psychobiology. Playing fast and loose with trauma threatens people's sense of security and stability. Our role is to understand, as best we can, how mindfulness interacts with this. Doing so opens the door to recognizing trauma, responding to it effectively, and preventing retraumatization—in other words, offering mindfulness in a trauma-sensitive way.

CHAPTER 2

Meeting the Moment:
Mindfulness and Traumatic Stress

---

*The practice of meditation is not a passive, navel-gazing luxury
for people looking to escape the rigors of our complex world.
Mindfulness and meditation are about deeply changing ourselves
so that we can be the change that we see needed for the world.*
                                                           —Larry Yang

I'd been seeing Tara and Nick for five weeks, and therapy had been pro-
gressing well. Tara, an introverted lawyer, was learning to make direct
requests; Nick, an outgoing, stay-at-home parent, was working on managing his anger. Like other couples I'd seen, the birth of their son, Connor,
four years earlier had placed significant pressure on their relationship.
They'd been fighting more frequently, watching more television, and
recently had stopped having sex. In sessions, they'd been able to confront
these issues with kindness—even humor now and again. But today something different palpably hung in the air.

"Do you want to start?" Tara asked Nick. It was more a statement
than a question. Nick nodded, staring into his glass of water. The night
before, he began, the entire family had been emotionally frayed. Tara was
overwhelmed by her caseload at work, Connor had been throwing tan-
trums all day, and the three of them had been passing around a cold for
weeks. At dinner, Connor fussed in his chair and was refusing to eat. Nick

became impatient, grabbing Connor's fork and holding it firmly in front of his face. Connor then let out a scream, picked up his plate, and threw it at Nick.

With spaghetti streaming down his shirt, Nick erupted. He stood up and threw a glass of water across the room, shattering it on the wall. Connor burst into tears as Tara recoiled sharply, and Nick made a quick retreat to his bedroom—dizzy, irate, and baffled by what had just taken place.

Sitting across from me, Nick and Tara were clearly shaken. Nick had lost his temper with Connor before, but he'd never been physically threatening. Tara was overwhelmed by the thought of needing to protect herself and Connor from her husband. "I feel like I've broken trust with my family," Nick said, leaning back into the couch and exhaling deeply.

With Tara triggered and Nick awash in shame, a new kind of conversation became possible. Crises like this often reveal issues that have been brewing under the surface. As if he couldn't hold the words in any longer, Nick started to open up about his traumatic past. He described growing up with a physically violent father who'd served in the Vietnam war. In his childhood, Nick and his younger brother would hide in the bathroom when their father returned home from work. If the front door closed gently, they'd emerge and greet him. If it slammed shut, they'd remain in hiding. Life was most unpredictable at the dinner table if his father had had a few drinks. There the blows came without warning.

Nick went on to say that he'd recently been experiencing flashbacks. Knowing that Connor was approaching the same age he was when facing the worst of his father's abuse, Nick was being flooded by images of the violence he had experienced: the image of his drunk father appearing in the hallway, or his brother's terrified face when they were hiding in the bathroom. He also felt a pervasive knot in his abdomen—a feeling that had been there since the beatings as a boy. Chronically edgy and agitated, he'd also been binge-watching television and drinking more than usual. By the end of our session, we'd all agreed that I would see Nick individually in the weeks that followed. Tara had already planned a trip with Connor to see her parents, and Nick was in search of strategies to help navigate these internal storms.

The first resource I offered Nick was mindfulness. With guidance, Nick began utilizing mindfulness to observe and tolerate the rage and terror that remained trapped inside. If a wave of intense anger rose up, he learned to stay present with the physical sensations rather than judge or avoid them. He also noticed that the feelings were shifting all the time—that they weren't as ingrained as he thought. Sometimes, the sensations and emotions even diminished to the point that he could take a deep breath and relax. With practice, Nick started to bring a quality of curiosity and compassion to his experience rather than reprimand himself, as he'd done for years. He realized that beneath his anger lay a scared, young part of himself that had been overwhelmed by the violence in his family.

Three weeks in, I asked how Nick felt about the mindfulness practices we'd been doing in sessions. "Whatever it takes," he responded, welling up with tears. "Connor means 'strong willed' in Irish, and he's definitely that kind of kid. But he doesn't deserve what I went through. I want the violence passed down through my family to end with me."

TRAUMA AND MINDFULNESS

Mindfulness is a power of mind that helps us recognize what's happening, without added commentary or judgment. It involves maintaining a moment-by-moment awareness of various aspects of our experience, including thoughts, body sensations, and feelings. As Nick experienced, it's a faculty that can help us be present with our inner world—even if what we find there is devastating.

Mindfulness is also a social trend. Originally utilized by Brahmans to memorize Vedic scriptures—and later by Buddhist monks seeking enlightenment—mindfulness has more recently been adopted into mainstream consumer culture. From classrooms to corporations, mindfulness is being practiced by a wide array of people—at times being marketed as a quick-fix solution to stress. Inside of this context, it can end up being difficult to speak about mindfulness without sounding smug or pretentious.

The instruction to "just be mindful" can seem dismissive of someone's legitimate distress and pain.

This is especially true with trauma. If we're not discerning, the invitation to be mindful can ride roughshod over trauma-based dread and shame. I've received countless e-mails from survivors who—despite actively struggling with traumatic symptoms—continued receiving the same counsel from mindfulness teachers who didn't have a strong understanding of trauma: take it back to the cushion. Keep practicing meditation. These teachers weren't lacking compassion, but in my view were underestimating the intensity of unintegrated trauma—and overstating the benefits of mindfulness.

At worst, mindfulness can also come across as elitist. Spoken of in hushed and harmonic tones—especially by someone with more privilege—mindfulness teachings can end up sounding condescending and entitled. They can end up unintentionally dismissing the complex realities of trauma and oppression. In my research, I heard stories from survivors whose experiences of systemic forms of trauma—of unrelenting homophobia or sexism, for instance—were ignored or brushed aside. They were encouraged to use mindfulness as a way to forgive others, open their hearts to the world, and simply accept things as they are. Again, these teachers didn't mean to cause harm. But they inadvertently discounted someone's experience of systemic oppression and missed out on an opportunity to acknowledge and address injustice.

At the same time, mindfulness can be an essential resource for survivors. Practiced with discernment, it can increase one's capacity to integrate trauma. As I'll demonstrate in this chapter, it does this by enhancing *self-regulation*—the ability to control our emotions, thoughts, and behavior. Whereas trauma is a dysregulating experience—often leaving us feeling disconnected from our bodies and out of control—mindfulness can help us regain a sense of agency. We practice focusing our attention, attuning with ourselves, and navigating our ever-changing emotional world. Using Nick's story as an example in this chapter, I'm going to focus specifically on the ways mindfulness and self-regulation can help survivors.

For those of us offering mindfulness to others, I believe it's helpful to know the benefits of mindfulness in relation to trauma. But in covering this material, I'm not intending to equip you to undertake trauma therapy. In fact, I want to dissuade you from thinking that mindfulness practice alone can heal trauma. As mindfulness practitioners, we need to resist the idea that mindfulness is a cure-all, or that we automatically know best. Instead, I believe our task is to respect the potency and complexity of trauma, and to learn what we can do to serve our students and clients who are facing it. This involves educating ourselves on the many dimensions of trauma—biological, psychological, and social—and the ways they intersect with mindfulness. Given the high prevalence of trauma I covered in the last chapter, this kind of self-education is central to offering mindfulness in a safe and transformative way.

DEFINING MINDFULNESS

Mindfulness is a modern translation of the word *sati* in Pali—a language native to India spoken during the time of the Buddha. The term has several meanings, including *presence of mind, memory,* and *clear awareness.* The definition of mindfulness I'll use comes from Jon Kabat-Zinn, a biologist whose pioneering research into the role of mindfulness in stress reduction paved the way for its remarkable popularity. Kabat-Zinn defined mindfulness as "paying attention in a particular way: on purpose, in the present moment, and non-judgmentally" (1994, p. 4).

Let's unpack this definition in the context of individual forms of trauma.

Purposeful Attention

The first component of mindfulness is *paying purposeful attention.* This means learning to intentionally direct and sustain our attention. It's akin to shining a flashlight in a dark room: without mindfulness, the light of our attention drifts randomly from corner to corner. With mindfulness, we can steady our flashlight on particular spots. This might involve paying attention to sensations connected to our breath, or observing a thought or emotion. Purposeful, mindful attention helps steady the wandering mind.

Traumatic stress has a wide range of effects on attention. People with posttraumatic stress will often reflexively track for trauma-relevant stimuli in their environment—particular sounds, smells, or sights associated with a traumatic experience. Nick became anxious around any man that looked like his father, for instance, as his body would brace. This is one reason mindfulness can be so powerful in the context of trauma: with practice, survivors can learn to direct their attention in purposeful ways that help support stability. Rather than being left at the mercy of their attention, they can steady their flashlight and regain a sense of agency and control.

In the Present Moment

The second element of Kabat-Zinn's definition of mindfulness is paying attention *in the present moment*. We practice grounding our attention in the here and now rather than becoming lost in thoughts about the past or the future. This, in fact, is the only moment we have—an "ongoing wave of passing time" (Gunaratana, 2011, p. 134). As Buddhist teacher Sylvia Boorstein wrote, "Mindfulness is the aware, balanced acceptance of present experience. It isn't more complicated than that. It is opening to or receiving the present moment, pleasant or unpleasant, just as it is" (1995, p. 60).

For survivors, the present moment is often rife with reminders of the past. As Nick experienced, unintegrated fragments of trauma—disorienting thoughts, agonizing memories, or vexing physical sensations—can encroach into one's field of awareness at any moment. These intrusions can cause survivors to experience the present moment through the lens of a painful history. With mindfulness, however, survivors can learn to keep their attention grounded in the present. As trauma specialist Babette Rothschild wrote in *The Body Remembers, Volume 2: Revolutionizing Trauma Treatment*, "The present-moment focus of mindfulness is an obvious natural antidote for PTSD, a condition where the mind and body of the trauma survivor are continually wrenched into memories of a terrifying past" (2017, p. 166). Of course, this doesn't make trauma recovery easy, nor does it avoid potential complications—something Rothschild herself notes. But learning to stay rooted in the present while reexperiencing an unintegrated element of trauma is an essential skill within trauma recovery.

Nonjudgmental Attention

The third component of mindfulness is *nonjudgmental attention*. This means bringing an attitude of curiosity and acceptance to our present-moment experience. Rather than judge or dismiss the mood we're in or memories we're having, we practice remaining open and inquisitive. This doesn't imply that we need to abandon critical thinking or adopt a laissez-faire attitude. Instead, we can utilize mindfulness to become less reactive and open the door to what's actually happening in our world. "Whatever experience we may be having," Buddhist monk Bhante Gunaratana wrote, "mindfulness just accepts it. . . . No pride, no shame, nothing personal at stake—what is here is there" (2011, p. 133).

Nonjudgmental attention can be a great challenge for survivors. As discussed, trauma of all kinds often creates shame and self-judgment. Survivors can come to believe they're to blame for their trauma, or that they're broken and unable to heal. Research has shown that the more severe their trauma symptoms, the more likely survivors are to engage in self-critical behavior.[1] While survivors may experience justified anger, resentment, or even rage toward the people or institutions that inflicted harm on them, it's more common for survivors to turn the force of their emotions inward.

Mindfulness offers a way to work with the judging mind. When survivors can meet their experience with curiosity—even self-compassion—they open the door to investigating the past and present with an open heart and mind. In one session with Nick, I suggested that he put his hand on the place where he felt rage, letting himself be curious about the

29

sensations and emotions that lived there. He often berated himself for having these feelings—as if he was to blame for the childhood abuse. But with mindfulness, he started directing more love and compassion toward himself as opposed to frustration and judgment, which opened the door to a more stable, balanced life. He rested his hand on his abdomen for a minute, taking a breath and softening his forehead.

SELF-REGULATION

The above three-part definition of mindfulness has appeared in hundreds of research studies examining the effects of mindfulness. In general, results have been positive: mindfulness has been shown to help treat a variety of conditions, including anxiety and depression, chronic pain, and eating disorders.[2] It has also been shown to improve mental and physical health overall. But reading through these findings, a natural question emerges: What is it that makes mindfulness so powerful? Why is mindfulness potentially as beneficial as, say, rigorous exercise, or taking a particular kind of medication?

In attempting to answer these questions, it quickly becomes apparent that mindfulness is difficult to operationalize—that is, to distinguish its components in a way that we can measure its effects. As mindfulness researchers Kathleen Corcoran, Norman Farb, Adam Anderson, and Zindel Siegel surmised, "Although the benefits of mindfulness practice are generally accepted, the specific mechanisms and processes that operate in their attainment are largely unknown" (2009, p. 339). Despite this, researchers have tried to isolate individual components of mindfulness for study: reduced arousal, for instance, or a more accepting attitude. One project even set up a "sham" meditation to control for certain variables, examining whether one's posture was correlated with benefits or the relationship with a skilled meditation teacher.[3] Researchers are still trying to decipher what it is that makes mindfulness so powerful.

The concept I want to highlight in this discussion is the notion that mindfulness is a process of enhanced self-regulation.[4] Psychology professors Joan Littlefeld Cook and Greg Cook defined self-regulation as "the ability to monitor and control our own behavior, emotions, or thoughts, altering them in accordance with the demands of the situation" (2005, p. 36). It's what helps us be self-responsive to the moment, whether putting on a sweater when we're cold to walking out of a movie because we're feeling overly disturbed. With mindfulness, researchers have suggested our ability to self-regulate is heightened, ultimately enabling us to respond to the world in flexible and adaptive ways.

Consider that people experiencing posttraumatic stress often have difficulty feeling in control. Constantly bombarded by disturbing thoughts, memories, and unbearable sensations, they find themselves behind the wheel of a ship they cannot effectively steer. With mindfulness, however, survivors can theoretically regain some agency, utilizing mindful attention to work skillfully with difficulty. They can observe and tolerate their inner world, and investigate thoughts and emotions with compassion rather than habitually avoid them. Those of us working as trauma-sensitive practitioners can also utilize mindfulness to be present with trauma in all its forms—both individual and systemic. Through enhanced self-regulation, we can more effectively tolerate the stories we bear witness to—whether it's the meditation student whose family member is being threatened with deportation, or the client facing memories of sexual abuse in their family. Mindfulness can support people experiencing trauma symptoms, including those who work with survivors.

Based on emerging neuroscience research, which I'll cover in Chapter 4, mindfulness has been proposed to support self-regulation in three particular ways: the regulation of attention, body awareness, and emotional regulation (see Figure 2.1).[5] To explore the relevance of these components to trauma, let's return to the case of Nick.

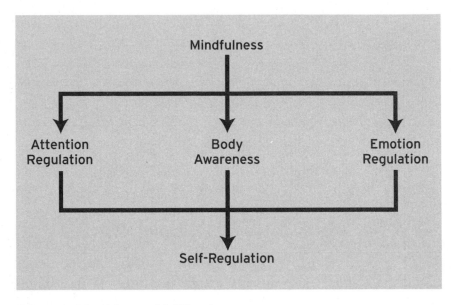

Figure 2.1. Mindfulness and Self-Regulation

ATTENTION REGULATION

While Tara and Connor were away visiting family, Nick was struggling alone at home. He kept replaying the memory of throwing a glass against the wall, and he couldn't escape the powerful ball of heat in his stomach. For Nick, these images and sensations were like a tractor beam, continually pulling his attention away from the present. At night when he'd crawl into bed, his mind would race for hours, churning over memories of his father and his fears about hurting Connor. He'd turn on the light and try to distract himself by reading a book, but he was exasperated. Beneath everything lay a sense of turmoil that refused to go away.

As I referred to earlier, people with posttraumatic stress often struggle with their attention. They're continually faced with traumatic reminders that come in the form of memories, sensations, and emotions. Before we started working together, Nick's attention was habitually and unconsciously drawn toward traumatic reminders that left him frustrated, overwhelmed, and out of control. He was constantly distracted and on edge. "I'm always checking my phone," he said, "distracting myself with random news clips I don't want to be watching. If I'm not doing that, I'm left with shitty memories and the feeling that I'm not okay."

With some guidance from me, Nick began working more purposefully with his attention. With the goal of supporting his stability and self-regulation, he began learning to use his attention like a flashlight, directing it to stimuli that helped him feel in control. Sometimes this would be an internal sensation that grounded him physically, like the pressure of his back against the sofa. Other times he paid attention to the fluttering leaves of a tree in the sun outside, learning to recognize the feelings of aliveness and warmth that arose in response to the scene. He was amazed to discover that where he directed his attention had a profound impact on his emotional state. "I didn't realize I've been focusing on things that scare me," Nick said. "I'm realizing how much I need to actually work with my mind."

BODY AWARENESS

The first time I asked Nick to pay mindful attention to his body, he shot me a confused look. "Why would you want me to do that?" he asked. "What I feel in my body is rage. Feeling that might cause me to throw a glass again."

Nick's avoidance of his body was an understandable strategy. It felt like a way to keep the overwhelming, unintegrated elements of trauma at bay. He'd cut his body out of his awareness in an attempt to manage his emotions. But by avoiding trauma-based sensations, he also became more vulnerable to suddenly being overwhelmed by them. Without warning, they'd take him over. The night he'd thrown the glass, he'd been avoiding the rage that had been building in his abdomen and chest all day.

Nick understood firsthand the way trauma is experienced through the body. Instead of being a place of refuge, the body is often the enemy for survivors. As trauma specialists David Emerson and Elizabeth Hopper wrote, "survivors experience an ongoing battle within their bodies. . . . They perceive their bodies as hurting them, because when they become conscious of the messages from their bodies, many of these messages express a sense of injury" (2011, p. 21–23). As a result of this, survivors often pull awareness away from sensations as an understandable way to cope with pain.

Mindfulness and meditation run counter to this tendency. They increase our awareness of subtle body sensations, which can have several benefits for survivors. First, they can help us connect with information about our moods, needs, or desires. When I worked with Nick, he discovered a myriad of signs that told him his stress was mounting—a tension behind his eyes, for example, or a sudden stream of frustrated thoughts. In the quiet of my office, Nick began turning his attention inside as if he were in a laboratory. These moments were humbling to witness, watching someone who'd avoided his inner world suddenly venture inside it. He discovered that the sensation of his feet on the ground made him feel more grounded and confident. Alternately, he found that if he focused too much attention on his stomach, he became overwhelmed. Simply paying attention to his body was a radical act for Nick.

Increased body awareness can also help survivors experience the fact that physical sensations are always changing. An exhale would shift the tension in Nick's stomach slightly, reminding him that his inner world was transient instead of fixed. Posttraumatic stress can convince us that we're stuck, and noticing even the subtlest movements can open up a new possibility—that we can be present with the thing that has scared us for so long. What was assessed as terrifying and unworkable becomes more possible to be present with.

With time and practice, Nick found that he could tolerate more discomfort, knowing that the troubling sensations inside would eventually shift—even if only slightly.* He moved out of a place of powerlessness and hopelessness and into one of possibility. "Damn," he said one session, opening his eyes wide after a mindfulness exercise. "I can actually

---

* In Chapter 4, I'll discuss the relationship between trauma-sensitive mindfulness and the four foundations of mindfulness as described in Buddhist teachings. This moment with Nick, for instance, is an example of the second foundation of mindfulness, *vedanā*, which refers to the range of pleasant, unpleasant, and neutral sensory experiences we can be mindful of.

feel this fireball in my stomach without it scaring the hell out of me. It actually settles down a bit when I'm able to just be with it." Nick's buoyancy was building; he was engaging his body in a new way. Up to this point, Nick had felt largely at the mercy of his trauma. He'd either been dissociating from his inner world or was overwhelmed by it. Now, he was starting to come more directly into relationship with it.

EMOTIONAL REGULATION

Two months after we'd started our individual work, Nick intercepted a wave of extreme agitation at home. He and Tara were on the couch having a discussion about whether they should have a second child, and Nick suddenly became triggered. He felt his face flush with heat and his heart rate begin to soar. Memories then flooded in: the image of his father slapping his younger brother, for example. The helplessness and terror he felt inside began to engulf him, and an internal narrative of self-blame took over: "I couldn't protect him; I couldn't protect him."

Nick stood up and walked to the window. Concentrating on the feeling of his feet on the ground, he was able to stay present—even curious—about what was happening. After a few breaths, he realized that he was feeling terrified. His churning stomach and anxious stream of thoughts had given it away. Noticing this, his desire to yell diminished, and he turned around and went back to Tara. "I want to talk about this," he said softly, meeting her eyes. "And, I'm also afraid. I suddenly started thinking of my father and what it means to have a bigger family. I'm scared of the pressure and just need a bit of time to work this through." Tara stood up and gave him a hug. She had endless patience when he could communicate this way.

Nick's progress reflects the connection between mindfulness and emotional regulation—our ability to influence how we experience our emotions and how they are expressed. We can do this in many ways, from deciding where we'll direct our attention to taking a deep, calming breath. All of these adjustments affect how we experience and express our emotions—and, by extension, how we experience life. Research has confirmed that mindfulness supports emotional regulation in multiple ways. By virtue of paying close, nonjudgmental attention to their inner world, people who practice mindfulness are more self-responsive to their own emotions, and can even have less emotional exhaustion.[6] Mindfulness also increases the capacity to be present with challenging emotions and thoughts without overreacting.[7] We practice recognizing our emotional state and responding to it with choice instead of reactivity.

In addition to these three components of mindfulness—attention regulation, body awareness, emotional regulation—there are two additional benefits of mindfulness for survivors that I'll introduce through Nick's story: dual awareness and exposure. These two benefits are a kind of emotional regulation but warrant their own explanations.

DUAL AWARENESS

When you're suffering under the weight of traumatic stress, it's hard to focus on anything else. Barraged by disturbing memories, gut-wrenching physical sensations, and traumatic reminders in the external world, survivors can end up hyperfocusing on stimuli that come to dominate their world. Think about a time you sprained an ankle or stubbed a toe, for instance. I'll bet that most of your focus was on the throbbing pain. For survivors, something similar happens. They come to fixate exclusively on particular stimuli. This could be a specific sound or smell that triggers an overwhelming sense of danger. Our attention is suddenly—and then continually—pulled in the direction of threat. When this happens, the present moment is experienced through the lens of trauma. Attention becomes myopic.

This is why dual awareness—the ability to maintain multiple perspectives at the same time—is such an important skill for survivors. Imagine a time when you were struggling with a difficult feeling, for instance, but could keep some perspective. Perhaps you became indignant after a driver cut you off, but laid off the horn because you had a sleeping child in the backseat. This is what survivors need when they're working with unintegrated trauma. They need to be able to pay attention to demanding stimuli while maintaining some awareness of a larger context. If they're having a flashback, they need to know they're reexperiencing a trauma from the past in the present moment instead of actually being there. This can give them just enough space to avoid continual overwhelm.

Let's come back to Nick. As he talked about his father, Nick's heart began racing uncontrollably. A minute later he couldn't focus on anything else. His breathing became rapid, he couldn't make eye contact, and he felt overwhelmingly scared and unsafe. He was back in time, in a situation that was terrifying. I asked Nick to look around the room and name different objects—the painting on my office wall, the bookshelf in the corner, the succulent by the window. This is an orienting technique intended to return survivors to the present. I then encouraged him to notice that his father was not in the room. Once he did this, I had Nick complete a series of sentences to help support his dual awareness. "Right now," Nick eventually said, "I'm feeling afraid and sensing my heart beating fast because I'm thinking of my father. At the same time, I'm looking around and see that there is no imminent danger to me in this moment."* Eventually he made eye contact with me and I could see that he'd returned. He knew he was in the present moment and that he'd been having a flashback. "This is what I experience at home," he said, "but I never get to stop and realize what's actually happening."

In her description of dual awareness, Rothschild distinguishes between the *observing self* and the *experiencing self*. The experiencing self is our internal sense of trauma—for survivors, often the stark, visceral signs of traumatic stress.[8] Nick's experiencing self was alarmed, with his heart racing and his breath shallow and rapid. The observing self, meanwhile, has some distance from an experience. We witness what's happening rather than becoming overwhelmed by it. Nick's observing self had come back online when he realized what was happening. He knew

---

* These are prompts from a protocol to halt flashbacks developed by Babette Rothschild (2000) that I'll return to in Chapter 5 to show you how to utilize.

that he wasn't in front of his father, but was in my office having a traumatic memory.

Mindfulness strengthens the observing self, and by extension, one's capacity for dual awareness. With practice, survivors can learn to witness their experience without becoming identified with it. By maintaining awareness of two things at the same time—and with the help of a skilled guide—they can experience traumatic stimuli while keeping one foot planted firmly in the present moment.

EXPOSURE

Left to our own devices, we typically move away from pain and toward what is pleasurable. It's a habitual, deeply wired response. But part of practicing mindfulness is deliberately exposing ourselves to whatever is happening in our field of awareness, both pleasant and unpleasant. Whether we're daydreaming about our next meal or feeling a sharp pain in our shoulder, we stay present. We let ourselves be impacted by whatever is happening—right here, right now. For many beginning meditators, this can seem counterintuitive, but mindfulness works differently. We practice turning toward what is arising instead of away from it.

Some writers have drawn parallels between this process and *exposure therapy*—a popular behavioral therapy technique developed to help people confront fear.[9] Developed by Edna Foa, a professor who specializes in the treatment of anxiety, exposure therapy involves exposing a client to a particular stimulus with the goal of overcoming excessive fear.[10] As with mindfulness, people are encouraged to face what is difficult. Someone who is afraid of dogs may practice imagining—or actually being exposed to—a dog. This often takes place on a continuum, where someone starts by imagining a dog, looking at pictures, and working their way toward *in vivo exposure*, which means directly facing a feared object, situation, or activity in real life.

Exposure therapy is one of the most frequently studied approaches to the treatment of PTSD. Research has shown it to be effective in treating PTSD, but the field is also controversial: dropout rates tend to be high, and only a third of participants who complete research studies show some improvement in their trauma symptoms.[11] Whether exposure therapy extinguishes trauma symptoms or simply blunts emotional sensitivity is also an important question.[12] What I want to point out here is that exposure plays a role in mindfulness practice, and can ideally expand one's tolerance for trauma-relevant stimuli that can help with integration.

At a playground one afternoon with Connor, Nick became triggered watching a father belittle his young son. Nick felt anger and fear well up in his stomach. He also felt an urge to walk over to the father and punch him in the face. But then Nick stopped. He took a breath and closed his eyes while sitting on the park bench. While the emotions and sensations were a lot to tolerate, they were bearable. "Stick with it," he told himself. "Don't run from these feelings."[13] He allowed himself to feel the heat in his stomach and the panic that was shooting through his shoulders. After a minute, he opened his eyes. He looked around the park and saw Connor playing happily. He felt shaken, but present. Mindfulness had seemingly increased his capacity to tolerate what were once excruciating feelings.

As I'll cover in Chapter 5, this kind of exposure is only useful when someone can tolerate what they're being exposed to. If Nick was mindful of his extreme anger and became overwhelmed by it, basic mindfulness instructions likely wouldn't have been the answer. He needed something different. But exposure can serve a constructive function for survivors when it's paired with mindfulness and a safe environment.

A DOUBLE-EDGED SWORD

Up until now, I've focused exclusively on the potential benefits of mindfulness for survivors. The three components of self-regulation—attention regulation, body awareness, and emotional regulation—and dual awareness and exposure all help increase our capacity to integrate trauma. But what about the risks of mindfulness, more generally? As I've alluded to, there are particular dangers embedded within mindfulness meditation practice that we need to be aware of when it comes to trauma.

To explore this, let's again return to Nick. Early one evening with Tara and Connor out visiting family, Nick sat down in his living room, wrapped himself in a blanket and decided to try solitary meditation. He started by following some basic instructions he'd found online: focus on his breath, and return there whenever his mind wandered. Ten minutes later, however, Nick was crawling out of his skin. He was being met by a series of familiar flashbacks of his father and the feeling he was in danger. He kept opening his eyes to confirm no one was there, but the troubling images would only return once he closed his eyes again.

Nick had been making progress with mindfulness. He was feeling increasingly compassionate toward himself and his family, and felt more in control of his life. He'd also expressed an interest in meditation, but given the intensity of his symptoms—his flashbacks, his intense anger—I'd suggested he hold off on any kind of solitary meditation practice. I wanted him to feel more stable before taking that step. But in Nick's mind, he was ready. He was convinced that more mindfulness practice could only lead to beneficial results. He also wanted to deepen his skills for the sake of his family.

Nick pressed on, committed to sticking it out despite the distress. He tried employing some of the practices we'd done in my office, shifting his attention in different ways. But he eventually realized he was stuck. Each minute he was spending in meditation was only ramping up his emotional activation. His breath was shallow, he was sweating, and he continued to have the feeling someone was about to hit him. Throwing his blanket across the room, he stomped into the kitchen filled with irritation. He cracked open a beer, turned on the television, and found himself flooded with shame.

Nick's experience reflects one of the traps of mindfulness for survivors: over-attending to traumatic stimuli. By paying mindful attention to what's predominant in their field of awareness, survivors naturally latch on to remnants of trauma. This can include upsetting flashbacks or particular sensations that connect to survival-based responses like fight or flight. It's hard to resist paying attention to these kinds of intense stimuli.

This can prove to be too much for survivors. To manage traumatic symptoms, people experiencing posttraumatic stress require more than basic mindfulness instructions to thrive. They need specific modifications to their mindfulness practice and, ideally, connection with a skilled trauma professional. Without this guidance, mindfulness meditation can become a setup for survivors. No matter how much sincerity they bring to their practice, they can end up being yanked into a vortex of trauma. They require tools to help them feel safe, stable, and having the ability to self-regulate.

A friend of mine told me a story that offers a metaphor for this issue. She'd taken a course in diving that trained students to respond to challenges underwater—running out of oxygen, for example, or one's mask popping off. Of all the different scenarios she might encounter, the most dangerous was becoming ensnared in a patch of seaweed. When this happens, the tendency for divers is to panic and make sudden, frantic movements. But this only makes matters worse. Struggling results in becoming even more enmeshed in the long tendrils of seaweed, leading to frightening—even deadly—consequences.

Trauma survivors who practice mindfulness can eventually find themselves in a patch of seaweed. By paying deliberate attention to their moment-to-moment experience, they naturally invite themselves into contact with traumatic stimuli—images or memories, or feelings of immobility and fury. These stimuli can unearth unspoken family secrets, legacies of traumatic violence, or any of the many other forms trauma can take. If survivors pay attention to their body and mind long enough, there's a good chance they will encounter the trauma that lives inside them.

This can be good news—*if* a survivor is adequately prepared. By becoming aware of traumatic stimuli, survivors can take a first step toward addressing it. But therein also lies a potential problem. If survivors find themselves in a patch of seaweed before they're equipped to work with traumatic stress, they can panic. Intrusive thoughts, physical symptoms, and unpredictable emotional reactions can ensnare and over-whelm them. Unless survivors have the tools to stabilize themselves and navigate their symptoms, they can become retraumatized and drown.

This isn't a new insight. Peter Levine wrote about it this way:

> To become self-regulating and authentically autonomous, trau-matized individuals must ultimately learn to access, tolerate, and utilize their inner-sensations. It would, however, be unwise to have one attempt a sustained focus on one's body without ade-quate preparation . . . Initially, in contacting inner sensations, one may feel the threat of a consuming fear of the unknown. Or, premature focus on the sensations can be overwhelming, poten-tially causing re-traumatization. (Levine, 2010, pp. 76–77)

This is why mindfulness is a double-edged sword when it comes to trauma healing. Direct, sustained contact with traumatic stimuli—without ade-quate preparation—locks survivors into a potentially debilitating loop. Mindfulness meditation can end up triggering traumatic symptoms that follow people into their lives. When this happens, it's easy for survivors to become discouraged or daunted. They might blame themselves for their distress and come to feel they are the problem. Sometimes they become hopeless and abandon mindfulness altogether. But in actuality, it is the way they're practicing mindfulness that is the problem.

This returns us to the seaweed metaphor. In my friend's course, being trapped in seaweed had a particular remedy: divers were taught to relax. Frantic, sudden movements only tighten the grip of the seaweed, often making things worse. Divers are also instructed to depend on others for help. Partnering with an individual or team is a regular safety practice with diving, improving people's chances of avoiding or surviving acci-dents. Both of these strategies extend to trauma. If we encounter trau-matic stimuli, fighting against ourselves only magnifies the intensity. In such moments, we need to learn how to self-regulate. Trauma survivors also need the guidance of skilled, compassionate teachers when they become caught in the weeds. We don't recover from trauma alone.

Given the high prevalence of trauma and the popularity of mindfulness, I believe we have a responsibility—as mindfulness practitioners—to be informed about how to work with survivors who become trapped in traumatic states. If we're unaware of the hazards mindfulness creates for survivors, we run the risk of people dysregulating or retraumatizing themselves under our care. But mindfulness can also be of enormous benefit to survivors and those bearing witness to trauma. Like Nick, it can change people's lives. This is why trauma-sensitive practice is so essential. The more we're informed about trauma, the more likely we can offer it in a way that's accessible to people who would benefit from its power. By offering an inclusive framework—along with particular, tailored modifications to help guide people's practice—we can help ourselves and our clients to face and integrate traumatic stress.

CHAPTER 3

Shaped by the Past:
A Brief History of Mindfulness and Trauma

History is not the past. It is the stories we tell about the past.
How we tell these stories—triumphantly or self-critically,
metaphysically or dialectally—has a lot to do with whether
we cut short or advance our evolution as human beings.
—Grace Lee Boggs

An understanding of psychological trauma
begins with rediscovering history.
—Judith Herman

Margaret was a social worker at a family services agency. A White, middle-class woman in her early forties, she'd grown up in a small Midwestern town where she worked. She loved her job, often traveling across the state to attend professional development workshops. Recently, she'd also registered for an online course about mindfulness after hearing about its benefits from a colleague. Believing it could help her practice, she began incorporating mini meditations into her sessions, and each morning felt inspired as she listened to a new mindfulness podcast on her way into work.

On a rainy Tuesday morning, Margaret met with Yvonne, a Black, middle-class woman in her mid-fifties who was seeking help for a series of panic attacks. Listening quietly as Yvonne told her story, she learned that the trouble had started six months earlier, after a new tenant moved into an apartment next to hers. He was a young, White college student in his senior year. The two had been friendly the first few weeks, saying hello when they passed in the halls. But one night this had changed.

It was close to 1:00 A.M., and the student was playing loud music adjacent to Yvonne's bedroom. Knowing she needed to be up early for work, Yvonne politely knocked on the wall before putting on her slippers to ring his doorbell. When the student appeared, Yvonne recoiled. He was shirtless and looking at her with disdain. When she explained the music was keeping her awake, he muttered something racist and slammed the door. Yvonne thought about calling the office manager or the police, but didn't trust that either would defuse the situation. She retreated to her apartment hoping this would be a one-time event.

But things grew worse in the coming months. The student continued to play his music loudly at night despite receiving complaints from other neighbors. He also whispered racial slurs under his breath when he passed Yvonne in the hall, playing innocent the one time she confronted him about it. At night, when she'd turn off her light and still hear him moving around, she felt a combination of rage and panic. She'd be flooded by memories of her lifetime's worth of experiences of racism— times she'd been harassed in particular neighborhoods or discriminated against when applying for apartments or jobs. Facing nightmares every time she fell asleep, she began binge-watching TV as a way to cope. Eventually she couldn't concentrate at work and stayed in at night out of fear of a confrontation. She'd lived in her apartment for 10 years, but began to consider moving out.

Then, unexpectedly, the neighbor left. Yvonne came home from work one evening to find his door open and contents emptied. She ordered celebratory take-out, left her front door ajar, and enjoyed the sunset. Part of her remained furious, but she was also relieved that she wouldn't have to deal with the neighbor again. She climbed into bed in anticipation of a good night's sleep and returning to a more normal life.

Yet her symptoms didn't go away. That first night, she lay in bed with her eyes open, braced for the sound of her neighbor. When she finally did fall asleep, the nightmares returned, and her insomnia persisted in the weeks that followed. She read magazines to distract herself, but she couldn't stop replaying scenes from the months prior. She'd reached out for help after having a few debilitating panic attacks at work.

When Yvonne fell silent, Margaret sat back in her chair. "That's terrible," she said, sighing heavily. "I'm so sorry you went through all that."

Yvonne nodded, awaiting a further response. But it didn't come. Margaret was actually having trouble relating to Yvonne's story. She felt empathic, but judgmental at the same time. Why hadn't Yvonne just ignored her neighbor, or put in earplugs at night? Why hadn't she asked other long-term tenants to join a protest to management? While the situation had been awful, why did it have such an intense—even traumatic—impact?

"Why don't we try a guided meditation?" Margaret asked, genuinely wanting to help and at a loss for other suggestions. "It's a way to help manage your stress, and it could help you with the panic attacks."

Yvonne paused. She'd heard good things about mindfulness and had come this far. She shrugged, figuring it couldn't hurt.

Adjusting her posture, Margaret asked Yvonne to close her eyes and pay attention to her breath. Yvonne immediately noticed that her heart was racing, clearly stirred up from having shared her story. A few minutes in, when Margaret directed her attention to her body, Yvonne found this made her even more anxious. She began to shift in her chair and a few times opened her eyes, appearing sensitive to the fluorescent lights. Seeing that Yvonne was having difficulty, Margaret encouraged her to continue being mindful. "Pay attention to your breath," she said, "and keep observing what's happening. Know that you are safe . . . safe in this office, and safe in this world. Mindfully rest yo—"

Yvonne's screeching chair interrupted Margaret's voice.

"I don't think this is working," Yvonne said, standing up and reaching for her coat.

Margaret's stomach sank. "Did I say something wrong?" she said as Yvonne opened the door.

"I can tell you're well intentioned," Yvonne replied in an exasperated voice. "But the world isn't safe for you and me in the same way. We both live in a very White town, and when I walk out this door, I have a very different experience from you. I'd need you to understand that if we were going to work together." Yvonne left, closing the door behind her.

Margaret was shocked, then embarrassed. The last thing she'd wanted to do was cause Yvonne more stress. She was someone who prided herself on being color-blind, and saw everyone as equal. She just didn't think much about race. But perhaps, she began to wonder, this was partly why the session had gone so poorly.

CONTEXTUALIZING TRAUMA AND MINDFULNESS

Why do we think about trauma and mindfulness the way we do? How does this inform the choices we make? And how can our understanding of the social conditions we—and our students and clients—have been shaped by help us to engage in powerful, accountable, trauma-sensitive work?

In this chapter, I'm going to explore the history of trauma and mindfulness in mainstream Western discourse—specifically the ways in which our contemporary definitions of both have been formed by the past. By studying history, we're offered a fuller understanding of ourselves and the domains in which we work. It allows us to critically examine the frameworks we've been offered, and be increasingly informed about our role. If we don't engage in this process, we run the risk of being less knowledgeable and effective.

Margaret offers one example of this. Because racial harassment wasn't a part of Margaret's definition of trauma, Yvonne's trauma was invisible to her. Based on her training, Margaret conceptualized trauma as a physically violent individual event, whatever the cause, and Yvonne had not been assaulted. But looked at through a different lens, Yvonne's traumatic experience makes more sense. Her earlier experiences of racism, and the ongoing social conditions of racial oppression, had amplified the threat she faced in one of the few places where she'd previously felt safe—her own home. Her foundational sense of security had been shaken, and the subsequent helplessness and isolation had exceeded her capacity for integration, creating symptoms of posttraumatic stress. Margaret had assumed an interpretation of "safety" that was not shared, and Yvonne's trauma had been largely invisible to Margaret.

This isn't meant to shame Margaret. Based on history—as well as our social context and prevailing cultural norms—we will simply be conditioned to perceive some people's experiences of suffering as traumatic, while others not. In her book *Trauma and Recovery*, Judith Herman (1997) explored this idea by examining the way that society's conceptualization of trauma arises out of a tension between two forces: political movements that call attention to particular forms of trauma, and systems that try to ignore, deny, and repress those violations. Women who experienced sexual violence, for instance, were historically silenced to the point of invisibility. They were blamed, shunned, hidden, rendered unmarriageable, or forced into marriage by rape. Yet the women's liberation movement of the 1970s challenged this. Through writing, research, and protest, the movement demanded that institutions—and by extension, the larger public—pay attention to the personal impact of sexual violence. By giving voice to women experiencing oppression, the movement helped legitimize a larger inquiry which ultimately changed mainstream definitions of trauma. And while these dynamics remain, our perception and understanding of trauma continue to change over time.

Margaret's understanding of mindfulness was also shaped by social and cultural context. Based on the popular versions of mindfulness she'd encountered, Margaret thought of mindfulness as a kind of quick fix for stress—a way to "calm down." The blog posts she read were often trying to sell mindfulness products, and they tended to overemphasize the benefits of meditation practice. Here the larger social context included a rich and complex history of religious and secular traditions, as well as capitalism. All of this influenced how Margaret thought about mindfulness and the way she'd offered it to Yvonne.

While this may be just one case of a mindfulness intervention gone awry, it's far from an isolated occurrence—RJ's teacher Marc being an example from Chapter 1. What's more, it's indicative of a larger issue. If we haven't explored the history of the traditions we're working with, we limit our effectiveness as practitioners. History adds depth and dimensionality to our work.

THE POLITICS OF TRAUMA

Through history, peoples and cultures have named and worked with trauma differently. Conceptions of both harm and health differ significantly over time, community, and place. In *Trauma and Recovery*, Herman identified three Western political movements that contributed to our current understanding of trauma: the nineteenth-century anticlerical movement in France, the antiwar organizing of veterans after the Vietnam War, and the women's movement of the 1970s. While these movements alone don't capture the full picture of how social movements have shaped this discussion, they do offer a window into the ways our contemporary orientation to trauma is influenced by historical events.

Let's begin with France. In the eighteenth and nineteenth centuries, Western medicine used the term *hysteria* to describe trauma. The word originates from the Greek word *hystera*, meaning uterus or womb. Hysteria was a gendered term, in this respect—a catchall diagnosis reserved exclusively for women. Symptoms included intense anxiety, insomnia, fainting, disturbances of vision and sleep, an inability to breathe, and muscle paralyses. The Catholic Church considered hysterical symptoms to be the "mark of the devil," an affliction that could "physically infect hundreds of others" (Herbermann, 1922, p. 545). It was also considered beyond the pale of serious science.

This changed with Jean-Martin Charcot. Widely regarded as the founder of modern neurology, Charcot undertook a wide-scale study of hysteria at the Salpêtrière—a famous Parisian hospital that, at the time of the French Revolution, was the largest in the world. Known partly for its massive infestation of rats, the Salpêtrière was a prison and asylum for people from the so-called lower orders: sex workers, poor people, and those labeled mentally and criminally insane. Charcot transformed this neglected institution into a renowned psychiatric facility, drawing ambitious—and later famous—students such as Pierre Janet and Sigmund Freud.

In Paris, Charcot presented his findings about hysteria in the form of weekly lectures. These gatherings, in which Charcot performed dramatic public examinations of his patients, were seen as theatrical events and were attended by a wide array of doctors, artists, and politicians. Charcot's approach was deeply objective and rationalist. He focused on neurological symptoms and had little interest in the inner lives of the women he treated. But his students—especially Freud and Janet—became obsessed with surpassing their teacher. Both wanted to discover the root cause of hysteria. In their quest, they adopted a revolutionary approach: they began *talking* to their female patients. As opposed to Charcot's more external focus, they studied hysteria by asking women questions about their lives. "For a brief decade," Herman wrote, "men of science listened to women with a devotion and respect unparalleled before or since" (1997, p. 12).

The political context in which this investigation took place is essential to understanding this story. Following the abdication of the Emperor Napoleon III in 1870, a struggle had emerged between traditional monarchists backed by the Catholic Church, and members of the French Third Republic, who advocated for science and secular democracy. Charcot, importantly, sided with the republic. As a prominent member of the emerging bourgeois, his work at the Salpêtrière—including his lectures—was partly a strategy to help undermine the monarchists as the church had dismissed hysteria as witchcraft. The anticlerical movement was providing a context to undertake a rigorous study of traumatic stress.

In their separate inquiries, Freud and Janet came to similar conclusions: hysteria was related to *actual traumatic events*. The women Freud and Janet interviewed had experienced repeated sexual assaults, incest, exploitation, and abuse. They were not malingerers, nor were they insane. They were traumatized.

Janet and Freud observed a division in the consciousness of these patients. A traumatic event had caused memories, physical sensations, or emotions to become split off and compartmentalized. It was these elements that then intruded back into their consciousness in disturbing and dysregulating ways. Janet referred to this phenomenon as *dissociation*: "Unable to integrate their traumatic memories," he wrote, "they seem to lose their capacity to assimilate new experiences . . . as if their personality has definitely stopped at a certain point" (1911, p. 532). This is one way to understand why Yvonne continued to have nightmares after her neighbor moved out. Unintegrated aspects of a traumatic experience kept intruding in the form of nightmares and panic attacks.

In the 1890s, Freud encountered a second, essential truth: sexual violence was endemic to women's lives. Working with wealthy Viennese families who could afford to send him patients for analysis, Freud heard repeated stories of sexual abuse, rape, and incest. These weren't the patients he treated at the Salpêtrière who were subject to unrelenting poverty and violence. These stories came from the bourgeois class. In a famous essay titled "The Aetiology of Hysteria," Freud put forward the claim that "at the bottom of every case of hysteria there are one or more occurrences of premature sexual experience" (1896, p. 203).

But this idea was unacceptable to the mainstream; the thesis too threatening to be rendered credible. Beyond the "pillars of society," most of Freud's medical colleagues pressured him to abandon this line of research. Absent a political context that could validate his claims— and given his own professional ambitions—Freud retreated. In the years following, he repudiated his theory. The truths he was speaking could not be received. Freud stopped listening to his female patients, leaving them once again silenced, ostracized, and repressed. Just as quickly as the door to the study of trauma and sexual violence had been opened, it slammed shut.

WAR AND TRAUMA

In the twentieth century, war drew the study of trauma back into the spotlight. Soldiers returned home from World Wars I and II with severe yet unexplained symptoms—flashbacks and paralysis, for instance. They would scream and weep uncontrollably, or become mute and unable to move. At first, these hysteria-like symptoms were thought to be entirely physical in origin. Civil War doctors had labeled the prevalence of nervous system and cardiac disorders *soldier's heart*. After the increased carnage and mechanization of warfare seen in the World Wars, terms such as *shell shock* and *combat exhaustion* appeared. It soon became evident that soldiers who weren't exposed to physical trauma also suffered from similar complaints. Under pressure to explain this phenomenon, medical experts began to acknowledge that the symptoms being exhibited by soldiers were not just physical, or made up. They were tied to extreme states of psychological distress.

Like women who'd been diagnosed with hysteria, these men were initially blamed for their condition. They were labeled weak, cowardly, and constitutionally inferior. U.S. General George Patton threatened to court-martial any "malingerers" suffering from combat fatigue. Traditionalist psychiatrists, Herman recounts, verbally shamed and physically abused soldiers who had developed trauma. Sometimes they subjected the soldiers to electric shocks.

But a group of more progressive medical professionals pushed back on this orientation. They argued that military trauma could occur to any person who was exposed to the horrors of combat. Psychiatrists who were influenced by Freud's psychoanalytic approach—famously named "the talking cure"—spoke respectfully with their patients to establish safety and trust. Their approach challenged the brutality of punitive treatments while advocating for more humane, relational forms of treatment. Over time, this work exposed the visceral impacts of combat trauma, including the unremitting terror soldiers experienced after returning home. By World War II, the American military establishment recognized that any soldier, no matter how valiant, could become traumatized.[1]

During this period, however, the study of combat neurosis was largely in the service of war. A primary goal of treatment was to return a soldier to combat. The military's incentive to have its psychiatrists provide empathetic listening was based on the higher success rates of this approach, which meant having a more deployable fighting force.

But this context changed following the Vietnam War. Unlike the so-called Great War, which had presumed the unified support of the nation, there was mass opposition to the Vietnam War both inside and outside the armed forces. Returning veterans were often suffering personally from their experiences at war, and many were also feeling sold out and unsupported by their government and fellow citizens. This painful rift also created the possibility for a powerful social movement to emerge. Veterans who felt abandoned organized not only to address their health and survival needs, but also to join and take leadership in the antiwar movement.

Through this powerful antiwar organizing effort, the study of trauma in service of the state was usurped by soldiers who had often been devastatingly impacted by a war they opposed. One of the most powerful organizing tools of the antiwar movement were "rap groups" formed across the United States. At these gatherings, returning soldiers were offered a forum to share their traumatic experiences, while also drawing public attention to the detriments of war. Because of this, a larger social context was created for the systematic study of trauma. In 1980, a group of soldiers with Vietnam Veterans Against the War successfully lobbied the American Psychiatric Association to create a new disorder reflecting their experiences—what eventually became known as PTSD. Psychological trauma became a "real" diagnosis, opening the gates to social legitimacy and continued research.

While I have focused here on two particular movements that have shaped mainstream definitions of trauma, I want to acknowledge that many scholars, activists, and healers with movements such as the American Indian Movement,[2] the Student Nonviolent Coordinating Committee of the Civil Rights Movement,[3] and the Healing Justice Initiative within Black Lives Matter[4] have been clear in their articulation of the traumatic impacts of colonization, genocide, and slavery. For those of us in the field of trauma-informed practice, this is part of our legacy as well.

THE WOMEN'S MOVEMENT

In the years leading up to the recognition of PTSD, a third political movement provided a context to once again study sexual trauma: the women's liberation movement of the 1970s in the United States. Often referred to as second-wave feminism, the movement focused on issues such as reproductive rights, domestic violence, equal pay, sexual assault, and entrenched legal inequalities—primarily for white women, as I'll discuss in a moment. Through writing, research, and collective action, the movement also helped reveal a striking fact: the most common form of trauma was not men's harrowing experience of war, but women's experience of sexual violence.

The women's movement challenged the idea that individual experiences can be understood outside of a social context. "The personal is political" became a central rallying cry.

The movement also challenged the shame, skepticism, contempt, and ridicule that women who spoke out about their experiences of sexual or domestic violence faced. The impact of sexism was designed to be borne in private. Race and economic class played a role in this as well, whereas class and race privilege tended to fence women more firmly into the privatized sphere of a nuclear family—with the concordant taboos around revealing one's personal life. For working-class and poor women, and for women of color, their options were often even more painfully limited when challenging sexual and domestic violence, facing more sources of institutional violence. This repression ensured that women stayed isolated while objectification and exploitation continued.

But the women's movement challenged this convention of secrecy. Like the rap groups formed by Vietnam veterans, feminists organized "consciousness-raising" groups to share their experiences of sexual and domestic violence—stories that held tremendous social stigma. Beyond individual healing, these groups aimed to create widespread social change. Women were encouraged to organize and take action together to challenge sexual oppression, and to "breach the barriers of privacy" (Herman, 1997, p. 29). Through speak-out groups and other organizing strategies, the public became increasingly aware of the issue of sexual violence. In 1975, the U.S. National Institute of Mental Health—in response to demands from the women's movement—created a center for researching the impact of rape. Large empirical studies in the 1980s revealed that sexual violence was indeed widespread: researchers found that one in four women had been raped in her lifetime, and one in three had been sexually abused in her childhood.[5]

Through interviews with survivors of rape, researchers also found that survivors were experiencing symptoms strikingly similar to combat trauma: nightmares, paralysis, dissociative episodes, flashbacks, intrusive thoughts, and extreme emotional distress. This investigation eventually expanded to include survivors of other forms of sexual assault, including children. Following the establishment of PTSD as a legitimate disorder, it became clear that symptoms experienced by survivors of sexual assault were similar to those of traumatized soldiers. After decades of study and advocacy, sexual violence was finally added as a core diagnostic criteria of PTSD in the DSM-5—115 years after Freud's recanted essay on women's experience of sexual violence.

This is no small thing. The DSM-5 definition of trauma has considerable impacts on people's lives, including who receives insurance coverage for trauma treatment. The definition also influences the public's perception of harm, including who is worthy of concern and care. As trauma-informed practitioners, we need to remember that institutional structures still commonly deny and repress trauma, and ignore or discount survivors. In Charcot's time, women with symptoms of sexual abuse were labeled insane. Soldiers returning home with traumatic symptoms a half century later were labeled dastardly and weak. Our definitions of trauma influence how we treat groups of people—both as a society and as individual practitioners.

It's important to note that as vital and innovative as the second-wave feminist movement was, scholars and activists have critiqued its centering of White, heterosexual women.[6] The movement marginalized the contributions of women of color, working-class women, and queer and transgender women, and adopted strategies that inadvertently perpetuated patriarchal and racist social structures. Third-wave feminism, which began in the 1990s, created an intersectional analysis that highlighted the interlocking nature of systems of oppression such as racism, sexism, homophobia, and classism.[7] The social and economic system we currently exist under concentrates wealth, dignity, and decision making in the hands of a few, and validates the harm and exploitation of others and the natural world. It's a type of "power over" system that depends on domination, violence, and extraction, and causes many forms of trauma. A third-wave feminist analysis invites us to center the experiences of the people and communities most impacted by oppression, and see the social and economic systems—as well as the solutions—through this lens.[8]

All of which leads us to our current historical moment. Who do we currently label as cowardly or "insane"? Whose experiences do we not listen to? What kind of harm do we ignore, repress, or label as unworthy of our collective attention? And who has the power to make these judgments in the first place?

TRAUMA TODAY

The Movement for Black Lives (M4BL) provides one powerful answer to these questions. Established in 2016, the M4BL network is made up of over 50 Black-led organizations including the Black Lives Matter national network. Through direct action, community organizing, campaigns, legal and policy work, writing, and other forms of resistance, organizations that make up the M4BL are calling direct attention to the systemic racism, violence, and ongoing trauma that Black communities face.

The M4BL is part of a movement that is creating the conditions for a deeper study of traumatic stress. A recent comprehensive report published by the McSilver Institute at New York University, for instance, details the traumatic impacts of racism and advocates for government-level policies and programs that target systemic racial oppression.[9] Dr. Joy DeGruy, author of the book *Post Traumatic Slave Syndrome*, has researched and documented the ways slavery has impacted African Americans through intergenerational trauma,[10] and Monica Williams has made a compelling case for an empirical investigation of the relationship between racism and trauma.[11] A recent wide-scale study also found that experiences of racial discrimination fuel generalized anxiety disorder—suggesting that the lived experience of racism may create lasting, cumulative effects that can lead to traumatic stress.[12] The study of systemic and intergenerational forms of trauma is on the rise.

As Herman shows us, such research can only flourish during a time of powerful anti-oppression organizing. Political movements create the container for truths to be told. "The study of war trauma," Herman wrote, "becomes legitimate only in a context that challenges the sacrifice of young men in war. The study of trauma in sexual and domestic life becomes legitimate only in a context that challenges the subordination of women and children" (1997, p. 9). Extending this argument, the study of trauma rooted in racial oppression becomes legitimate only in a context that challenges White supremacy—the belief that White people are superior and should therefore dominate non-White people.[13] As one movement challenging White supremacy, the M4BL is providing a context in which our understanding of trauma can be advanced. But there are no guarantees that this political moment will alter contemporary definitions of trauma. For those of us who live as "White" in the United States, we are still deeply conditioned *not* to see the ways that racism—especially subtler forms—can be traumatic. It's the prevailing narrative of the day.

This, I want to suggest, is one of the main reasons that Margaret struggled in her session with Yvonne. She failed to make connections between racism and trauma. Based on her social context, she had been shaped to invalidate Yvonne's experience of race, and therefore racism. She considered herself "color-blind." But being color-blind is a dynamic in which a dominant group—in this case, White people—denies the actual dynamics of social power and privilege. It's an aspect of racism. Through her clinical training, she'd also been conditioned to see racism as traumatic only when associated with a physically traumatic event. The social context she lived in—and the institutions she'd learned from—had molded her in a particular way. She hadn't considered the way racism in its many forms could have exceeded Yvonne's capacity for psychological integration, or her own denial of racism.

Trauma-sensitive practice involves engaging with this conditioning. Each of us will approach this from a different personal and social context, but it is imperative that we ask the question: How have we come to conceptualize traumatic harm? What institutions and social norms formed our understanding? Do the books, teachers, manuals, or communities we learn from have an analysis of systemic oppression? If not, why not? Are we aware of the ways that modern-day political movements are currently influencing a larger study of trauma? Given our socialization (race, class, gender, sexual orientation), what did we learn to see, or not see? Who did we learn to validate or invalidate? Just as mindfulness is a deep practice of awareness, engaging a deep reflection of social conditions is as well.

A CHOICE

Trauma-sensitive practice presents us with a choice. It is a choice you may reject or find controversial, but is central to our conversation.

When we commit to working with trauma, we come to bear witness to suffering. Whether it's a one-time conversation with a student or a longer-term relationship with a client, we enter into relationship with other people's traumatic pain. When the trauma we witness is the result of an accident or a natural disaster, it's generally easy to empathize. The tragedy could happen to anyone. But when the events we encounter are interpersonal and rooted in social and economic oppression, the dynamic becomes more complicated. We become caught in a conflict between perpetrator and victim.

In these moments, we become forced to choose a side. There is no room for neutrality. Why? Because any attempt at impartiality simply reinforces the status quo. To not choose means we've already chosen. "If you are neutral in situations of injustice," the archbishop and peace activist Desmond Tutu said, "you have chosen the side of the oppressor."[14]

I have struggled with this personally. As someone who was raised to please others, I default to neutrality. I attempt to dodge conflict by attempting to remain detached and objective—something that was reinforced by having been raised male and occasionally within my mindfulness training. As a White heterosexual man raised with class privilege, I've also been shaped to not see or acknowledge oppression when it happens. If I witness sexism, for instance, I distance myself from the situation rather than engage it. "Boys will be boys," we've all heard, or it's just "locker-room talk." Avoidance and normalization become the easier choice. But this attempted impartiality only buttresses oppressive systems. If I don't intervene, I've effectively communicated that I'm okay with what's taking place. Pleasing some people generally happens at the expense of others, and sometimes I haven't been aware of who has borne the outsourced burdens.

For many of us, the pull toward neutrality will be quite strong. Herman describes it this way:

> It is very tempting to take the side of the perpetrator. All the perpetrator asks is that the bystander do nothing. He appeals to the universal desire to see, hear, and speak no evil. The victim, on the contrary, asks the bystander to share the burden of pain. The victim demands action, engagement, and remembering. (1997, pp. 7–8)

Trauma-sensitive practice asks a great deal of us, in this respect. It is not simply a box we can check, but an orientation to working with systemic harm.

In the context of mindfulness, the pull toward inaction can become an issue. Mindfulness is sometimes cast as neutral, in that it involves observing things as they are. As Bhante Gunaratana wrote in his classic book *Mindfulness in Plain English*, "Mindfulness is an impartial watchfulness. It does not take sides" (2011, p. 133). We need to differentiate here between the mind state of mindfulness and taking mindful action in the world. In the context of trauma, we can't brush off responsibility to choose a side just because we're practicing mindfulness.

And so, as with trauma, we need to ask: How has history molded our understanding of mindfulness?

MINDFULNESS AND BUDDHISM

The history of mindfulness in the West weaves together two separate approaches: a 2,500-year-old historical tradition in Buddhism and a more recent 25-year-old tradition within modern science.[15] Both are relevant to trauma-sensitive mindfulness.

Often referred to as the heart of Buddhist meditation, mindfulness is among the original teachings of Siddhartha Gautama, also known as the Buddha, who is believed to have taught in the eastern part of India in the fourth century BCE.[16] To support the cultivation of mindfulness, the Buddha offered a meditation technique known as *vipassana*, which is often translated as "clear seeing." Vipassana involves techniques that help practitioners refine their attention. The Buddha asserted that the cultivation of single-pointed, refined concentration—a state his contemporaries were highly accomplished in—was not the most important thing in contemplative practice. Instead, he encouraged practitioners to develop a receptive, observational quality of attention known as mindfulness to focus their minds on investigating their moment-to-moment experience. Within a larger discursive framework, this technique helped facilitate an awareness of the true nature of reality (impermanence, suffering or unsatisfactoriness, and the realization of non-self), and ultimately a release from suffering.

Buddhist teachings on mindfulness are also embedded within an ethical framework. While meditation is often thought of as the foundational practice of Buddhism, ethics are designed to support the development of wisdom and compassion and considered by many to be the first step on the path to insight. The Buddha actually established over 200 precepts, or behavioral guidelines, for monastics—monks, nuns, and those living under religious vows. When lay people go on Buddhist meditation retreats, they typically follow 5 of these 200 precepts: the commitment not to harm or steal, and the abstention from sexual misconduct, unwise speech, and the misuse of intoxicants.

Buddhist ethics have interesting applications for trauma-sensitive practitioners. Rather than being harsh, authoritative rules, precepts are intended to be standards that can support mindfulness practice and the cultivation of safety. A client of mine who'd experienced sexual trauma attended a residential Buddhist meditation retreat and found that the precepts created safety and stability for her. Knowing she wouldn't be approached romantically ultimately supported her trauma recovery work.

Modern interpretations of mindfulness come largely from the *Satipatthana Sutta*, a traditional Buddhist discourse that describes mindfulness as a path to discovering the true nature of our existence. There are said to be four primary means by which one can develop mindfulness, known as the four foundations:

- Body (the flow of transient physical sensations)
- Feelings or sensations (vedanā; the tone of pleasant, unpleasant, and neutral sensory experiences, including mental and emotional experiences)[17]
- Mind (citta; emotions and mental states; one's mindset or state of mind)
- Dharma (broadly speaking, the interrelation of all things; patterns over time)

Each of these foundations can be a focus of mindful awareness. We can be mindful of the breath, for instance, or the tone of pleasantness or unpleasantness of a mental or emotional experience. In Buddhist teachings, foundations 1–3 involve noticing what is—witnessing the arising and passing away of thoughts and sensations, and learning that no pain or pleasure defines who you are. The fourth foundation involves looking at foundations 1–3 as they appear over time. "The power in foundations 1–3," Buddhist teacher and trauma professional Tempel Smith (2016) wrote, "is having the courage not to intervene—to rest into a deep acceptance and intimacy with life as it is. The power of the fourth foundation is to look at how different patterns arise, how they behave, how they disappear, and learning how to skillfully intervene" (personal communication, April 28, 2017).

Throughout this book, I focus on the first three of these foundations of mindfulness—body, feelings, and mind—for survivors.[18] The fourth foundation, Dharma, takes us into aspects of Buddhist teaching that lie beyond the scope of this project.

A SECULAR APPROACH

My decision to focus on these first three foundations of mindfulness is partly a personal limitation—I'm not a religion scholar—but it also reflects a debate about the division between religious and secular approaches to mindfulness that's an important part of its contemporary history.[19] In 1975, Harvard professor Herbert Benson published a book titled *The Relaxation Response*—a stripped-down version of a *transcendental meditation* (TM) technique that came out of Hindu yogic tradition. TM was created by the famous teacher Maharishi Mahesh Yogi, who is perhaps best known in the West as the guru of the Beatles. In conducting research with TM practitioners, Benson was amazed to find that 20 minutes of meditation caused a decrease in blood pressure, anxiety, heart rate, and hormone production. It effectively reversed the sympathetic fight-or-flight response.[20]

At the time, Benson was concerned that the Eastern roots of TM could diminish his professional scientific reputation. In this, we see an example of how cultural racism shapes the legacies we inherit. Benson decided to substitute the word *relaxation* for meditation—stripping TM of any potentially religious underpinnings. He argued exclusively for the health benefits of focused attention. In doing so, he also found commercial success: to date, his book has sold more than four million copies and is in its 64th printing.[21]

Four years later, in 1979, the aforementioned Jon Kabat-Zinn developed a program called Mindfulness-Based Stress Reduction (MBSR). Developed at the University of Massachusetts Medical Center, MBSR utilizes a combination of mindfulness meditation, body awareness practices, and simple yoga postures in an intensive eight-week program that consists of weekly group classes, 45-minute guided meditations at home using a recording, and an all-day retreat on the sixth week of the course. Like Benson, Kabat-Zinn presented a traditional Eastern meditation technique—this time drawn largely from the Buddhist vipassana tradition—as a secular health intervention. And, like TM, MBSR was an immense success: it has been shown to be successful in treating a range of medical conditions, including cancer, HIV/AIDS, heart disease, Parkinson's, depression, and chronic pain.[22] Today, more than 1,000 certified MBSR instructors teach the program in 720 medical settings in over 30 countries.

MBSR played an important role in mindfulness becoming a mainstream success. In 1993, Kabat-Zinn appeared on Bill Moyers's Emmy award–winning series *Healing and the Mind,* shifting the focus to its more general benefits. Mindfulness is now central to a number of psychotherapeutic approaches,[23] and mindfulness-based programs have been incorporated into elementary and high school curriculums—including research and teaching centers in major universities such as Duke, Brown, UCLA, and the University of Wisconsin. Major corporations such as Apple, General Motors, Reebok, IBM, General Mills, and Safeway offer mindfulness training programs to their employees, and it is increasingly being offered in prisons as well.[24]

Mindfulness, in this respect, is its own movement. A quick search on Amazon reveals 19,646 books about mindfulness and a dizzying number of mindfulness-related products capitalizing on the trend.[25] As a reflection of its mainstream acceptance, Kabat-Zinn was featured as a primary part of a cover story in *Time* magazine in 2014 titled "The Mindful Revolution," detailing the rise of mindfulness as a mainstream approach to health and well-being.[26]

PUSHBACK

But this revolution has proven complicated. With its explosive growth in popularity and disconnection from its Buddhist roots, mindfulness can be marketed as a no-risk, easily mastered self-help technique. As senior editor Mary Sykes Wylie wrote in an article for the *Psychotherapy Networker* titled "The Mindfulness Explosion: The Perils of Mainstream Acceptance":

> While few critics quarrel with using MBSR as a way to alleviate suffering in mind or body, they're disturbed by how much meditation in America appears to have been individualized, monetized, corporatized, therapized, taken over, flattened, and generally co-opted out of all resemblance to its noble origins in an ancient spiritual and moral tradition. (2015, p. 24)

Because of this dynamic, mindfulness can end up being described as a technique to achieve any desired goal—relaxation, career success, sexual confidence, or happiness in general.[27]

This amounts to what I refer to as the *panacea problem*—the tendency to look to mindfulness as a remedy to all difficulties. Given the fact that mindfulness has been a huge success in multiple domains, this is an understandable issue. Further, there is little evidence to suggest that mindfulness can be problematic. How dangerous can meditation really be?

Yet the potential risks of meditation are becoming increasingly well known. An important development in this area is the Varieties of Contemplative Experience project started by Willoughby Britton, assistant professor of Psychiatry and Human Behavior at Brown University.[28] The project has examined the range of challenging experiences that can arise in the context of Buddhist meditation—experiences that can resemble psychological dissociation, depersonalization, and the reexperiencing of traumatic memories. In a recent study that documented a range of meditation-related challenges experienced by Western Buddhist practitioners,[29] the authors documented 59 different categories of experiences based on interviews with nearly 100 meditation students and teachers.[30] "Many effects of meditation are well known, like increased awareness of thoughts and emotions, or improved calm and well-being," said the study's lead author, Jared Lindahl. "But there is a much broader range of possible experiences. Exactly what those experiences are, how they affect individuals and which ones show up as difficult is going to be based on a range of personal, interpersonal and contextual factors" (Orenstein, 2017, p. 1). Without diminishing the benefits from those who experience them with mindfulness meditation, the study does caution against wide-reaching claims that dismiss the potential pitfalls of mindfulness practice.

Margaret's session with Yvonne is a good example of the panacea problem. When Margaret sensed that her session with Yvonne wasn't going well, she wanted to offer something of value. Everything she had heard about mindfulness was positive, and she couldn't imagine a scenario where anything could go wrong. But this didn't turn out to be the case. Based on her limited understanding of mindfulness, Margaret offered it as a relaxation technique, effectively trying to cover over Yvonne's stress. In combination with Margaret's failure to recognize the potential impact of systemic racism, the meditation ended up leaving Yvonne more disoriented and anxious than when she'd come in.

This reflects one of the liabilities behind the exploding popularity of mindfulness. Excited about the benefits of mindfulness, Wylie wrote, "the media cherry-pick newsworthy scientific results and ride roughshod over cautiously worded research findings, typically reducing them to a one-sentence factoid" (2015, p. 44). News outlets end up exaggerating its positive effects. If we're excited about mindfulness, it can be tempting to internalize these positive headlines and allow them to form our view.

Trauma-informed practice asks us to consider these underlying forces.

I'm not suggesting that each mindfulness talk needs to come with explicit warnings, but I do believe it is important that we continually inform ourselves about the potential drawbacks of mindfulness and meditation. Trauma-informed mindfulness involves tempering our enthusiasm.

THE PAIN PARADOX

There is one more idea in Buddhism and MBSR that shapes our orientation to mindfulness: the notion that our avoidance of suffering can exacerbate it. Mindfulness experts John Briere and Catherine Scott referred to this as the *pain paradox*—the observation that our natural tendency to escape, deny, or withdraw from pain only intensifies and prolongs the distress.[31] What we resist, the saying goes, persists.

This paradox was key to Kabat-Zinn's introduction of MBSR to the medical community. When he originally approached doctors with the idea of having patients meditate, Kabat-Zinn was advocating for a fundamentally different approach to suffering—one that lay at the heart of the Buddhist tradition he'd trained in. "From the perspective of mindfulness," he wrote, "nothing needs fixing. Nothing needs to be forced to stop, or change, or go away."[32] Perhaps not surprisingly, this idea raised eyebrows. Western medicine was built largely on helping alleviate people's pain, offering interventions such as medication or surgery. Mindfulness ran completely counter to this paradigm. How could paying closer attention to one's pain alleviate it?

Yet doctors were also open to the idea. Each of them had patients they couldn't cure and who were resistant to conventional treatment approaches. Doctors and their patients had little to lose. The first MBSR studies thus began with those who were suffering from chronic pain. Kabat-Zinn wanted to see whether they could mobilize their own internal responses to the suffering they were experiencing. "We invited them, paradoxically," he said, "to put the welcome mat out for whatever sensations they were experiencing, just to see if they could attend to them moment by moment and 'befriend' the actuality of their experience, even briefly."[33]

The results were successful. Patients found that their relationship to pain shifted positively when they practiced mindfulness. At times, their pain even disappeared. Patients also reported discovering that the vexing sensations that lived inside them were transient and shifting.[34] Rather than being constant throughout their day, the pain was shifting over time—a huge realization for those who felt perpetually burdened by their bodies. Mindfulness was helping people relate to their pain differently. For some, it was even opening a door to a freedom they had forgotten or had previously not known.

Based on this history, many of us will be conditioned to think of mindfulness as an effective tool for the pain paradox. Mindfulness has been successful with a broad range of physical and psychological ailments, and it's entirely natural to think that it can help anyone struggling with pain. Given that avoidance is a primary symptom of posttraumatic stress, it's also logical to assume that the success of MBSR would extend to people experiencing traumatic stress. But trauma is a different kind of pain. The positive empirical findings mindfulness has garnered don't automatically extend to posttraumatic stress. While avoiding traumatic stimuli can prolong suffering, it is also an intelligent, survival-based response to managing it. Simply asking someone to pay more attention to their traumatic pain—without nuance or guidelines—may invite them into a vortex they can't escape.

This was the second trap Margaret fell into. When she noticed that Yvonne was becoming progressively anxious, she assumed that having her pay more attention to her discomfort could only be a good thing. This had been Margaret's experience with mindfulness meditation, so why wouldn't it work for Yvonne? Yet one of the most irresponsible things we can do with traumatic stress is to invite people deeper into their pain.

One way we can improve our ability to recognize trauma is to study how the brain and body respond to both trauma and mindfulness—and it is to this we'll now turn.

CHAPTER 4

The Brain and Body in Trauma and Mindfulness

*The brain is a world consisting of a number of unexplored
continents and great stretches of unknown territory.*
—Santiago Ramon y Cajal

*If the human brain were so simple that we could
understand it, we would be so simple that we couldn't.*
—Emerson M. Pugh

On a chilly Saturday afternoon, Tim was doing what he loved best: taking pictures. An increasingly successful local photographer, he'd been hired by a local dance troupe to take promotional shots for an upcoming show. The light was perfect in the old warehouse district they'd chosen, and Tim, swept up in the moment, shifted and moved with the dancers to capture the unique beauty of their choreography.

But then the movement stopped. Through his camera lens, the dancers' expressions of joy turned to fear; one pointed behind Tim and shouted "look out." Slowly turning around, Tim came face to face with two men—one with a gun pointed toward his chest. Terrified, Tim raised his hands overhead. Without revealing any sense of panic, Tim began to speak in a low, calm voice, but was quickly interrupted when one of the men motioned him toward an alley. For a split second, Tim felt the sudden, overwhelming urge to run. But he obeyed, walking cautiously as the two men ushered him out of sight of the dancers. There, the men pushed him roughly against a wall, grabbed his camera, and fled.

Tim was filled with shame as he walked back to the dancers. They tried to reassure him, but he was humiliated that he hadn't fought back. As he drove home, he felt hollow, dazed, and in disbelief about what had just taken place. This continued into the next day, when he found he couldn't shake what had happened. He felt jittery walking through his apartment, and images from the attack kept skittering through his mind. He'd hardly slept, and his hands shook as he struggled to fill out the insurance claims online.

In search of relief, he decided to attend his weekly mindfulness meditation class—a practice he had taken up a year earlier at the recommendation of a friend. He hoped it would soothe him as it had done in the past. But halfway through his sitting practice, he could hardly stay on his cushion. His mind was fixated on images from the robbery, his heart was beating rapidly, and his mouth was unusually dry. When the meditation ended, he discovered he'd sweated through his shirt. He considered saying something to his teacher, but he quickly convinced himself he must be getting sick.

Yet Tim didn't have an infection. In the weeks following, he continued to feel tense and disoriented, coping with these feelings by reediting photos, drinking more wine than usual, and deflecting the conversation if anyone asked about the robbery. He found himself swinging between states of detachment and anxiety, and took up smoking after 10 years of abstinence. When he did leave his apartment, he reflexively braced whenever he saw men walking in pairs. In his meditation practice at home, his mind filled with scenes from the robbery—images that left him terrified and unable to focus or take a full breath. The practice wasn't helping him relax—it was only heightening his disquiet. Desperate, he e-mailed his teacher. What did she think was happening? Was this common? Was he practicing incorrectly? And did she have any suggestions about what he could do?

LINES OF DEFENSE

For practitioners, the first challenge of trauma-sensitive mindfulness is recognizing the signs of trauma. If we're approached by a student like Tim, what should we look for? How can we tell that someone is experiencing posttraumatic stress?

One answer to these questions arises from *neurophysiology*—a branch of neuroscience concerned with the functioning of the nervous system. Understanding how the body and brain respond to both trauma and mindfulness provides important context for our trauma-sensitive work. Why was Tim sweating and short of breath? Why couldn't he concentrate? And inside of all this, how could mindfulness help? This chapter offers a brief overview of what we currently know about the neurophysiology of trauma and how this relates to trauma-sensitive mindfulness.

Let's go back to the moment Tim realized he was being robbed. When he turned around and saw the robbers, a sequence of survival-based strategies was set in motion. Commonly known as fight, flight, and freeze, these protective responses are activated through the autonomic nervous system (ANS)—the part of the nervous system that regulates involuntary bodily functions such as breathing and heart rate. The ANS is fundamental to how we experience both safety and danger, and is composed of two main branches: the sympathetic nervous system (SNS), which mobilizes the fight or flight response, and the parasympathetic nervous system (PNS), which promotes functions such as rest and digestion. Described as the accelerator (SNS) and the brake (PNS), these branches work together to regulate how we expend or conserve energy.

The complex interplay between the SNS and the PNS is critical to understanding trauma. In his book *The Polyvagal Theory*, neuroscientist Stephen Porges (2011) described three hierarchically organized subsystems of the ANS that function during our involuntary responses to threat: the ventral vagal complex (VVC), the sympathetic system, and the dorsal vagal system. These three subsystems are effectively lines of defense developed throughout the course of evolution, with the more primitive systems becoming activated as more evolved systems fail.

In the moments before the robbery, Tim's VVC was active. He was present, open, and connected to himself and the dance troupe. The VVC is named for the ventral (front) branch of the vagus nerve, the longest nerve of the ANS, which connects the brain with the throat, heart, and lungs. It is also the part of the PNS that initiates the relaxation response. When the VVC is activated, we have access to what is known as the *social engagement system*—one of the most sophisticated and evolutionarily advanced systems in our bodies. This system allows us to communicate with others by regulating social gestures. It is what lets us wink at someone with whom we've shared a joke, for instance, or raise our head from a book when a friend walks in the room. It is also this system that allowed Tim to work so effectively with the dancers, moving in sync with their intricate patterns and feeling a sense of connection and joy.

Tim still had access to his social engagement system when the robbers confronted him. Even with the possibility of danger, he was able to turn his head slowly to avoid startling the attackers, and he could control his emotional expression and vocal muscles so as not to communicate threat. But once it became clear that reasoning with the men would be ineffective, Tim had the overpowering impulse to run. He'd perceived a new level of danger, and a chain reaction of internal events took over as his SNS went into high gear: epinephrine, or adrenaline, was released in his body, along with the stress hormone cortisol. Tim's social engagement system had given way to fight or flight, and his body's next line of defense was activated.

The power that can be generated in sympathetic, survival-based responses cannot be overstated. It is what allows us to perform otherwise impossible feats of strength, such as lifting a car off a child. To mobilize a quick burst of energy, blood flow to Tim's muscles increased, temporarily diverting it away from nonessential areas such as the digestive tract. His blood pressure and heart rate soared to supply extra short-term energy to the muscles, supplying extra speed and strength. All processes that weren't vital to his survival also became inhibited, including hearing and his ability to salivate and cry.

If Tim had been able to run to safety, he would likely have returned to equilibrium relatively quickly after the danger passed. His body would have been able to metabolize the threat-based neurochemicals that had been released, and sprinting would have reduced his arousal—allowing his nervous system to return to homeostasis. But running wasn't an option. He had a gun pointed at his chest, and any quick movement might have startled one of the men into shooting.

THE FREEZE RESPONSE

Standing in the alley, Tim froze. He didn't struggle as the men pushed him into the wall and grabbed his camera. His last line of defense, the most primitive of the three ANS subsystems—the dorsal vagal system—had kicked in. This back (dorsal) branch of the vagus nerve extends down to the stomach and lower gut. The heart "drops" as the heart rate plunges, we can't breathe, and we become immobile or faint.

Freezing has deep evolutionary roots. Formally referred to as *tonic immobility*,[1] it is an adaptive survival function in mammals—most famously the possum. While certain predators will instinctively attack a moving creature, the freeze response can negate this aggression, tricking a predator into believing their prey is already dead and possibly rotten. If a predator drags their prey to a protected area for later consumption, freezing offers a window of escape. And if all else fails, freezing releases a cascade of endorphins that block pain. When we can't escape, dissociation allows us to get away, helping make "the unbearable bearable" (Levine, 2010, p. 50).

When Tim had e-mailed his mindfulness teacher, he could no longer deny that something was wrong. He was vacillating between impassivity and agitation, had difficulty completing the simplest projects, and was filled with overwhelming shame. He avoided the area of town where the photo shoot had taken place, and he wasn't returning calls from the dance troupe. There was also a pervasive ache in his legs that stretching didn't seem to help—a trembling edginess deep inside his bones.

Tim was experiencing posttraumatic stress. While his response to the robbery had protected him, he had become trapped in a dysregulated state. The dynamic interplay between his SNS and PNS had fallen out of balance. Because his SNS was on overdrive, he was sweating more often, his mouth was dry, and his heart rate was elevated. He hadn't fully integrated the traumatic event. He was reliving it in images in meditation, actively evading external reminders of the robbery, finding himself inundated with negative self-talk, and being plagued by chronically high levels of arousal. The men may have walked away, but Tim had effectively remained stuck in place.

WHEN INTEGRATION FAILS

Tim's response to the robbery returns us to the central concept of integration. As discussed in Chapter 1, integration means that parts function well together to create a harmonious whole. Posttraumatic stress is a failure of integration. An event, or series of events, is too much for us to metabolize. Using the lens of integration, consider the strength of the survival-based response that lay unintegrated in Tim's body. When he was accosted, his legs had surged with energy as he prepared to run. But faced with a gun, he'd frozen. His gross motor skills—running—had been enlisted, but not employed. He didn't discharge his physiological urge to flee, and his body had become fixed in an immobility response.

Peter Levine—whom I focus on in Chapter 6—has explored the potentially negative implications of longer-term immobility.[2] Levine studied animals in the wild to understand how mammals cope with life-threatening events. What he saw is that animals frequently discharge a freeze response through physical actions such as shaking or trembling. We humans often do this too—crying, sweating, trembling, or shaking in the aftermath of a threat. These reactions help us integrate the event and return us to a state of balance.

A teacher of mine whom I mentioned earlier, Staci Haines, tells a story about seeing this process in action. In San Francisco one afternoon, she noticed a caregiver and five children approaching an intersection.

When they were well into the street, a car ran a red light and the caregiver and children ran to avoid being hit. One young boy, in particular, dove onto the pavement to survive. She gathered the children on the other side of the street, and the young boy began to cry, wimper, and shake. The mother then grabbed his shoulders, demanding he stop. Staci saw the boy grip his jaw, hold his breath, and tighten his small chest to keep from sobbing.

This story isn't meant to shame the mother. Staci could see that she was terrified herself, with her anger being one way to release her fear. But I do want to draw attention to two things: first is the fact that containing this kind of survival-based energy—either because we couldn't run away or we couldn't cry and shake afterward—can provoke long-term complications. If we can't release our sympathetic response, energy that was meant to help us fight or flee remains bottled up. The trauma that began outside our body becomes lodged inside, engendering symptoms of posttraumatic stress. Second, emotionally expressing survival-based energy can run counter to social convention. Some of us will have been taught to shun rather than encourage intense emotional expression such as crying and screaming. When the parent at the intersection scolded her son, she herself was frightened. She didn't know that allowing her son to discharge his shock and fear would have helped him integrate the experience.

As trauma-sensitive practitioners, it is crucial that we recognize and respect the dormant energy that lies at the root of trauma. Traumatic stress isn't simply a negative emotional experience. It's an incomplete, survival-based response. All of which returns us to the basic question with trauma: Why do we get stuck? Why don't we simply move through traumatic events and come back into balance?

EXAMINING THE BRAIN

When Tim was experiencing posttraumatic stress, he felt troubled and unsafe. At any moment, he'd feel like an attack was imminent. He'd look around and know he was safe, but some part of him communicated otherwise. This was actually true: a part of Tim *was* continuing to signal threat—in this case, a particular area of his brain. From the perspective of neurophysiology, we can understand what was happening in Tim's body and brain during (and after) the robbery, including reasons he was held in trauma—and how mindfulness can help.

The brain can be viewed as having three parts: the neocortex, the limbic system, and the reptilian brain. This three-part division—called the triune (three-part) brain theory—comes from the work of Paul D. MacLean (1990), the late neuroscientist who adopted an evolutionary approach to his work. MacLean highlighted the fact that our brains are built from the bottom up. Beginning at the lowest part of our brain, right where our spinal cord enters the skull, we have the *reptilian brain*—the most primitive part of the brain we share with turtles, lizards, and crocodiles. This part of the brain is responsible for all of the things we can do when we're born: sleeping, eating, crying, breathing, urinating, and defecating. Right above the reptilian brain lies the more advanced *limbic system*, or *mammalian brain*—the part of the brain we share with animals who live communally and nurture their young. The limbic system supports a variety of functions, including long-term memory and our emotions. It also initiates protective responses such as fight, flight, and freeze.

Taken together, the reptilian brain and limbic system make up what neuroscientist Joseph LeDoux (1998) has termed the *emotional brain*—a part of our brain primarily responsible for our survival and overall well-being. The emotional brain tracks for both danger and opportunity in our environment: it might compel us toward someone we find attractive, for instance, or away from food that smells rancid. Working in generalities to produce quick, survival-based results, the emotional brain has the first say in interpreting incoming stimuli. LeDoux here offers the example of seeing what looks like a snake and quickly jumping back—only to realize a moment later that it is a branch. The emotional brain swiftly initiates preprogrammed defensive responses before we have the chance to think about them.

Atop the emotional brain we find the youngest and most advanced part of our brain—the *neocortex*, or *rational brain*. This area of the brain allows us to use language, engage in abstract thought, empathize with others, and make choices based on an imagined future. Compared with other mammals, humans rapidly develop frontal lobes in this area of the brain beginning in the second year of life. Our prefrontal lobes also give us some executive control over our bodies, behavior, and emotions—key for learning to navigate a nuanced social world. We learn that we don't need to yell every time we feel angry with someone, or pull the car over the minute we have to urinate. We can see a bigger picture and make decisions that support our short- and long-term goals.

Ordinarily, our rational and emotional brains work together. The moment before the robbery, Tim felt engaged, fluid, and content while taking pictures (his emotional brain), while simultaneously assessing which angles would work best (his rational brain). He also felt mildly hungry (emotional brain), but knew he'd be eating in an hour and could exert executive control to keep working (rational brain). These are generalities, but provide a sense of how our emotional and rational brains continually coordinate.

With posttraumatic stress, this coordination falls out of balance. While it's one thing to cope with hunger pangs, it's another thing entirely to navigate the intense, visceral sensations that accompany traumatic stress—agitation, aching, or the nausea Tim felt in his stomach. His rational brain told him that the robbery had ended, but it couldn't suppress the impulses from his emotional brain. Something inside him kept sounding the alarm. But why was this happening? Why couldn't Tim's rational brain restore order?

Research using functional magnetic resonance imaging technology has shown that powerful emotional states such as fear or anger reduce activity in several parts of the rational brain. If this happens, our ability to modulate or inhibit our emotional responses is diminished. "When the alarm bell of the emotional brain keeps signaling that you are in danger," van der Kolk wrote, "no amount of insight will silence it" (2014, p. 64). If you think about it, this dynamic makes evolutionary sense. If a car is speeding directly toward us, it doesn't serve us to think rationally. We must act. Yet if we can't disable or subdue the alarm sounding inside once the emergency is over, we face longer-term consequences. We keep responding to threat as if it's live, even if we "know" the alarm is false. It's a terrible tug-of-war.

To understand why this happens—and how it relates to mindfulness—we need to explore three smaller, more specific brain areas: the amygdala, the hippocampus, and the prefrontal cortex.

THE LOW ROAD AND THE HIGH ROAD

The *amygdala* is an almond-shaped set of neurons located in the limbic area of the emotional brain. Referred to by van der Kolk as the body's "smoke detector," the amygdala's central function is to assign emotional interpretations to sensory information, identifying what is most relevant to our safety and survival. For the amygdala, speed is of the essence: we can respond to stimuli before we consciously recognize what it is. Hearing a close friend's voice on the phone, we may smile and relax a few milliseconds before realizing who has called. Or, returning to the example of the branch and snake, the amygdala expeditiously interprets the shape of the branch as a potential threat, sending an instant message down the brain stem to release stress hormones (e.g., adrenaline) that activate a whole-body response—all before we notice it's just a branch.

Another structure in the limbic system, the *hippocampus*, plays an important role in memory. Among other functions, it registers and then informs the rational brain about the time sequence of an event, assigning it a beginning, middle, and end. Think of an experience you had yesterday, for instance—an errand you ran, or a conversation you had. The fact that you know this is a memory indicates that the hippocampus is doing its job.

A third area important for understanding trauma is the *prefrontal cortex*, which is located in the rational brain, directly above our eyes. The prefrontal cortex offers a view from on high, helping us understand what's happening and making decisions about the best path forward. I live in an earthquake zone, for instance, and loud grumbling noises usually elicit an automatic startle response. Milliseconds later, my prefrontal cortex helps me assess the situation. Do I need to run from my apartment, or should I check my phone to see if there are any earthquake warnings? Unlike the amygdala, which makes snap judgments before the rational brain weighs in, the prefrontal cortex can assess the situation and help us calm down—especially if the amygdala's response was a false alarm. This helps us keep the emotional brain in check and prevents us from flying off the handle every time we detect some kind of threat.

With posttraumatic stress, the integrated process between these three brain areas above goes awry. We keep responding as if a threat is still taking place. One way to understand this rests in two neural pathways proposed by LeDoux[3]: the "low road" (a faster route where the amygdala's messages bypass the rational brain) and the "high road" (a second, slower route in which information is sent to the rational brain to be sorted through). When trauma remains unintegrated, stress hormones continue to circulate in the body, causing survival-based emotional reactions to cycle indefinitely. This was why Tim experienced bouts of anxiety and hypervigilance in the weeks following the robbery: his amygdala was continuing to sound the alarm via the low road.

Ideally, this is where the high road comes in. By receiving information from the hippocampus that an event has passed, the prefrontal cortex can inhibit the emotional reactions of the amygdala and restore the body to balance. But if our stress levels are strong enough, the stress hormones cascading through the body will disable the hippocampus. This means that the time sequence of a traumatic event isn't accurately recorded, and the event remains devoid of a beginning, middle, and end. The rational brain never gets the message that the traumatic event has ended, and fails to inhibit the amygdala.

This is known as *hippocampal failure*. On the day of Tim's robbery, powerful stress hormones (adrenaline, cortisol) released in his body had temporarily disabled his hippocampus, preventing his prefrontal cortex from receiving the news that the robbery was over. His amygdala was continuing to sound the alarm and creating problems. As neuropsychologist Rick Hanson (2009) writes in his book *Buddha's Brain: The*

Practical Neuroscience of Happiness, Love, and Wisdom, "It's a bad combination for the amygdala to be over-sensitized while the hippocampus is compromised: painful experiences can then be recorded in implicit memory—with all the distortions and turbo-charging of an amygdala on overdrive—without an accurate memory of them" (p. 57).

Again, this makes evolutionary sense. When faced with a threatening experience, it's critical that we be able to act quickly and instinctively (the low road) instead of relating it to past events and rationally thinking it through (the high road). But this hippocampal failure is meant to be short lived. Following a traumatic event, the hippocampus is meant to come back online, informing the rational brain about the time sequence—especially the ending—of the event. The rational brain can then instruct the amygdala to stop sounding the alarm, bringing the body back into its natural state of equilibrium. But when an event exceeds our capacity for integration, survivors can end up confined in an abyss where their emotional brains keep responding as if the trauma were still happening.

It's imperative to keep this dynamic in mind when we ask people to be mindful. Survivors are often coping with disintegrated thoughts, emotions, images, and physical sensations that relate to a traumatic experience. It's easy for them to become triggered. In fact, simply asking a survivor be mindful of traumatic stimuli can actually reinforce them—one of the reasons trauma survivors require particular kinds of support.

WORKING WITH A TRAUMA PROFESSIONAL

I first sat down with Tim a month after the robbery described at the beginning of the chapter. He'd been referred to me by his meditation teacher, and as he sat down, he appeared to be in an aroused SNS state: his muscles were tense, his pupils were dilated, and his face was pale. After I invited him to take a few deep breaths, his color began to return. He also began making more eye contact as we spoke—indicating his social engagement system was online—so I began asking him a few questions:

What had he experienced in meditation? What had he done in response? And were these symptoms relevant to something that had happened in his life?

Tim welled up with tears. He'd been trying to hold things together since the robbery and was grateful to finally be talking to someone about what was happening. He told me about the robbery, including the symptoms he'd been having ever since. Since meditation was clearly making matters worse for Tim, I recommended he temporarily stop meditating until we had helped his nervous system process enough of the trauma so he could return safely to practice.

Our initial sessions partly focused on psychoeducation—a process of providing information and support. It is helpful for many clients to understand what is happening in the brain and body and to realize that their responses are normal. It can also lessen self-blame, an important factor for Tim and many other survivors. "If I were a real man," Tim said during our first session, "I would have punched those assholes in the face." He judged himself for being a coward and for not being "over it" yet. Once he understood what was happening in his nervous system, he was able to bring more compassion to his experience.

As he progressed, I looked for signs that Tim could safely return to his meditation practice. When I'd ask him to become mindful of what was happening in his body, he could notice fear in his stomach or nervousness in his legs without becoming overwhelmed. We agreed that Tim could also begin experimenting with mindfulness practice at home— limited to 5 to 10 minutes. The bottom line was that any practice had to *improve* Tim's symptoms rather than exacerbate them. In fact, I wanted Tim to be able to return to his meditation community, which we agreed would be a positive thing. My one request was that he check in with his teacher at the end of each class.

Tim's teacher's awareness of trauma had been crucial to his recovery. She recognized that he needed individual support to process his trauma—not simply more meditation instruction. Another teacher, well meaning but not trauma-informed, might have interpreted Tim's experience as ego dissolution—a natural loss of an attachment to a sense of self. They might have even assured Tim this was progress on his path and encouraged him to continue—potentially traumatizing him further. Alternately, a teacher hearing about Tim's difficulties with concentration might have recommended more frequent practice in order to steady his mind. Fortunately, Tim's teacher had the awareness and curiosity to inquire more deeply into Tim's experience, and had a network of trauma professionals to which she could refer him.

MINDFULNESS AND THE BRAIN

So how is it—from a neurophysiological perspective—that mindfulness can be a resource for trauma survivors? What does neuroscience research tell us about the relationship between mindfulness, trauma, and the brain? We're still in the preliminary stages of understanding how mindfulness affects trauma survivors, but contemporary findings offer us some answers to these questions, specifically through the three brain areas we explored earlier: the amygdala, the hippocampus, and the prefrontal cortex.

One of the better-known findings is that mindfulness meditation correlates with thicker middle prefrontal areas in the brain. In an oft-cited study, Harvard professor Sarah Lazar and her colleagues (2005) used functional magnetic resonance imaging technology to discover that people who practiced mindfulness meditation have greater activation in the prefrontal cortex.[4] Given that the prefrontal cortex helps us observe our experience—and exert executive control over compulsions from the emotional brain—the relation to mindfulness makes sense: mindfulness allows us to witness thoughts, sensations, and emotions without being identified with them. We can assess our situation rather than reflexively react to it. While much more study is needed, it's possible that mindfulness meditation, practiced over time, could lead to enhanced neural function in executive areas of the brain.

Mindfulness practice has also been associated with decreased volume of gray matter in the amygdala,[5] which decreases reactivity to trauma-relevant triggers.[6] In an eight-week study, individuals who participated in a mindfulness-based program were reported to have significantly less perceived stress and reductions in the amygdala gray matter density. In other studies, meditators have shown decreased physiological reactivity after being exposed to a stressor,[7] and a lower amygdala response to emotional stimulation during meditation.[8] Following in the footsteps of these researchers, the group found that these changes transferred to nonmeditative states—that the decrease in amygdala activity occurred following meditation as well.[9]

More generally, mindfulness meditation has also been shown to activate areas of the prefrontal cortex involved in emotional regulation.[10] There are several theories as to why mindfulness decreases amygdala activity and improves emotional regulation, including the idea that our enhanced ability to regulate attention is an important resource when we're confronted with stressful events. If we have some control over what we focus on, we can cope more effectively with our emotions and behaviors. The above findings offer us some clues as to why mindfulness has been shown to diminish stress and emotional reactivity, and improve overall health. But great gaps in understanding remain.

INTEGRATING TRAUMA

After six weeks of working together, Tim and I had a particularly powerful session. He came to the session feeling open and centered, and was ready to explore the terrifying sensations he'd been feeling in his stomach. I invited him to look inside, and Tim began to feel the shape and texture of the knot in his stomach, remaining as nonjudgmental as he could. He began to feel like he was back in the alley, petrified and helpless as the men snatched his camera from his neck.

"It was scary," he said, burying his face in his hands and letting himself begin to cry.

"That's right," I said. "It *was* scary. And, it's something that happened in the past. See if you can keep noticing that you're here in my office. Feel your feet on the ground. Try to keep noticing that you're safe, here, right now."

Tim couldn't hold back. He began to sob and shake. Images and memories came in waves over the next half hour, each bringing a new emotion to release. During this time, I stayed attentive, making eye contact when he needed it to help activate his social engagement system. I helped provide him with a safe and reassuring place to attend to what was happening inside his body. He began to feel his legs tremble with fear, and though it was unnerving, he let the shaking happen. My presence, containment, and encouragement supported this release. Helping Tim feel he was not alone made it safer for him to experience the overwhelming feelings that came up after the robbery.

After a while, Tim looked around the room. He was drenched in sweat and had gone through half a box of tissues. Yet he also felt resilient, relieved, and full of life. He began to laugh, and then he sighed deeply. His body was experiencing a kind of equilibrium that had become unfamiliar. It was like the robbery was over, he said—as if something had completed.

In many ways, it had. In the presence of someone he trusted, the experience that had been too much for him to process had become bearable. He was able to begin processing the survival-based responses, memories, and emotions that he had compartmentalized but now felt in the present. The sense of alienation he had been feeling inside himself was washed away as survival-based responses ran their course, discharging through shaking, sweating, and crying. While Tim still had difficult memories and emotions from the robbery, they didn't hold the same power. They were more integrated into his consciousness. He imagined there might be more waves to come, but he felt like he was returning to normal.

Under the right conditions, trauma *can* be integrated. This isn't an explicit goal of trauma-sensitive mindfulness, but it's important to realize the potential of this. This returns us to a fundamental question: What modifications can we adopt to ensure that mindfulness is helpful—and not harmful—to trauma survivors? In other words, what are the "right conditions" we can put in place?

In Part II, I'll present the basic principles and the specific practices that can make our approach to mindfulness trauma-informed.

PART II

THE FIVE PRINCIPLES OF TRAUMA-SENSITIVE MINDFULNESS

CHAPTER 5

Stay Within the Window of Tolerance:
The Role of Arousal

---

*Everything that exceeds the bounds of
moderation has an unstable foundation.*

—Seneca

At the age of 29, Prince Siddhartha—later known as the Buddha—
renounced his material life. Born and raised to a life of abundance, Siddhartha left his family palace to follow the path of the ascetic, practicing
severe self-discipline and—as the traditional stories tell us—limiting
his diet to one grain of rice per day. Six years later, however, all of this
changed.

Meditating on the banks of a river one day, Siddhartha overheard
a musician teaching a student how to tune a sitar. "Tighten the strings
too much," the teacher said, "and it will cause them to snap. Leave them
too loose, however, and they will cease to make a sound." Hearing this,
Siddhartha had a revelation. He'd experienced the extremes of both
sensual indulgence and abstention, but neither had led to any kind of
lasting peace. In that moment, he committed to walking a more moderate path—one that occupied a middle ground between luxury and self-
denial. In Buddhist teachings, this became known as the Middle Way.[1]

The Middle Way is highly relevant to trauma-sensitive mindfulness.

As we've learned, traumatic stress creates extreme mental, emotional, and physical states. A fight-or-flight response mobilizes a powerful burst of survival-based energy, while a freeze response effectively traps that remarkable force. In posttraumatic stress, this energy remains uninte-grated, causing a wide range of complications. Someone who witnessed a horrific assault might become chronically hypervigilant, for instance, unable to regulate their emotions. Or a person who grew up in an abu-sive home might become chronically dissociated and unable to feel many physical sensations. Trauma survivors can vacillate perilously between states of intense agitation and outright numbness.

The aim of trauma-sensitive mindfulness is to help people cultivate a practice that avoids these extremes. We want to ensure that trauma sur-vivors can safely observe and tolerate the range of their experience. One way to do this is to teach students and clients to stay in the *window of tolerance*—a term coined by Dan Siegel.[2] The window of tolerance is an internal zone of support for survivors and a starting point for all trauma-informed practice. It's a way to help ensure people aren't exceeding how much they can handle. When people are in their window, they're more likely to feel stable, present, and regulated. When they're outside of this zone, they're more likely to feel triggered, out of control, and dysregulated. Unless survivors can stay in their window during mindfulness practice, they can simply end up recreating traumatic states.

This brings us to the first principle of trauma-sensitive mindfulness: *stay within the window of tolerance*. As trauma-sensitive practitioners, we want to make certain that—at a minimum—survivors are practic-ing in a safe and stabilizing way. This means helping people enhance their ability to self-regulate rather than having them spin out of control. The window of tolerance offers a framework to do this, and can inform our interventions with students and clients. We can learn the signs that someone may be exceeding their window of tolerance, and begin to offer common-sense modifications—described at the end of this chapter—that can help people thrive in their practice, and help ensure they avoid retraumatization.

BROOKE

Fifteen minutes into our first therapy session, Brooke realized she hadn't taken off her jacket. It was our first meeting, and she'd launched into her story the moment she'd sat down. She paused and took a breath, and an apologetic smile passed over her face. It had been a difficult year.

Four months earlier, Brooke had lost her seven-month-old daughter to sudden infant death syndrome. Waking up that terrible morning, she'd immediately sensed that something was wrong. She reached for her daughter in her bedside crib but felt no response when she went to pick her up. Yelling for her husband to call an ambulance, Brooke felt helpless, torn between sprinting to the hospital and waiting for the medics to arrive. Eventually she collapsed to the floor, holding her daughter close and rocking back and forth as she heard the sirens approach.

In the weeks that followed, Brooke managed as best she could. She'd taken a brief leave of absence from her work as a nurse and went to stay with her parents for a few weeks. Some days she felt manic, running errands from the moment she opened her eyes until falling exhausted into bed. Other days she felt hopeless, depressed, and detached from the world. "I was living someone else's life," she said of these days, attempting to keep her head above water and hoping the pain would eventually recede. Two months after her daughter's passing, she'd gone back to work and the structures of her life began to return. She even started thinking about the possibility of having another child.

Around this time, at the encouragement of her husband, Brooke decided to attend a weekend meditation retreat. She'd had a meditation practice on and off for years, and both of them thought the time away would be restful and healing. At first she was grateful for the silence and the practice, unable to remember the last time she'd felt relaxed. But near the end of the first day, disturbing memories began to engulf her. When she closed her eyes, she saw her daughter's pale face from the morning she'd died. Other moments she swore she could hear ambulance sirens in the distance. While she tried to bring her attention back to her breath in practice, these images and sounds were like a black hole, pulling for her attention. Rather than feeling the expansiveness she'd experienced in the past, she felt trapped.

For the next hour—in both sitting and walking meditation—Brooke swung uncontrollably between anxiety and dissociation. Tears streamed down her cheeks as she sat. While the grief felt appropriate to her, being alone on retreat also made it unbearable. She felt isolated, and the lack of contact with others was excruciating. "All I wanted was to feel my husband's arms around me," she said. "I would wrap my arms around myself to mimic his touch, but I couldn't feel him. It was so awful." Seeing the backs of people's heads in the meditation hall left her feeling even worse, surrounded by fellow meditators but completely alone with all of her pain. The first evening, she spoke with one of the leaders of the retreat, who listened compassionately and encouraged Brooke to continue to be mindful of the images and noticed when they shifted. But Brooke felt hopeless, waking up dejected the next day and deciding to leave the retreat early. She left a note to the teachers telling them she had the flu.

In the month since her retreat, Brooke had been on an intense roller coaster. "I'm startled by the slightest noises," she said. "I'm having trouble concentrating at work and I can hardly sleep." One moment she'd be feeling angst-ridden and hypervigilant—eyes wide, speaking rapidly, pupils dilated—and the next she'd be listless and numb, her eyes glazing over. She felt estranged from her husband and had little interest in talking with him at the end of the day. At the hospital where she worked, hearing ambulance sirens brought her back to the morning she lost her daughter. Her heart would race, she'd break out in a sweat, and she occasionally felt like collapsing into a ball on the floor. The sirens had been difficult before the retreat, but now they were agonizing. Oscillating between hopelessness and dread, she wondered if she'd be able to continue working as a nurse—or if she'd ever find release from her sorrow.

DYSREGULATED AROUSAL

Why was Brooke experiencing such intense fluctuations between paralysis and panic? How, if at all, was mindfulness exacerbating them? And if we encounter someone like Brooke as a mindfulness practitioner, how can we work with them in a trauma-sensitive way?

To address these questions, we need to unpack a few theoretical concepts related to the window of tolerance. The first has to do with the notion of a middle path between two extremes. Examples of this kind of dynamic are everywhere. As you're reading this, for instance, your body is engaged in the complex task of keeping your core temperature in a relatively safe zone around 98°F—a region between extreme heat and cold. There's also something known as a "zone of proximal development" that supports your learning. [3] If I bombard you with information, you'll become overwhelmed; too little information, and you'll become bored.

Siegel's (2010) image for this optimal zone in mindfulness is a body of water running between two riverbanks (see Figure 5.1). On the top riverbank, we find chaos—life is turbulent and unstable, and we tend to feel out of control. On the bottom riverbank, there's rigidity. Life is stagnant, fixed, and we tend to feel stuck. In between these two banks is a river that strikes a balance between these two extremes. There we find harmony and equanimity, and our lives can flow freely. Siegel refers to this as a *River of Integration* (see Figure 5.1)—a zone between chaos and rigidity that, as I will show you in a moment, is tied directly to the window of tolerance.

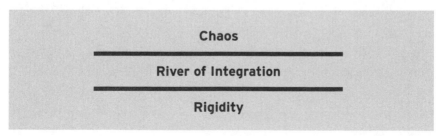

Figure 5.1. The River of Integration

In trauma-sensitive mindfulness, the variable we're interested in here is *arousal*—defined as our basic readiness for life. Arousal originates in the brain stem, activates our ANS, and helps us respond to the demands of the world. If we need energy to do something, such as get out of bed or pick up our child, arousal increases; when we rest, it decreases. Trauma, meanwhile, creates acute arousal. With fight or flight, our bodies hit the accelerator. We experience a burst of exceedingly high arousal. If we then freeze, our bodies slam on the brakes. With posttraumatic stress, arousal can end up fluctuating wildly between these two extremes. Both pedals effectively remain slammed to the floor.

This is known as *dysregulated arousal*—a state where our ability to self-regulate becomes seriously compromised. Overly sensitized to traumatic reminders, we end up experiencing too much arousal (*hyperarousal*) or too little arousal (*hypoarousal*), or swing uncontrollably between the two. It is a precarious state, and one of the brutal costs of trauma. When we're hyperaroused, there's too much energy in the system: we can be plagued by intrusive thoughts, are anxious and easily overwhelmed, and can find it hard to relax or focus. This is the upper riverbank in Siegel's model. When hypoaroused, we experience a lack of energy that leads to an absence of sensation, a lack of concentration, and a sense of immobility—the lower bank. There, people report feeling passive, disinterested, unmotivated, and numb.

When Brooke came to see me, she was describing dysregulated arousal. "I feel out of control," she said in our first session, placing her head in her hands and slowly running her fingers through her hair. "It feels like my body just isn't mine anymore." Brooke was waking up each morning not knowing what state she'd find herself in. One day she'd be profoundly hypervigilant, and the next she'd be numb, absent, and withdrawn. She was either in chaos or rigidity, and it was wearing on her. "I feel like I can't show up in my marriage or at work," she said, her voice cracking. "Something just keeps taking me over and nothing seems to make it better."

As Brooke discovered on retreat, mindfulness and meditation can be exceptionally challenging for someone with dysregulated arousal. Although mindfulness can enhance self-regulation, as I discussed in Chapter 2, meditation practice can also exacerbate dysregulation. By paying close attention to traumatic images and memories, as Brooke was doing, she was ending up increasing her arousal, which was proving unhelpful. Seeing her daughter's face over and over again made her more anxious, and the fact that she was alone and in a new place only made things more raw and painful. She couldn't depend on the calming, regulating contact of her husband, or the familiar sights, sounds, and smells of her home. In this case, meditation had aggravated her trauma symptoms and pushed her outside her window of tolerance.

TEACHING THE WINDOW OF TOLERANCE

This brings us to the window of tolerance—a zone that lies between the two extremes of hyper- and hypoarousal (see Figure 5.2). When we're hyperaroused, we tend to be oversensitive to sensations or sounds, hypervigilant to our surroundings, and experience high emotional reactivity. Life there is chaotic. When hypoaroused, we can experience an absence of sensation and apathy. Things are rigid. When we're inside our window of tolerance, however, we're more equipped to tolerate the full range of our experience. Our arousal naturally ebbs and flows, and we're more likely to feel alert, relaxed, and engaged.

The window of tolerance is tied to cognitive processing. With hyperarousal, our cognitive processing tends to be disorganized and in disarray. There's too much stimulation, and it often becomes difficult to pay attention. With hypoarousal, our cognitive processing becomes disabled. It's hard to think clearly, and people often report feeling spacey, removed, and unable to concentrate. This is one reason trauma survivors can have difficulty functioning in their daily lives: disorganized and disabled cognitive processing makes everyday tasks difficult, especially those that involve executive skills such as planning, decision making, and organizing daily activities. I've worked with clients who, in the aftermath of a traumatic experience, felt like they'd lost their ability to manage and control their minds and lives.

	Increased Sensation
	Emotional Reactivity
	Hypervigilance
	Intrusive Imagery
Hyperarousal Zone	**Disorganized Cognitive Processing**
Window of Tolerance	
Optimal Arousal Zone	
Hypoarousal Zone	**Relative Absence of Sensation**
	Numbing of Emotions
	Disabled Cognitive Processing
	Reduced Physical Movement

Figure 5.2. The Window of Tolerance (Ogden, Minton, & Pain, 2006, p. 27)

This is a primary reason survivors can run into difficulty in mindfulness meditation. As I covered in Chapter 4, posttraumatic stress causes particular areas of the emotional brain to continue signaling threat. The rational brain can't restore order. When a survivor is outside their window of tolerance (as happens with dysregulated arousal), paying mindful attention is troublesome—if not impossible. No matter how hard they might try, survivors can end up following basic mindfulness meditation instructions yet remain incapable of regulating their attention. It's a frustrating setup for those struggling with posttraumatic stress.

When I began working with Brooke, I started by introducing her to the window of tolerance. Sketching the window on a piece of paper, I explained that the swings of arousal that she was experiencing were normal in the wake of the tragic event she'd been through. We talked about the way trauma creates dysregulated arousal, and the specific ways it was wreaking havoc in her life. I wanted to empower Brooke to understand how to work with her body and mind, finding that this kind of knowledge often helps normalize clients' experience and they sometimes feel more regulated right away.

Once I'd introduced Brooke to the window of tolerance, we began working together to identify signals that told her whether she was inside or outside of her window. If she was feeling foggy, listless, and numb, she was likely experiencing hypoarousal. If she felt hypervigilant and anxious, and noticed that her heart was racing, she was probably hyperaroused. In between these zones was her window of tolerance—a zone where her eyesight was clear, she could take a full breath, and she could also feel her feet on the ground. I wanted Brooke to be able to notice when she left her window and eventually develop the skills to move back into it. Before any other work, it was essential for her to regain a sense of agency—to sense that she had the power and skills to exert some control over her nervous system. If she couldn't, further work risked reinforcing her trauma rather than resolving it.

"This is a relief," she said, her eyes softening. "When I came in here," she added, "I assumed I'd have to be reliving the terror all over again."

I hear statements like this often. People assume that, in order to heal, they have to dive headfirst back into their trauma. But that's not true. Emotional catharsis—an intense purgation of emotions—doesn't necessarily mean someone is integrating trauma. Often it can just end up pushing someone outside of their window of tolerance. To find stability, survivors can begin tracking their window so they can self-regulate. They need to learn what they can stay present for, and, conversely, what they can't tolerate.

It is important to recognize that people's window of tolerance varies. Sometimes it is wide, meaning they can tolerate and stay present with large swings of arousal. At other times, a window is more narrow, meaning it doesn't take much to trigger a reaction. Before Brooke lost her daughter, she could handle most stressful situations with ease, in part because of her training as a nurse. At the hospital where she worked, she was known for being steady in a crisis. After the death of her daughter, however, it didn't take much for her to become unhinged. The slightest stress could cause her to buckle at the knees or suddenly feel painfully incompetent. Many days, she said, it was hard to make it to lunch without crying.

The width of our window of tolerance is also tied to our *threshold of response*—the amount of stimulation required to provoke arousal.[4] If our threshold is low, arousal occurs with minimal input—it doesn't take much to elicit a response. If our threshold is high, more input is required to provoke a reaction. Those suffering from posttraumatic stress often have extremely high or extremely low thresholds of response. Brooke had a particularly low threshold, so that the slightest noise would startle her. She'd be hyperaware even when she was home alone and her environment was calm. Another client of mine had a high threshold of response. When a serious car accident took place outside his apartment, he barely responded. His neighbors called for help, but he remained quiet, still, and calm.

Thresholds also apply to the concept of *triggers*—stimuli that can set off memories or flashbacks related to a traumatic event. Triggers can include people, places, things, situations, and internal experiences. Each is personal and unique. No matter how hard we might try to create a trigger-free environment, it's difficult to do so. A smell, a memory, an interpersonal dynamic—any one of these might push a survivor outside their window of tolerance. Brooke became especially sensitive to the sound of ambulance sirens, for instance, often feeling faint or hypervigilant. Sometimes she'd be bombarded by memories of the moment of her daughter's death, while other times there wasn't a conscious memory associated with the feeling—just a jarring uncertainty that caused her to feel more out of control.

As trauma-sensitive mindfulness practitioners, we can track people's window of tolerance as best we can. Survivors we work with will each have distinctive thresholds, individualized triggers, and varying breadths to their window of tolerance. If someone you're working with is clearly outside their window, basic mindfulness instructions won't necessarily be enough to bring them back into their window. We need to be alert, sensitized to the window, and committed to attending to people's well-being.

AROUSAL ZONES AND THE POLYVAGAL HIERARCHY

If you look back to Chapter 4, you can begin to see the outlines of the theory underlying trauma-sensitive mindfulness. The three zones of arousal—hyperarousal, hypoarousal, and the window of tolerance— correspond directly to the three subsystems of the polyvagal hierarchy we discussed in the last chapter (see Figure 5.3). As we saw with Tim, the photographer who was robbed, these subsystems—the VVC, the sympathetic system, and the dorsal vagal system—serve as our primary lines of defense in response to traumatic experiences.

Here is an example to remind you of how these systems interact: Imagine you're biking down a street and hear a dog barking loudly from a nearby yard. You've already passed by when you hear a gate bang open. Looking back, you see the dog is chasing you. It's big and angry, and you don't hear anyone calling its name. In this situation, you want your blood to flow to your limbs instead of your brain. You don't need to know what words or signals the dog might respond to (the VVC). You just need to pedal as fast as you can (the sympathetic system). If you're able to escape, your body will ideally return to an optimal zone of arousal once you realize you've escaped the dog. You'll burn through the energy generated by your sympathetic response and return to your window of tolerance. Your social engagement system—mediated by the VVC—will come back online, and you can integrate the experience by talking to a friend.

In posttraumatic stress, survivors often lose access to their social engagement system. They continue to feel threatened and remain stuck

Figure 5.3. The Three Arousal Zones and the Polyvagal Hierarchy (Ogden et al., 2006, p. 32)	
Hyperarousal Zone	Sympathetic "Fight-or-Flight" Response
Window of Tolerance Optimal Arousal Zone	Ventral Vagal "Social Engagement" Response
Hypoarousal Zone	Dorsal Vagal "Immobilization" Response

Figure 5.3. The Three Arousal Zones and the Polyvagal Hierarchy (Ogden et al., 2006, p. 32)

in a sympathetic or immobilization response—outside the window of tolerance. What makes this especially difficult is that the social engagement system helps regulate the ANS. When a survivor is outside of their window of tolerance, it ends up being much harder to get back in.

Why is this the case?

When we perceive that we're safe, our PNS is in charge, slowing the heart rate and lowering the production of the stress hormone cortisol. If we look around and notice we've escaped the dog that was chasing us, we can let down and rest. If we assess threat, our more primitive sympathetic system—the accelerator—kicks into gear. When our sympathetic system remains active well beyond the overwhelming event—as happens with posttraumatic stress—we lose the capacity to self-regulate. We can't necessarily return to a relaxed state. We end up having flashbacks to the dog and can't calm down. As Levine wrote, "The social engagement system is intrinsically self-calming and is, therefore, built-in protection against one's organism being 'hijacked' by the sympathetic arousal system and/ or frozen into submission by the more primitive emergency shutdown system" (2010, p. 94).

How might this affect how we teach mindfulness in a trauma-sensitive way? Consider again the potential complications of asking someone with dysregulated arousal to meditate. If they're hyperaroused, they may be facing intrusive imagery, traumatic sensations, and disorganized cognitive processing. If they're hypoaroused, they may experience an absence of feeling, dissociation, and disabled cognitive processing. No matter how sincere an effort they may be bringing to meditation, the practice itself can become a setup for further distress.

My client Brooke, for example, lost her ability to self-regulate on her meditation retreat. She'd felt stable for most of the first day, but then started to experience intense vacillations in her arousal. The invasive imagery she'd been struggling with grew worse, and she felt alternately overstimulated and dazed. Brooke was outside her window of tolerance. Because the group setting offered her so little social support, self-regulation also became even more difficult. She'd spiraled out of control and couldn't bring herself back into her window.

RELATIONSHIP WITH SELF AND OTHER

Losing access to our social engagement system affects our relationship with others and ourselves. One of the most heartbreaking dynamics for families and friends of trauma survivors is the way their personalities can change so drastically after a traumatic event. A partner suddenly begins lashing out uncontrollably, a friend becomes absent and withdrawn, or a family member turns to substances or behaves recklessly. In the month following her meditation retreat, Brooke felt distant from her husband and uninterested in physical or emotional intimacy. "Most of the time, I don't want to touch or be touched by him," she said to me in our second session. "And it's not that I don't love him—I just don't feel right inside. When I look into his eyes before bed I feel nothing. It's awful."

It's vital for us mindfulness practitioners to know that interpersonal relationship is often difficult for those experiencing traumatic stress. Under the surface, a survivor is likely struggling with a loss of control— the sense that they may reexperience their trauma at any moment. In the attempt to handle this unrelenting terror and instability, relationships become difficult. Those who have experienced trauma based in oppression and interpersonal violence struggle with even greater violations of safety. In Chapter 8, I'll be talking more about the essential role of relationship in the context of trauma-informed practice, and until then want to stress that trauma impacts one's ability to feel safe and nourished in connection with another.

Trauma can also impact our relationship with *ourselves*—including our ability to cultivate mindfulness. In his book *The Mindful Brain*, Siegel (2007) explored this connection through the perspective of psychological attachment—the study of how interpersonal relationships shape our social, emotional, and cognitive development. Siegel proposed that mindfulness may harness the same neural circuitry as our social engagement system: that we use the social engagement system to relate not only to other people, but also to ourselves. As Daniel Hughes, a psychologist specializing in childhood trauma, suggested: "The social engagement system might also reasonably be called the *mindful engagement system*, whether the engagement is social, or in relation to a flower, the traffic noise, or our own breathing" (2013, p. 21).

Cultivating mindfulness, in this respect, is much harder if we're outside our window of tolerance. If our access to the social engagement system is compromised, we have more difficulty *relating* to the present moment—whether it's our breath, a thought, or another object of consciousness. All which makes common sense, if you think about it: within their window of tolerance, survivors are more likely to be alert, relaxed, and in a state that supports mindfulness. When they're caught in fight, flight, or freeze, the brain centers that support mindfulness are shut down.

How, then, can we help survivors stay within their window of tolerance while practicing mindfulness? For the remainder of this chapter, I'm going to offer you eight modifications of basic mindfulness practice designed to support the window of tolerance. Please keep in mind that these modifications are not meant to be prescriptive, static instructions to be applied carte blanche. Instead, they are suggestions that can be tailored to the people you're working with. Think of them as tools you can adapt and use as you—and the people you work with—see fit.

STAY IN A WINDOW OF TOLERANCE: TRAUMA-SENSITIVE MODIFICATIONS

(1) WATCH FOR DYSREGULATED AROUSAL

Before we can respond to trauma, we first need to recognize it. Sometimes a new student may disclose their trauma history to us in conversation, or the information might appear on an intake form. But for those of us teaching mindfulness meditation, it's up to us to notice nonverbal cues that someone may be approaching or exceeding the boundaries of their window of tolerance.

Because of the way mindfulness meditation is generally practiced, this presents a unique challenge. If you're a meditation teacher who offers a weekly class to a group of students, how can you track the arousal of each individual? Mental-health professionals can assess a person's arousal through direct conversation—reading facial expressions and noticing nonverbal cues—but silent meditation practice minimizes such contact.

Those of you teaching mindfulness to groups will be relying chiefly on observation. The following are some of the basic internal and external signals that suggest someone may be outside of their window of tolerance. These are not necessarily indicators that a student or client is actively experiencing traumatic stress, but they are signals that suggest an intervention of some kind is warranted:

- Muscle tone extremely slack (collapsed, noticeably flat affect)
- Muscle tone extremely rigid
- Hyperventilation
- Exaggerated startle response
- Excessive sweating
- Noticeable dissociation (person appears highly disconnected from their body)
- Noticeably pale skin tone
- Emotional volatility (enraged, excessive crying, terror)

In conversation or interviews:

- Disorganized speech or slurring words
- Reports of blurred vision
- Inability to make eye contact during interviews/interactions
- Reports of flashbacks, nightmares, or intrusive thoughts

In Chapter 8, I'll talk about how to utilize interviews and intake forms to assess for active trauma symptoms. For now, watching for the above symptoms can serve as an invitation to request a conversation with a student or client. We might say, for example, "I noticed during meditation that you were sweating a lot, and it looked difficult for you to stand up after practice. Can we talk?" Or, "In our group interview, it appeared you were having difficulty focusing, and you got a bit spacey. Could we sit down and talk about how practice is going for you?"

(2) FOCUS ON STABILIZATION AND SAFETY: A PHASE-ORIENTED APPROACH

As a new therapist, I sometimes encouraged clients to go deeper into intense emotions with the assumption that only good things could happen. Whether they were sobbing or hitting a pillow, I assumed they must be having some kind of breakthrough. But catharsis doesn't necessarily mean that a survivor is integrating trauma. One week later, the same client was likely to come back stuck in similar symptoms. It was a bit like digging a hole in the sand only to have the ocean come and wash all progress away.

As I described with Brooke, one of the first tasks of trauma-informed work is to create a sense of stability and safety. I didn't begin my first session with Brooke by asking her to tell me every detail of the morning she lost her daughter. I was more interested in helping her develop the capacity to be present. A trauma-sensitive approach to mindfulness adopts a similar approach. Our first priority as mindfulness practitioners is to ensure that people are safely strengthening their faculty to be present for life—not just cycle through stretches of dysregulated arousal. As we saw in Chapter 4, simply recounting and reexperiencing a trauma can reactivate and reinforce the alarm systems located in the emotional brain. If we learn or assess that someone we're working with has experienced trauma—or is actively experiencing symptoms—our foremost concern is that they remain stable and safe. Our initial job isn't to help them recount and integrate trauma memories, but to make sure that they aren't retraumatizing themselves in practice. In time, mindfulness can help people increase their capacity to stay present with trauma-relevant stimuli, which tills the soil for trauma resolution.

This emphasis on stabilization and safety reflects something known as a *phase-oriented approach* to trauma. This idea originated with Pierre Janet, the French psychologist whom I discussed in Chapter 3. In a treatise published in 1898, Janet proposed that there were three fundamental phases necessary for trauma recovery:

- Phase I: Stabilization and Safety
- Phase II: Remembering and Processing Trauma Memories
- Phase III: Integration with Family and Culture, and Normal Daily Life

Phase I of this framework aims at helping trauma survivors establish a sense of stabilization and safety both internally and in relation to their environment. Phase II work involves more actively processing traumatic memories, which can involve reviewing and reappraising traumatic incidents. In Phase III, integration becomes the focus, ensuring that the healing work is woven into the many domains of the survivor's life, including body, mind, family, and community.

Rothschild suggested that Janet's framework offers a *common-sense approach* to trauma recovery work.[5] If we can make sure that individuals have some semblance of control over their symptoms before attempting to process traumatic memories, they are more likely to move at a pace that supports their overall recovery process—even if that pace is slower than they might prefer. Because working with trauma can be a destabilizing experience, survivors need to learn how to stay present with themselves before moving into potentially destabilizing states. Said another way, they need to stay in their window of tolerance. Anything else can become a setup for failure and heightened pain.

This is why prioritizing the window of tolerance is so important in trauma-informed mindfulness. Focusing on stabilization and safety increases the likelihood that one's mindfulness practice will be safe, sustainable, and successful. While it may be tempting to speed people along into Phases II and III, the necessity of establishing safety and stability in Phase I cannot be underestimated.

(3) EDUCATE OTHERS ABOUT THE WINDOW OF TOLERANCE

As we saw in the case of Brooke, the window of tolerance can serve as a guidepost when working with students and clients. If we assess that a meditation student is hyperaroused, we might choose to encourage them to take a break from practice. Or we might decide to have a conversation with them about what is happening in their practice, asking how we can best support their stability.

This holds true for students and clients themselves. We don't need to keep the window a secret, but can talk to others about how the window applies to them and ways they can work with it skillfully. This can involve educating those who comes to mindfulness practice about the relevance of the window of tolerance. It assures that all meditators—especially those new to practice—have a basic understanding of the relationship between trauma and arousal, and can make informed choices about how they want to practice. As I mentioned earlier, I sketched out the window of tolerance on a piece of paper when Brooke began working with me. Although I was working with her as a therapist, one on one, I could also have done this as her mindfulness teacher.

Educating students and clients about the window of tolerance aims to empower them. It also interrupts the idea that we, as mindfulness teachers and mental-health professionals, automatically know best. We want to have all practitioners develop trust in their minds and bodies. Over time, survivors can begin to notice signals such as those in the first modification above: that they are hyperaroused (e.g., a tight jaw, repetitive thoughts), hypoaroused (e.g., numbness, apathetic thoughts), or actually in their window of tolerance (e.g., deep full breathing, an ability to focus). This can help them track themselves more effectively, stop, or practice making adjustments to stay within their window of tolerance and steer clear of retraumatization.

(4) USE MINDFUL GAUGES

Beyond providing students with a theoretical understanding of trauma-sensitive practice, we want to offer them practical tools as well. One of these is a *mindful gauge*—a way to evaluate one's response to different stimuli in the present moment. A term coined by Rothschild,[6] mindful gauges can help survivors reestablish agency and self-regulation in the aftermath of trauma.

Mindful gauges can include body sensations, moods, feelings, or thoughts. In my work with Brooke, I described these domains and asked her to notice which "gauge" was strongest and most accessible to her. After some experimentation, she found that paying attention to her breath—specifically whether it was deep or shallow—was her most powerful gauge. Brooke then began paying mindful attention to her breath throughout the day. If her husband asked whether she wanted to go for a walk, Brooke would check in with her breath. If her chest was open and she could breathe easily, it was a signal that a walk would be positive for her. If her chest constricted, she took that as a sign she needed to do something else. Working with these kinds of low-risk decisions, Brooke began to establish a sense of inner guidance that she had lost in the aftermath of her daughter's death. Her gauge was helping her to self-regulate.

Mindful gauges have their root in *somatic markers*, a concept developed by neuroscientist Antonio Damasio.[7] During an investigation into the experience of people with damage to the prefrontal cortex, Damasio found that they had little or no awareness of bodily sensations—in particular, internal sensations. They had difficulty feeling what was happening inside. As a result, they had trouble identifying their emotions and making decisions. Without sensations as a guidepost, they were often unsure about their mood and the best path forward. This caused Damasio to conclude that one's bodily and emotional awareness are critical to making choices. He proposed that experiences we encounter leave "pleasant and unpleasant traces inscribed in our bodies—somatic markers—that help guide our future decision making" (Rothschild, 2011, p. 13). This means that we don't have to go through an experience to determine if it's the best choice for us. We can notice the "pleasant and unpleasant traces" a decision evokes and follow sensations as the lead.

Mindful gauges, in this respect, can help survivors make decisions that encourage self-regulation. In meditation, they can utilize a gauge to evaluate whether a practice is right for them. This might include a decision about whether to go on a silent retreat, or whether to take a solitary walk while the larger group is meditating. For survivors who may have lost this capability in the wake of trauma, finding one's unique gauge can be a route back to self-regulation.

(5) RECOGNIZE WHEN TO APPLY THE BRAKES

It's imperative that students and clients know that they can work with trauma gradually, at a pace that works for them. *Applying the brakes* is a way to stay within one's window of tolerance so that mindfulness doesn't become retraumatizing. Coined by Rothschild,[8] applying the brakes means that survivors purposefully slow the pace of their mindfulness practice in order to feel safe and stable. Given that trauma so often leaves survivors feeling out of control, it's important that they be fortified with strategies to self-regulate in the face of traumatic stimuli—to "brake" if they're accelerating uncontrollably. At a minimum, we want to make sure survivors are not exacerbating their experience of dysregulated arousal in meditation.

There are many ways to apply the brakes:

- Open one's eyes during meditation practice.
- Take structured breaks from mindfulness practice (e.g., walking, stretching, unstructured time).
- Take a few slow, deep breaths.
- Engage in a soothing form of self-touch (e.g., hand on heart).
- Focus on a resourceful, external object in one's environment (detailed more in Chapter 6).
- Engage in shorter practice periods.

Each of these above suggestions will differ for each person we work with—after all, what's resourceful to someone can be triggering for another. Our work is to remain responsive to the individual needs of the people that we're working with, encouraging them to apply the brakes when things become overwhelming.

These strategies are not meant to facilitate an "anything goes" approach to mindfulness meditation. Each of you will have different structures and traditions you work within, and we want to advocate some structure in practice and hold people accountable to their aspirations. But as I've offered through many examples, mindfulness requires a deft and delicate touch when we're working with trauma. A strict approach to the structure of practice may benefit some, but it runs the risk of dysregulating people who are experiencing posttraumatic stress. Our work is to galvanize students and clients to be self-responsive to their window of tolerance, and in all cases to use common sense.

(6) UTILIZE THE BREATH

As Ogden (2015) points out in her guide to working with trauma, breath intervention can be a valuable resource for people working with trauma. It offers survivors the means to increase or decrease their arousal, depending on what will support their window of tolerance. While working with the breath is not an across-the-board solution to dysregulated arousal, it's a practical tool teachers and professionals can offer to someone struggling with hyper- or hypoarousal.

The basic guidelines in utilizing the breath are relatively straightforward: if someone is hyperaroused, they can take slower, deeper breaths to see if that supports self-regulation. If they are hypoaroused, they can gently increase the pace or intensity of the breath to support their window of tolerance. As Brooke stabilized in her Phase I work, for instance, she asked me about restarting her meditation practice at home. Given that she tended to experience hyperarousal in practice, I recommended that she try taking four to six deep, long breaths to begin her practice, or anytime her gauges were signaling that she was hyperaroused. I didn't want her to control her breath rigidly, but to slow her respiration to decrease her arousal and buoy her meditation practice.

Utilizing the breath comes with certain caveats. First, it's important that people don't alter their breath too intensely, either speeding up enough to cause hyperventilation or slowing their breath to a crawl. This kind of change invites catharsis, which can push people outside of their window of tolerance and undermine their attempt to find stability. A client of mine who was chronically hypoaroused took the invitation to increase his breathing too far: one night he lay on the floor and took big, deep breaths for 10 minutes. While this certainly created an emotional shift—it filled him with a sense of aliveness and electricity—it also put him out of his window of tolerance, leaving him dysregulated and over-energized the rest of the night. Second, not everyone will benefit from this modification. As Ogden and Fisher wrote, "issues such as heart problems, asthma, emphysema, diabetes, migraines, or anger management can all be contraindications to breath work" (2015, p. 370). Breath interventions are not a blanket prescription but must be tailored to the individual and used moment to moment.

(7) UTILIZE AROUSAL SCALES

As we covered earlier in the chapter, each person has a specific scope to their window of tolerance. Some have wide zones, meaning they can tolerate a lot of stimuli, while others have narrower zones, so that it takes less input to create dysregulated arousal. When people know if they're in or outside of their window of tolerance, they can more successfully self-regulate and make informed decisions about their lives.

One tool that students and clients can use to track arousal—and report to you, as a mindfulness practitioner—is an arousal scale ranging from 0 to 10.

Figure 5.4. An Arousal Scale to Assess Range

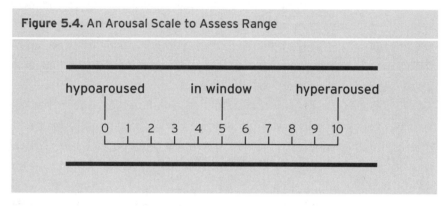

Figure 5.4. An Arousal Scale to Assess Range

On the low end of the scale, people may experience extreme fatigue, lethargy, and even immobility (hypoarousal). At the higher end, they can experience extreme agitation and heightened emotional reactivity (hyperarousal). While the actual numbers students and clients report are slightly arbitrary, using the scale enables them to track and determine their level of arousal, gives them an ongoing reference point about the breadth of their range, and enables them to self-report to teachers or clinicians on their level of internal arousal.

Arousal scales can be utilized in many different ways. A meditation teacher working with a traumatized student can ask them to share an "arousal number" before and after meditation sessions, for instance. This gives the student two chances to check in with themselves, and it provides the teacher with information about how the student is responding to practice. Such check-ins also create the opportunity to talk about approaches for maintaining one's window of tolerance that can be employed within meditation.

(8) STAY WITHIN YOUR OWN WINDOW

Imagine a student approaching a teacher at the end of a meditation to disclose a history of trauma. If the teacher is within their window of tolerance, they will be more likely to have access to their social engagement system, communicate more effectively, and serve as a regulating force. If the teacher is outside their window, they will more likely be triggered by the traumatic content, have less patience, and potentially lose *their* ability to communicate clearly and effectively.

As a person in a position of influence, you must remember that the width of your own window of tolerance impacts the quality of your relationships with students and clients. Our level of emotional and physical activation sends messages about what material is safe for people to bring up and explore, and in turn what content is more likely to be disavowed. Effective teachers and therapists often have wide windows of tolerance, in this respect. They have the ability to be present with a broad range of stimuli in their internal and external environments. Those looking for healing and guidance will often instinctively feel this capacity.

A friend of mine who had been attending a weekly, introductory meditation course told me a story that underscores the importance of this modification. In her third class, she decided to approach one of the teachers to ask how to work with memories of sexual abuse that were arising in practice. The first teacher she asked appeared startled, proceeding to ask a series of inappropriate questions that provoked a sense of shame (e.g., "Where did this person touch you, exactly? Why wasn't there anyone around to protect you?"). Sensing that the teacher was triggered—and likely out of her window of tolerance—my friend wisely cut the conversation short. She later approached the other teacher in the room and felt a palpable difference: the teacher maintained comfortable eye contact, thanked my friend for letting her know, and normalized the experience of such memories arising in meditation. My friend felt understood, and following the conversation left with some practical suggestions—and an ally.

To maintain a wide window of tolerance, we can engage in practices of self-care—deliberate interventions that support our overall health and bolster our ability to offer effective, competent care. These practices can include:

- Monitoring our own range using the 0 to 10 scale as a way to assess the level of our internal resources
- Engaging in personal activities that foster well-being and resilience (e.g., exercise, time in nature, social action)
- Meeting regularly with other colleagues to offer peer support and exchange ideas and challenges

When working with trauma, it's also useful to remember that engaging with someone's pain doesn't mean we assume it as our own. Activist and social worker Laura van Dernoot Lipsky (2009) refers to this as *trauma stewardship*—a practice of purposefully opening to another's hardship while not assuming their pain as ours. Whether we're a mindfulness educator, mental-health practitioner, or a person who practices mindfulness, we can develop a quality of presence in the face of trauma that allows us to be touched and impacted, but not overtaken.

The modifications I've covered here endeavor to protect and support trauma survivors practicing mindfulness. Offering people ways to modulate the intensity of mindfulness meditation is a way to empower them in practice. Adopting a moderate approach—returning, consistently, to the middle way—is a foundation of trauma-sensitive practice upon which the remaining four principles rest.

CHAPTER 6

Shift Attention to Support Stability: Avoiding the Fear/Immobility Cycle

*Unrestricted mindfulness toward any and all elements can
activate disturbing intrusions and overwhelming arousal
for people with PTSD and thus is often met with dismay,
judgment, self-criticism, and further dysregulation.*

—Pat Ogden

In his book *In an Unspoken Voice: How the Body Releases Trauma and
Restores Goodness*, Peter Levine referenced the myth of Medusa to illustrate the relationship between trauma, the body, and attention.[1] In the
myth, Medusa is depicted as a fearsome monster—a winged creature with
live, venomous snakes in place of her hair. Those who look at her face
become immobilized and turned to stone. Perseus, a Greek hero whose
task was to defeat Medusa, calls upon Athena, goddess of knowledge, to
ask her advice. Athena counsels Perseus that he must never look directly
at Medusa but use his shield to reflect her gaze. Adopting this strategy,
Perseus enters Medusa's cave and successfully slays the monster.[2]

Levine was apt in using Medusa as an analogy for trauma. Recall that
immobility is central to traumatic stress: if we're unable to flee or fight, we
freeze and—metaphorically, at least—turn to stone. With posttraumatic
stress, this freeze can force us into continually reliving unintegrated elements of trauma. We might lie awake in bed at night haunted by intru-

sive thoughts, or suffer under the weight of crushing sensations in our chest that signal we're in danger. With trauma, the horror that began outside of our body ends up trapped within.

This creates a dilemma for survivors practicing mindfulness. By following basic meditation instructions, survivors will eventually encounter traumatic stimuli—the invasive thoughts or gut-wrenching sensations that never seem to go away. While learning to observe and tolerate these stimuli is a key part of recovery, paying them *too much* attention can end up intensifying trauma symptoms. Sustained attention on traumatic stimuli—for reasons I'll cover in this chapter—can cause dysregulation, retrigger traumatic states, and land one outside of their window of tolerance. Absent the advice that Athena offered Perseus, survivors can come to fixate on traumatic stimuli over and over again—stimuli that need more than just mindful attention to heal.

This brings us to the second principle of trauma-sensitive mindfulness: *shift attention to support stability*. To support their window of tolerance, survivors must learn they can shift their focus away from traumatic stimuli during mindfulness practice. This might involve opening their eyes and paying attention to the surrounding environment—a tree outside the window, for example, or an object in the room. Or, rather than beginning meditation by concentrating on the breath, a survivor might choose anchors of attention that are more stabilizing for them, such as the feeling of their feet on the ground. We want our students and clients to be self-responsive and shift their attention in ways that support their window of tolerance. If someone is being pulled to look into Medusa's eyes, we want them to know how to purposefully shift their view.

DYLAN

Dylan began opening up about his traumatic past halfway through our first session. A shorter, soft-spoken young man from North Carolina, Dylan was transgender—an important part of his story. "I never really fit into boxes," he'd said the first time we met, pushing his glasses up his nose and adjusting his baseball cap. "I was raised as a girl, but it never fit. When I cut my hair and started dressing differently, people didn't know what to do."

When he was 15, Dylan asked his teachers and classmates to change his gender pronoun—to refer to him as "he" instead of "she." That, he said, is when the harassment really began. For the final two years of high school, a small group of students made his life a living hell, trolling him on social media, catcalling him, and threatening him physically while he'd walk with his head down in the hallways. "By the end of my school week," he said in a quiet, unsteady voice, "I could hardly take it anymore. Sometimes I didn't know if I was going to make it."

Thankfully, he did. He'd moved away four years earlier and loved his current life. He'd surrounded himself with a supportive community he felt safe with, and had a dog, Milo, who was a steadfast companion. But disturbing aspects from his past had followed Dylan from his hometown. He was having chronic nightmares about the bullying and flashbacks when he'd pass a high school. Even when he was safe at home he felt a visceral sense of threat. This had become especially true since North Carolina had passed a "bathroom bill" known as HB2—a law that bans people from using public bathrooms that don't correspond to the biological sex listed on their birth certificates.[3] For weeks, Dylan had been obsessively reading every piece of news he could find, his stomach sinking each time he read a story from back home. He knew his father supported the law, and he kept replaying some of the hurtful, disparaging things he had said to him as a teen. When he closed his eyes at night to sleep, he was inundated by voices of his father, classmates, or the news reporters he'd been watching.

The hardest part for Dylan was managing his attention. He was a meditator—the reason he'd reached out to me—and found that his attention was impossible to control. In general, he said, he'd often felt uncomfortable in his skin—the sense that he'd been born into a body that didn't feel congruent with his gender. But he was now constantly gravitating to a churning in his stomach, and other times a tingling on the back of his neck—a sensation that made it feel like someone was about to strike him. He'd open his eyes knowing that no one was there, but still felt menaced. Sometimes he'd freeze during this intensity and was unable to move. In his meditation practice, paying attention to his taut muscles only seemed to make him more afraid. Outside of his meditation practice, Dylan had started compulsively tracking for a particular shade of blue when he was walking down the street—the same blue that one of his high school assailants wore when harassing him. Dylan couldn't help watching for it and was flooded with anxiety anytime he saw that color.

"I'm so pissed these bullies are still inside my head," Dylan said, his jaw clenched and his eyes full of frustration. "I moved to get away from it, but it's still with me. I feel like some part of me was taken, and I want it back."

COMING TO ATTENTION: THE ORIENTING RESPONSE

Attention comes from the Latin word *attendere*—meaning, literally, to *stretch toward*—and connects to the Old French word *atendre,* which translates into *directing one's mind or energy.* A basic premise here is that energy follows attention. As you're reading these words, for example, you're investing energy in the topic of trauma-sensitive mindfulness. Alternatively, you could shift attention to a part of your body, feeling for the quality of contact it is making with your environment. Or you could turn your attention to someone you love and concentrate on their virtues. How we focus our attention shapes our mood and dictates where we devote our energy.

Each of us has hardwired, automatic impulses with attention. We direct it in predictable ways. Imagine that while reading these words, you heard an extremely loud noise. Quickly, a whole series of events would take place: your head and body would likely turn slightly toward the sound, your pupils would dilate, and the electrical properties of your skin would change in response to the subtle increase in arousal. Your attention would be compelled to the source of the noise. These aren't things you'd have to think about doing—they'd happen instinctively, as part of an automatic process.

This is known as an *orienting response*—a reflexive narrowing of consciousness to help us gather information about a novel stimulus. Orienting takes place in ways that are both visible and invisible to the naked eye. In response to a noise, for instance, we'll make external, physical adjustments to help us assess the situation, squinting our eyes, slowing our physical movements, or cocking our head in a way that we can hear more clearly. We can also make internal, mental shifts that are more difficult to see: we can alternate our attention between what is happening outside our bodies—the area where the noise came from—and internal feelings, such as tension in our face. These are known as overt (visible) and covert (invisible) orienting responses.

What does this have to do with trauma-sensitive mindfulness? People struggling with trauma will tend to *reflexively orient toward trauma-relevant stimuli*. This can include external stimuli, such as certain sounds or images, or internal stimuli, such as sensations associated with a traumatic experience. Often it will be a combination of both. In Dylan's case, he started to compulsively track for a certain color of blue in his environment, or the tingling in his neck. Meditation was underscoring the fact that he wasn't able to regulate his attention, and it was leaving him troubled and exasperated.

Dylan's knee-jerk orientation to trauma-relevant stimuli was an intelligent survival strategy. Though it was exhausting for him, deploying his attention toward perceived threats was an attempt to secure safety. He was tracking for danger to try to ward off a potential threat. Besides his traumatic experiences in high school, Dylan had good reason to be concerned for his well-being: as a transgender person, he was physically less safe than nontransgender people. In the United States, disproportionate violence against transgender people starts at an early age, and transgender people are at a higher risk for multiple types of traumatic violence.[4] As I've pointed out, an ongoing sense of threat is very real for people who are targeted by systems of oppression.

Inside of this, the kind of reflexive orienting that Dylan was doing was also preventing him from being able to accurately evaluate safety in his present-moment environment. Trapped in a body that was experiencing the present moment through the lens of a traumatic past, he was hyperfocusing on cues that—while once extremely relevant to safety—were not pertinent in the same way. In Dylan's case, the bullies were not present and his father was many time zones away. But his emotional brain was sounding the alarm, and Dylan was compulsively orienting to trauma-relevant stimuli—maintaining an internal sense of threat.[5]

In my sessions with Dylan, we worked with his attention in order to establish an internal sense of safety and stability. I started by helping him find areas of attention in his body that helped him feel comfortable and grounded. Sometimes this was the feeling of his back and buttocks against the sofa, specifically the feeling that he could rest his full weight there. Other times he'd focus on flowers in my office followed by the way his chest expanded in response to looking at them. This wasn't just a way for him to avoid his pain or endlessly distract himself. He'd eventually need to work with his unintegrated trauma. But in service of Dylan's window of tolerance, I wanted him to first viscerally experience the fact that his attention could be helped with self-regulation. He needed to get back some control over his life.

THE FEAR/IMMOBILITY CYCLE

In his study of traumatic stress, Levine observed that animals in the wild rarely become stuck in a long-term freeze, or immobility, response.[6] Recall that freezing increases the likelihood of survival for mammals: it can reduce a predator's urge to kill, buy time, or create a state of numbness that protects against extreme pain and terror. What Levine observed is that after a life-threatening encounter, animals typically discharge a freeze through shaking or running. They release the survival-based energy that was mobilized inside. As detailed in Robert Sapolsky's (1994) book *Why Zebras Don't Get Ulcers*, animals in the wild are skilled at integrating exceedingly stressful experiences.

A remarkable example of this can be seen in footage captured of a polar bear being ensnared in the wild. In the video, scientists in a helicopter can be seen tracking a polar bear whom they shoot with a tranquilizer dart—a kind of artificial freeze.[7] When the polar bear regains consciousness, its body begins to shake and discharge the survival-based energy that had been activated during the chase. In slow motion, you can actually watch the polar bear's legs mimicking the act of running—the strategy it had used to try to escape. After this shaking, the bear takes a few deep, regulating breaths—discharging survival-based energy—and comes back into balance.

Exiting immobility, as I discussed at the end of Chapter 1, is often much harder for humans. Emotions such as fear and shame can keep us from discharging survival-based energy and integrating a traumatic experience. An added focus for Levine here is the relationship between immobility and terror. When we're exposed to trauma, we can end up experiencing both simultaneously—becoming "scared stiff." If this happens, Levine suggested, sensations related to immobility become paired with those related to acute fear and helplessness. Like Pavlov's dogs, who came to associate the sound of a bell with food, we become conditioned to associate sensations related to immobility with terror, and vice versa. Levine refers to this as the *fear/immobility cycle*—a conditioned sequence in which our experience of one stimulus begets, and then reinforces, the other.[8] If we feel our lungs start to constrict, for instance—a part of the immobility response—we can start to feel intense fear. This fear deepens our freeze and our lungs constrict further, which then begets more fear. It's a vicious cycle.

What the fear/immobility cycle reveals is that paying attention to traumatic stimuli can actually retrigger traumatic states. By feeling fear, we can trigger—and deepen—a freeze. Dylan offered an example of this: When he was sitting in meditation, he became aware of a pit of fear in his stomach. If he brought mindful attention to these sensations, he'd sometimes enter into a mildly frozen state. He'd feel a subtle sense of paralysis when it was hard for him to move or take a breath. These sensations were not only uncomfortable for Dylan, but frightening. He wasn't in control of his body. By paying close attention to his present-moment experience, he ended up intensifying the symptoms he was trying to alleviate.

This brings us to what I refer to as *the Medusa problem*—the tendency to over-attend to traumatic stimuli in meditation. By asking survivors to pay close, sustained attention to their experience, we invite them into contact with unintegrated remnants of trauma: the sensation of being unable to breathe, for instance, or a jaw that's tightened in terror. This, importantly, can spark the fear/immobility cycle. Survivors become locked in a self-perpetuating loop that leaves them more helpless, isolated, and alarmed. In following basic meditation instructions, they lock eyes on Medusa and end up immobilized—essentially turned to stone.

The fact that attention can retrigger traumatic states is vital knowledge for us as trauma-sensitive practitioners. If we understand this—and the fear/immobility cycle—we can more effectively prevent people from retraumatizing themselves in practice. Rather than someone leaving a mindfulness class humiliated for having made their symptoms worse, we can normalize their experience. Like Athena to Perseus, we can offer practical, grounded suggestions to help survivors work skillfully inside of their practice and take steps toward integrating trauma.

SHIFT ATTENTION TO SUPPORT STABILITY: TRAUMA-SENSITIVE MODIFICATIONS

(1) EDUCATE OTHERS ABOUT MEDUSA

Offering students and clients basic psychoeducation about the role of attention—including the Medusa problem—can empower their practice. We want survivors to be informed about potential pitfalls of mindfulness. Like the window of tolerance, Medusa is a basic frame we can offer people to guide their overall practice.

In my second session with Dylan, I spoke to him about the Medusa problem. He was frustrated that his meditation practice—which had been grounding and vitalizing for several years—was making things worse. In our first conversation, my goal was to empathize with Dylan and normalize his experience. He'd gone through something traumatic, and his mind and body were responding in ways intended to keep him safe. I wanted Dylan to know how much respect I had for the parts of him that were trying to protect him, even though I knew they were causing him distress.

"I hadn't thought of it that way," Dylan said in our conversation, surprised by what I'd covered. "I thought I needed to get over this problem, not appreciate it." In the coming weeks, Dylan developed compassion for the way he was constantly tracking for danger. We talked about what it meant for him to be transgender, and given his history, why it was understandable he'd be compulsively searching for safety. He also grew to understand why he had to be careful with his attention in meditation, and why it could dysregulate him if moved outside of his window of tolerance.

Talking to students and clients about Medusa can be tricky. We don't want to make survivors more afraid of their inner world then they already are. But we do want them to have a framework for the strategies they adopt—a kind of scaffolding for the modifications we offer them. We want them to know why they're doing that as opposed to just applying rote techniques. Explaining the basic theory behind modifications— rather than leaving it a mystery—educates and empowers the people we're working with.

(2) ESTABLISH STABLE ANCHORS OF ATTENTION

Mindfulness meditation typically involves something known as an *anchor of attention*—a neutral reference point that helps support mental stability. An anchor might be the sensation of our breath coming in and out of the nostrils, or the rising and falling of our abdomen. When we become lost in thought during practice, we can return to our anchor, fixing our attention on the stimuli we've chosen.

But anchors can also intensify trauma. The breath, for instance, is far from neutral for many survivors. It's an area of the body that can hold tension related to a trauma and connect to overwhelming, life-threatening events. When Dylan paid attention to the rising and falling of his abdomen, he would be swamped with memories of mocking faces while walking down the hallway. Other times, feeling a constriction of his breath in the chest echoed a feeling of immobility, which was a traumatic reminder. For Dylan, the breath simply wasn't a neutral anchor.

As a remedy, we can encourage survivors to establish *stabilizing anchors of attention*. This means finding a focus of attention that supports one's window of tolerance—creating stability in the nervous system as opposed to dysregulation. Each person's anchor will vary: for some, it could be the sensations of their hands resting on their thighs, or their buttocks on the cushion. Other stabilizing anchors might include another sense altogether, such as hearing or sight. When Dylan and I worked together, it took a while until he could find a part of his body that didn't make him more agitated. He eventually found that the sense of hearing was a neutral anchor of attention. At my office, he'd listen for the sound of the birds or the traffic outside, which he found to be stabilizing.

"It's subtle," he said to me, opening his eyes and rubbing the back of his neck with his hand. "But it is a lot less charged. I'm not getting riled up the same way, which is a huge relief."

In sessions together, Dylan's anchor was a spot he'd rest his attention on at the beginning of a session or a place to return to if he felt overwhelmed. If he practiced meditation at home—I'd recommended short periods if he could stay in his window of tolerance—he used hearing as an anchor, or "home base" as he called it.

"I finally feel like I can access a kind of refuge," he said quietly, placing his hand on his belly. "My body hasn't felt safe in so long. It's a relief to finally feel like I'm learning how to be in here."

Anchors of attention you can offer students and clients practicing mindfulness—besides the sensation of the breath in the abdomen or nostrils—include different physical sensations (feet, buttocks, back, hands) and other senses (seeing, smelling, hearing). One client of mine had a soft blanket that she would touch slowly as an anchor. Another used a candle. For some, walking meditation is a great way to develop more stable anchors of attention, such as the feeling of one's feet on the ground—whatever supports stability and one's window of tolerance. Experimentation is key.

Using subtler anchors does come with benefits and drawbacks. One advantage to working with the breath is that it is dynamic and tends to hold our attention more easily. When we work with a sense that's less tactile—hearing, for instance—we may be more prone to drifting off into distraction. The more tangible the anchor, the easier it is to return to it when attention wanders.

(3) REORIENT ATTENTION

Another way to support one's window of tolerance—and avoid the Medusa problem—is to reorient attention in practice. If paying attention to the breath is causing someone to become too agitated, we want them to know they can open their eyes and attend to something different. Pushing oneself to stay mindfully focused on a particular stimuli is not necessary—nor helpful—for survivors. We want people to stay self-responsive and learn to shift attention if they're becoming dysregulated. But shifting attention away from traumatic stimuli isn't necessarily easy. It may run counter to a survival-based strategy. During a guided mindfulness practice I was offering Dylan to begin our third session, his face began to tense and he suddenly felt far away. "I can't feel anything," Dylan said. "I can't even feel you here, it's like I'm drifting away on an iceberg."

"That was a really smart response in the past, Dylan. And in this moment with me, see if you can stay here," I said kindly, but firmly. "Feel your feet on the floor; see if you can shift your attention to something different." He started shaking his head. I asked him to open his eyes. The fear on his face was striking—he looked like a young, scared adolescent. "This kid that used to mess with me all the time, Jake, a senior, I can't get him out of my head."

"Is there an area of your body that feels stable right now?" I asked. Dylan looked at me for a moment, and then said it was his feet. Maintaining eye contact with him, I had him spend a few minutes concentrating on the feeling of his feet on the floor. I wanted him to notice what felt good about it, and ground his attention there.

"I went away there for a minute," he said, clearly back in the room. I nodded. Again, my direction of Dylan's attention wasn't in the service of him forever evading traumatic memories. But we were still in an early stage of building safety and stability, and I wanted to make sure he could stay in his window of tolerance.

Redirecting attention is much harder in solitary meditation practice. When I was working with Dylan, I could track his arousal and help interrupt dysregulating habits of attention. It's simply more challenging to do this without a guide. Ideally, we want survivors to be able to redirect their attention competently and confidently, both in practice and their lives. If they feel themselves becoming dysregulated because of what they're paying attention to, we want them to be able to shift, purposefully attending to something else for a period of time. But one needs time and practice to train in how to do this, and most often it will be with the help of a trauma professional.

At a minimum, we don't want to drive survivors to pay repeated mindful attention to something that's destabilizing them. There's a good chance this will take them out of their window of tolerance. Instead, we want people to feel permission to be creative with the anchors of attention they use and be mindful in ways that support stability. There are also times when a survivor simply shouldn't be meditating without direct supervision. If someone is unable to consistently stay in their window, they should seek the guidance of a trauma professional. Survivors suffering from dysregulated arousal benefit from direct supervision, guidance, and support.

(4) ATTEND TO THE ENVIRONMENT

Building on the above modification, survivors can support their window of tolerance by orienting to their surrounding environment. This can be as simple as opening one's eyes during meditation and looking around. Whereas trauma wrenches us into the past, orienting to one's surroundings is a powerful, practical way to connect to the present moment.

Dylan practiced this often—both in my office and in meditation practice at home. If he started to become overwhelmed by a memory or sensation, he'd open his eyes and look out the window. Viscerally connecting to his environment was a way to remind his neurophysiology that he was safe—at least in that moment. If he was having a flashback to the bullying, for instance, he would look at the landscape outside and consciously register he was in a different city than he'd grown up in. Dylan knew that his vigilance was justified given the oppressive realities of the world. But he also used his environment as a way to find stability and safety, claiming the power he felt he'd lost in high school.

Attending to one's environment is straightforward with mindfulness. If one is in seated meditation with their eyes closed, they can open their eyes. One can also orient to the environment through touch or listening to sounds in their surroundings. People can also choose to label the objects that they are observing or sensing in the room (e.g., chair, window, traffic noise, or tree).

(5) FOCUS IN, THEN WIDEN OUT

Mindfulness practice typically draws upon two forms of attention: *focused attention*, which involves the voluntary and direct focus of attention on an object, and something known as *open monitoring*, which involves observing our experience without trying to focus our attention.[9] With focused attention, we focus on one thing only. In open monitoring, we let ourselves be aware of what's happening without trying to direct or control our attention. Mindfulness meditation uses both of these forms, beginning with focused attention—on the breath, for instance—and then opening the aperture of attention to monitor whatever is predominant in our field of awareness.

Of course, we can't predict how someone will respond to mindfulness. Focused attention will create stability for some survivors while dysregulating others. Here, the basic instruction is to progress from focused attention to open monitoring if it supports one's window of tolerance. We can have students and clients begin with focused attention on the breath—and then gradually widen their attention to include increasingly more stimuli—but we want them to track their own window. If one has a stabilizing anchor, the progression from focused attention to open monitoring can work especially well.

After a few months of working with me, Dylan had new knowledge and tools to bring to his meditation practice, which he'd resumed at home. We came up with a structure together that would keep him in his window: He would start his meditation by focusing on the anchor of hearing, then expand his attention to include physical sensations and then thoughts. If traumatic memories or intense sensations surfaced, he'd shift back to hearing. If unsuccessful in self-regulating, he would open his eyes and orient to his surrounding environment. If this didn't work, he'd call for his dog, Milo—which leads us to the final modification for this chapter.

(6) FOCUS ON RESILIENCE

Another way to work with attention is to focus on *resilience*—a counterbalance to trauma. "Resilience," Staci Haines wrote, "is our inherent capacity to see beauty, find connection, commune with something larger than ourselves, and create—even in or after horrendous experiences" (personal communication, June 20, 2016). It reflects our capacity to cope effectively with adversity and stress, and has a strong connection to both mindfulness and trauma.[10]

Resilience can involve purposefully turning our attention toward what brings us energy and joy. Neuropsychologist Rick Hanson (2009) refers to this as "taking in the good"—a practice we can purposefully engage in to internalize positive experiences. Recalling who or what we love is an example of resilience. So are self-care practices, or community events that nourish us. It helps remind us that our own bodies can be a source of pleasure as opposed to only trauma and pain. Communities can also engage in collective resilience practices in the face of trauma and oppression. Cara Page, a Black, queer activist and healer who is currently director of the Audre Lorde Project,* defined collective resilience as:

---

* The Audre Lorde Project is a Lesbian, Gay, Bisexual, Two Spirit, Trans and Gender Non Conforming People of Color center for community organizing, focused on the New York City area in the United States. For more information, see alp.org.

"Being able to transform inside of perhaps the worst conditions, but still on a cellular level being able to respond to intervene or transform what has been done to us or on us. . . to remember that that we deserve dignity, honor and a way to look at how we can sustain our well being, in a society that has almost normalized our physical, emotional and spiritual degradation. That in and of itself is collective resilience."[11]

In trauma-sensitive practice, resilience involves imagining a place, activity, or memory that connects us to a sense of well-being—a practice I learned from Staci Haines. This can be cultivated by introducing a brief intervention during mindfulness practice or by practicing a separate guided meditation. Once people feel they can stabilize their attention on the resilient stimuli—the feeling of being somewhere safe, or a positive memory—we can then guide them to feel physical sensations that correspond with the resilient object of attention.

Dylan's dog, Milo, was a good example of resilience. If Dylan was having trouble feeling settled and stable when he practiced at home, he would look across the room at Milo. Just seeing his warm, content face made Dylan feel softer inside. If he was in my office, he would imagine running with Milo in a park near his house. When he did this, Dylan's breathing would typically deepen and a feeling of aliveness would rush through his legs. He'd then bring his attention to the pleasant sensations that were running through his lower body, making an explicit connection between his body and mind.

Resilience isn't meant to be a way to bypass areas of pain in our life. It also isn't meant to be a practice to cover over inequities or oppressive violence. Instead, resilience increases our capacity to be present with life as it is. The modifications in this chapter are meant to support this ability when it comes to trauma. By helping survivors be strategic with their attention, we can help them utilize mindfulness to find stability in the midst of traumatic symptoms.

CHAPTER 7

Keep the Body in Mind: Working With Dissociation

---

*Trauma victims cannot recover until they become familiar with
and befriend the sensations in their bodies. . . . Physical self-
awareness is the first step in releasing the tyranny of the past.*
—Bessel van der Kolk

*Racism is a visceral experience. . . . You must never look
away from this. You must always remember that the sociology,
the history, the economics, the graphs, the charts, the
regressions all land, with great violence, upon the body.*
—Ta-Nehisi Coates

Reginald Ray paused and looked out over the crowd. A popular Buddhist teacher, Ray was reading from his book *Touching Enlightenment*,
an exploration of the relationship between Buddhist practice, the body,
and transformation.[1] It was a warm fall evening, and most of us in the
audience were settling in for a lecture. Ray, meanwhile, had other ideas.

"Everyone, please lie down," he said. The audience remained still.
"No, really," he said with a mischievous smile. "I'm serious. Please find a
place to lie down."

Ray had a reputation for challenging convention, but even this was
unexpected. The auditorium was packed, and it was impossible to lie

down without making contact with a complete stranger. Awkwardness filled the space, but we all made our way to the floor. If anything, Ray had our undivided attention.

"After four decades of meditation practice and teaching," he said, reading from his book, "many things have surprised me, but none more than the growing and somewhat anguished realization that simply practicing meditation doesn't necessarily yield results" (2008, p. 4). The audience grew quiet. "My experience," he continued, "suggests that our problem is very simple: we are attempting to practice meditation and to follow a spiritual path in a disembodied state, and this is inevitably doomed to failure."

The air left the room. Here was a respected Buddhist teacher—one of the people responsible for the popularity of mindfulness in the West— questioning the very effectiveness of a practice at the core of his tradition. But Ray wasn't suggesting that our efforts weren't up to par. It was that people were *thinking* about their bodies instead of practicing inside them. And this was the reason we were lying down: to connect to our internal world in a less conceptual way.

Ray isn't alone in this pursuit. The body has emerged as a central focus in psychology and is increasingly seen as essential to healing and transformation. This is especially true in the field of trauma. A brief scan of popular book titles—*The Body Keeps the Score*,[2] *The Body Remembers*,[3] *The Body Bears the Burden*[4]—reveals that trauma is now understood to be a physical as much as a mental experience. Posttraumatic stress lives on in our minds, but it also lives on in our bones, cells, and tissues.

For those suffering from posttraumatic stress, the body often becomes a minefield—a harbinger of sensations related to horrific, overwhelming events. It's the theater in which the agony of trauma is played out. In response, survivors will often dissociate from their bodies, pulling attention away from their inner world. They cut off from the visceral warning signals that they're constantly being bombarded with. This helps survivors manage traumatic symptoms, but it also comes at a significant price: by disconnecting from physical sensations, survivors also lose touch with the sense of being fully alive.

This makes the body an important domain in working with trauma. In the process of recovery, survivors eventually need to come back into connection with their bodies. They are asked to befriend their inner world in order to regain a sense of agency and control. Mindfulness can help with this, boosting our awareness of inner body sensations and our power to observe and tolerate what's happening within. But this isn't an easy task. Connecting with sensory information related to trauma is often intense and frightening. The instruction to "be mindful of the body" can be loaded and complex for survivors, and often they need particular suggestions and modifications to thrive.

This brings us to the third principle of trauma-sensitive mindfulness: *keep the body in mind*. As mindfulness practitioners, we want to ensure people are working skillfully with the body in mindfulness practice. This means understanding the risks and rewards of paying close, sustained attention to one's inner world—including practices such as body scans. We also want to create a physical environment that is conducive to the needs of survivors. By doing so, we can help make sure that survivors feel safe, dignified, and in control of their bodies when they're practicing mindfulness.

GINA

"What are you noticing right now?" I asked. It had felt like my client Gina had drifted away. A quiet, introverted woman in her mid-40s, she often sat with her hands clenched while pressing one thumb into the other.

"I'm not sure," Gina said, opening her eyes slowly and gazing at a bookcase across the room. "I think I went away."

I nodded, trying to normalize her experience. "I had that sense too. Do you know where you went?"

Gina paused and reflected. "I went *up*," she said, pointing her finger to the ceiling.

"That's great that you know that," I replied. "Does it feel familiar?"

Gina nodded, blinking away tears. Her tendency to float away was one of the main reasons she'd come to see me.

Four years earlier, Gina had been raped by an intimate partner. The two had been experimenting sexually, introducing bondage and role-play in ways that involved domination and submission. One night, Gina's partner had taken this too far, and she'd frozen in fear and had been unable to cry out—leaving her angry, ashamed, and dysregulated.

Gina had been struggling ever since. Despite that fact that she had broken up with her partner, her body continued to signal danger when she was safe and alone in bed. She also found herself dissociating and checking out in her life—especially when she got physically close to a new person she was dating. She was exhausted and afraid she'd never be able to be close to anyone again.

At the suggestion of a friend, Gina had taken up mindfulness meditation. She sought out a local sitting group, hoping that the practice could help extinguish or at least diminish the internal threat she felt. She wanted to better manage her emotions so she could once again date. At first she'd enjoyed the practice, finding stillness inside in a way she never had before. She began feeling more present in her life, and loved the community of people she was practicing with. But mindfulness meditation, she found, could also be excruciating: she'd become aware of a feeling of dread in her stomach, even after opening her eyes during the meditation and seeing that nothing menacing was there. The dissonance this created was frustrating and humiliating. "I know I'm safe," she'd say, "I'm surrounded by people who welcomed me and treated me kindly, but then I get scared for no good reason." After a few months she considered giving up.

Desperate to heal, Gina decided to attend a daylong meditation retreat to see if the sustained practice could shift something. In the afternoon of the daylong, she'd become absorbed in what felt like a powerful state of tranquility and concentration—everything became acutely quiet and still. When the bell rang to signal the beginning of a walking meditation period, she felt no impulse to move. Gina then sat though the walking period—and the following meditation sessions—until dinner. In total, she'd sat motionless in meditation for three hours, which she'd never done before. At the end of the day, the teacher praised her for her concentration, suggesting she come back the next month. Gina left feeling proud, accomplished, and hopeful that she was taking some practical steps toward her healing.

That night, however, Gina feared she'd dissociated on retreat. She felt spacey and distant, and could hardly feel the warm water on her skin while taking a shower before bed. In the days afterward, she'd felt foggy and disoriented, and had trouble stringing sentences together. She also loved mindfulness, and wanted to learn how to practice in a way that assisted with her recovery. When she reached out to me, she was determined to learn how to practice in a way that worked for her.

THE BODY AND TRAUMA

Our bodies are staggeringly compact and complex systems. Our small intestine is about 3.5 times longer than the length of our body—about seven meters long.[5] Our brains house approximately 100 billion neurons, which, if stacked like single pieces of paper, would stretch 5,000 miles upward.[6] Our cardiovascular system—arteries, capillaries, veins—if stretched from end to end, would extend out for 60,000 miles, circling the earth two times over.[7] As a teacher of mine, Richard Strozzi-Heckler, has said, our bodies house billions of years of evolutionary wisdom.[8]

This wisdom comes to us largely in the form of physical sensations—a steady stream of information about who we are in the present moment. To illustrate this further, as an experiment try asking yourself: What is my mood right now?

Now, how did you arrive at that answer? Did you think about it or search somewhere inside your body for clues? Typically, we assess our emotional state based on a constellation of internal sensations. A tight throat, aching shoulders, and shallow breath may translate into anxiety, or an open chest might correspond with happiness. Physical sensations inform our experience, help us navigate the world, and assist us in cultivating a sense of self.

Traumatic stress often makes it difficult to trust sensations. While we can usually depend on physical cues to help us self-regulate—knowing when we're hungry or needing to rest—trauma often leaves us with unreliable and inconsistent data. Because our emotional brain is continuing to sound the alarm, our bodies continue to respond in ways that suggest threat is imminent, even if it isn't. As Chicana writer and queer theorist Gloria E. Anzaldúa wrote:

"We are taught that the body is an ignorant animal intelligence dwells only in the head. But the body is smart. It does not discern between external stimuli and stimuli from the imagination. It reacts equally viscerally to events from the imagination as it does to real events" (1987, p. 37).

This process—of the body responding to threats ensnared in the mind—can make it hard for survivors to trust what they're feeling inside.

Take Gina. Lying awake in bed at night, she'd often have the feeling that something terrible was about to take place. For no apparent reason, her heart would be racing, her stomach would be clenched, and the back of her neck would tingle—all cues to her that suggested threat was impending. Sometimes she'd walk around her apartment and consciously check to make sure she was alone, but it never seemed to soothe her. She'd crawl back into bed and reexperience the same sensations she'd had the night of the assault.

When she dated someone new, being physically close to them often led to panic. She'd start to sweat and try desperately to hide the terror she was feeling. Even worse, she wasn't sure whether this information from her body was accurate. Should she trust her gut feeling that something was amiss? Or trust the person was safe and stick it out? Sometimes she'd dissociate entirely, having trouble moving and speaking during the date. The next day she'd often feel ashamed for her response and discontinue speaking to the person.

This is what makes trauma so cruel. Instead of integrating a traumatic experience, we become forced to reexperience it—over and over again—through the body. What was meant to be an adaptive, short-term response to threat becomes maladaptive and problematic over time. Our main navigational system—our inner body sensations—becomes compromised, and our ability to correctly assess the present moment vanishes. Our ability to detect what's safe versus what's threatening is lost, and we can come to mistrust our own experience.

EXTEROCEPTIVE AND INTEROCEPTIVE SENSATIONS

There are two kinds of sensations especially relevant to understanding trauma: *exteroceptive* and *interoceptive* sensations.[9] Exteroceptive sensations are those that help us relate to what is happening outside of our body. Exteroceptors, as they're called, are nerves related to the five senses of touch, taste, smell, sight, and hearing. We use exteroceptive sensations to gather information about the temperature of a bathtub by placing our hand in the water, for example. Interoceptive sensations, meanwhile, aid our perception of what's happening inside our bodies. Interoceptors are nerves that relate to what is happening for us internally, helping provide us with an embodied sense of self. Our guts, especially, provide us with tremendous amounts of interoceptive information that influence our entire organism. The neural network in the intestines, for instance, houses over 500 million neurons, helping to explain the terms *gut feeling* or *gut instinct*.[10]

Ideally, we're able to integrate exteroceptive and interoceptive sensations. Our internal experience lines up with our external experience, allowing us to make effective decisions about our behavior. We look out at a beautiful sunset and notice our chest warming and expanding, and in feeling this decide to take an extra minute to stop and watch it. Or we might have an uneasy feeling in our stomach when a friend walks in the room, prompting us to check in with them about their day. We depend on exteroceptive and interoceptive sensations to maneuver through the world.

With trauma, the integration between intero- and exteroceptors can go awry. Years after a traumatic event, interoceptors continue signaling that danger is forthcoming, even if exteroceptors don't reveal any source of threat. Gina's case is one example. Although information from her exteroceptors suggested her environment was harmless (e.g., no visual or auditory indications of threat), her interoceptors told her something was wrong (e.g., her stomach doing barrel rolls). It was a merciless dynamic that created understandable confusion, frustration, and distress.

People experiencing posttraumatic stress tend to place a disproportionate amount of attention on interoceptive sensations. They become compelled to attend to the alarming signals taking place inside their bodies. This creates problems when internal sensations are used exclusively to judge one's surroundings. As Rothschild wrote, "[Trauma survivors] are often so overwhelmed by the disturbing interoceptive input of their internal reality that they mistake it for external reality. This results in jumping to conclusions or judgments about the environment based on interoceptive experience rather than evaluating the actual circumstances via exteroceptors" (2017, p. 57).

Consider the setup this creates in mindfulness meditation. By asking people to close their eyes and focus internally, mindfulness practice encourages survivors to pay an inordinate amount of attention to interoceptive sensations. This isn't necessarily a problem, but it can be if one's inner world is constantly communicating threat. Gina ran into this problem when she started meditating. She'd close her eyes and discover internal cues conveying threat (e.g., a clenched stomach) but her external world didn't line up with what she was experiencing inside.

In my work with Gina, the key to resolving this dynamic was to help her develop dual awareness—a concept I covered in Chapter 2. Dual awareness means we can maintain multiple perspectives at the same time, including being able to balance awareness between our internal and external reality.[11] If I noticed that Gina was focused solely on interoceptors, I would jump in to refocus her attention to help her take in information about her surroundings (exteroceptors). One time I did this, she looked up at me, surprised. "This is exactly what I wasn't doing in meditation," she said. "I was just continuing to focus on the threat inside, and eventually I'd just check out."

In the initial stages of trauma recovery, survivors often require direct coaching and guidance to work with interoceptive and exteroceptive sensations. Trying to navigate them alone is an exceptionally difficult task. In the next chapter, I'll talk about the benefit—even the necessity—of working with trained trauma professionals in the context of mindfulness. At the very least, survivors require trauma-sensitive tools and modifications in mindfulness practice to ensure they are practicing safely. Without these, the basic practice of mindfulness can end up amplifying an already challenging experience, creating confusion, disappointment, frustration, and dysregulation.

DISSOCIATION

One common strategy to cope with dysregulating sensations is to dissociate—cutting away from one's physical and emotional experience. When our sensations are continually sending us threatening information, disconnecting from our bodies is a way to help us minimize stress. It is a smart, survival-based strategy that we can learn to recognize, honor, and address as trauma-sensitive practitioners.

Like trauma, dissociation exists on a spectrum.[12] It ranges from a mild detachment from our surroundings to a complete severing from our lives. We all daydream, for example, which we could call a "normal" dissociative state. You also might have driven your car somewhere and realized you'd spaced out the entire way. Most of us will have a dissociative experience that's noticeable but not necessarily clinically significant. Yet dissociation can also come in more potent forms, involving extreme psychological numbing,[13] amnesia, and the sense that the self or the world is unreal. Often these experiences are unexpected, inexplicable, and very unsettling.

Dissociation will often be correlated with traumatic experiences.[14] Trauma survivors will sometimes talk about the feeling of leaving their bodies or experiencing something known as *depersonalization*—witnessing oneself while having no control over the situation.[15] This is especially common in the case of child abuse that begins at an early age, with the level of dissociation having been found correlated with the severity of the abuse.[16] In the midst of a traumatic event, dissociation can help us handle unbearable sensations; in its aftermath, it can help us mitigate or tolerate traumatic sensations. Dissociation helps us get away when we can't.

In their book *Coping with Trauma-Related Dissociation*, Suzette Boon, Kathy Steele, and Onno van der Hart (2011) define dissociation by focusing on its opposite: integration. Recall from Chapter 1 that integration is crucial to understanding trauma: when we're integrated, we can make connections between thoughts, emotions, and historical experiences to gain a stable sense of who we are. Different systems in our body coordinate together well. Dissociation, meanwhile, is a failure of integration. We cut away from certain aspects of our experience—feelings or thoughts—which ends up disrupting our sense of self. This is an intelligent, protective strategy for many survivors, helping them self-regulate as best as they can. The problem is that the strategy also keeps survivors stuck over the long term, causing them to compartmentalize their pain and impairing their ability to integrate trauma.

This was the troubling bind Gina was in. Her dissociation was helping her endure the tumult she felt inside, but it was also keeping her stuck. She didn't want to dissociate, but didn't yet know how to stay. This was also the reason mindfulness meditation was so perplexing for her. Sometimes it felt like the practice was helping her feel more present, allowing her to observe sensations such as her breath. Other times, like on the daylong retreat, she'd dissociated and felt detached for the rest of the day. Even more baffling was the fact that her teacher had praised her for being able to sit still in meditation for so long. "Am I making progress?" she asked me, "or am I just checked out?"

In our work together, I encouraged Gina to become mindful about the particular ways she dissociated—the way she went "up," for instance. Once Gina knew how she was dissociating, it would be easier for her to return. We also tracked for triggers that caused her to dissociate, such as the feeling of fear in her stomach. With practice, she began to notice the moments when she'd dissociate, becoming compassionate toward herself when she did. "It makes sense that you want to leave," she would say silently to herself, placing her hand on her heart. "What happened was awful, but it's safe to be here now."

It's imperative that trauma-sensitive practitioners respect dissociation. We don't want to override a survival-based strategy—especially one directed toward managing agony. Rather than shame someone for not being able to stay present in meditation—or trying to force them back into the present moment—we can become curious about how dissociation is affecting their practice, and enter into a conversation about how we can best be of support.

So how can we best work with dissociation in the context of mindfulness? What strategies support survivors in working with potentially dysregulating interoceptive and exteroceptive sensations? For the rest of the chapter, I'm going to offer you 10 modifications intended to help survivors work with the body in mindfulness practice.

KEEP THE BODY IN MIND: TRAUMA-SENSITIVE MODIFICATIONS

(1) LEAVE PEOPLE IN CHOICE

Nobody chooses to experience trauma. Whether it's a natural disaster, a devastating accident, or an act of interpersonal violence, trauma often leaves people feeling violated and absent a sense of control. Because of this, it's vital that survivors feel a sense of choice and autonomy in their mindfulness practice. We want them to know that in every moment of practice, they are in control. Nothing will be forced upon them. They can move at a pace that works for them, and they can always opt out of any practice. By emphasizing self-responsiveness, we help put power back in the hands of survivors.

The body is central to this process. Survivors need to know they won't be asked to override signals from their body, but to listen to them—one way they'll learn to stay in their window of tolerance. We can accomplish this, in part, through our selection of language. Rather than give instructions as declarations, we can offer invitations that increase agency. Here are a few examples:

- "In the next few breaths, whenever you're ready, I invite you to close your eyes or have them open and downcast" (as opposed to "Close your eyes").
- "You appeared to be hyperventilating at the end of that last meditation. Would you like to talk to me for a minute about it?" (versus "You looked terrified. I need to talk to you").

In all of our interactions, we can tailor our instructions to be invitations instead of commands.

Another way to emphasize choice is to provide different options in practice. We can offer students and clients the choice to have their eyes open or closed, or to adopt a posture that works best for them (e.g., standing, sitting, or lying down). Any time we are offering different ways people can practice, we can also work to normalize any choice they make—one way is not superior to the other.[17] While we can encourage people to stay through the duration of a meditation period, we also want them to know that leaving the room—especially if they are surpassing their window of tolerance—is an option that is always available to them.

Providing choice was an indispensable part of my work with Gina. Any time that we did a mindfulness practice, I gave her a number of options: having her eyes open or closed during practice, for example, or working with anchors of attention besides her breath. The problem was that Gina believed there was a "right way" to practice mindfulness. She felt like a failure if she wasn't sitting cross-legged with her eyes closed, attending to her breath. She wanted to heal so desperately that she was often hard on herself, pushing herself in ways that didn't aid her healing. Over time, however, Gina began to see that being self-responsive—and respecting her window of tolerance—was a way she could honor her body and still work with mindfulness.

Emphasizing choice and autonomy isn't about coddling trauma survivors. As I mentioned earlier, there's still room for structure and rigor in trauma-informed practice. But while we want to encourage people to stick with structures that will support their transformation, we never want to force structures upon them. We can extend survivors the trust that they know what is best for themselves at any given time, conveying an attitude of curiosity and respect in our instruction.

(2) INCORPORATE MOVEMENT INTO PRACTICE

Asking a trauma survivor to attend to their body is no small thing. It invites them into direct contact with potentially harrowing feelings that are reminders of traumatic events. But we also want to support survivors in cultivating their capacity to observe and bear these sensations. We want them to be equipped with tools that will help them inhabit their bodies in mindfulness practice.

Incorporating physical movement into mindfulness practice is one way to accomplish this. For some survivors, it will be much easier to stay present with sensations while moving—either in walking meditation or stretching. In most mindfulness-based programs, walking meditation is a key aspect of practice: participants alternate between periods of still practice and structured walking meditation. Here I want to advocate for even more optional movement in mindfulness practice—if and when it supports individual survivors' facility to cultivate mindfulness. Sometimes a few minutes of optional preliminary movement before a seated meditation can be an effective doorway into connecting with the body. Or a mindful walk can be much more powerful for a survivor than a static meditation session. Intentionally sensing both interoceptive and exteroceptive sensations while moving freely through space can be very regulating.

Being able to move during mindfulness practice became very important for Gina. If she found herself dissociating while practicing mindfulness at home, she'd gently press her hands into her legs to remind herself to feel her lower body. Other times she'd massage her feet during meditation as a way to ground herself in the present moment. Sometimes Gina needed to give herself permission to walk outside instead of practicing.

She'd mindfully concentrate on the feeling of her feet on the ground or shift her attention between interoceptors (the feeling of her lungs expanding and contracting) and exteroceptors (the sounds of birds in the trees). Sometimes she'd just let herself space out in thought, knowing she couldn't always be mindful. It was whatever she needed that day and in that moment—an important skill for survivors to develop.

The relationship between trauma and movement has been studied in depth at the Trauma Center at Justice Resource Institute in Massachusetts. Researchers there have explored the particular relationship between yoga asanas, or postures, and a biological marker called heart rate variability—a way to measure the integrity of one's arousal system. Research has shown that a modified, trauma-sensitive yoga program may in fact regulate arousal and positively impact PTSD symptoms.[18] David Emerson and Elizabeth Hopper's (2011) *Overcoming Trauma Through Yoga* describes this program in detail and offers useful insights about trauma-informed practice in the context of movement.

(3) WATCH FOR SIGNS OF DISSOCIATION

It's important for trauma-sensitive practitioners to watch for signs of dissociation in our students and clients. This isn't to make a formal diagnosis but to identify people potentially struggling in practice. If we notice that a student or client is dissociating, we can gently invite them into conversation and discuss the best options moving forward—more supervised practice, or perhaps working more closely with a trauma professional. We enter into a collaborative process to help determine what will serve them best.

Below are some possible signs of dissociation. Given that it's difficult to detect dissociation purely by watching someone in meditation, I've included signs that can appear primarily in conversation:

- Fogginess, appearing disconnected from their body.
- Automated movements and intensely flat affect.
- Person reports feeling they are a long way away.

- Person cannot hear our voice and/or constantly asks others to repeat questions.
- Person is staring off into space without blinking and not responding to any questions.
- Person loses sense of time and cannot remember what happened previously.
- Consciousness appears to fluctuate—you notice the person "isn't there" or seems preoccupied with internal distraction.
- Person cannot maintain a continuity of story or experience in conversation (e.g., jumping from topic to topic).
- In conversation with the students or client, you yourself begin to feel foggy, confused, or like you're floating. This can be a sign that the person you're connected with is dissociating.

It can be challenging to distinguish dissociation from intense periods of deep concentration. Different contemplative traditions have different explanations and assessments for out-of-body experiences. If Gina had continued on with her teacher, for instance, he may have encouraged her for years to continue on in the vein she was working. This can end up being a case of *spiritual bypassing*—a term coined by teacher and psychotherapist John Welwood to explain the use of spiritual or contemplative practice as a way to avoid difficult emotions and developmental tasks.[19] Used in this way, practice ends up being a place where people stunt their growth. But it can also be tricky to ascertain when someone is dissociating because it exists on a spectrum. Ultimately, I believe this gets back to letting individuals decide what's best for them. When in doubt, we can also contact a trauma professional in order to receive support and consultation (see Chapter 8).

(4) UTILIZE EXTEROCEPTIVE SENSATIONS FOR GROUNDING

If a student or client is dissociating, having them focus on exteroceptive sensations can be a useful grounding technique. The five senses of touch, taste, smell, hearing, and seeing can help a survivor arrive back in the present moment, supporting the window of tolerance. Here are some examples:

- **Touch**: You can encourage a survivor to find (or bring in) an object that feels grounding and stabilizing to touch. This might be a soft blanket or another object. It could also be placing a hand on a solid floor. You can also have survivors make contact with their own bodies (e.g., the feeling of hands pressing together, one's tongue pressing into the roof of the mouth, or gently rubbing oneself on the chest).

- **Taste**: A survivor who tends to dissociate during practice can carry a small food item that has a pleasant, intense taste.[20] This can be a piece of candy or lozenge that can retain one's focus and ground them in the here and now. As trauma-sensitive practitioners, you can also have these items on hand and offer them when appropriate.

- **Smell**: Similar to taste, survivors can equip themselves with items they can use to reground themselves in the present, such as a small bottle of essential oil or hand lotion. If someone is feeling spacey, this can help bring them back to the present moment. These items conflict, however, with a suggested modification below on creating scent-free spaces, so it is recommended that people use these items outside instead of in a shared space.

- **Hearing**: Survivors can use sounds around them to ground themselves in the present moment if they find themselves dissociating. Whatever the sound, it can be used as an anchor to return to the here and now.

- **Seeing**: Like Modification 4 in Chapter 6, we can encourage survivors to notice and name objects in the surrounding environment to ground attention in the present moment and support integration. This can be a particular piece of furniture, color, or object that one finds supportive to look at. Naming this object internally (e.g., "couch; the color blue") can also be a valuable way to come into the present moment.

In *Coping with Trauma-Related Dissociation*, the authors recommend a combined sequence of these above senses. An individual can notice three different objects for each sense door (e.g., three objects that are visible in the room) and then linger on each one. In going through this sequence with other exteroceptors, a person can concentrate on the fact they are noticing these objects in the present moment in the room they are in, utilizing touch or smell, for example.

(5) BE CAUTIOUS WITH BODY SCANS

A body scan is a technique utilized in programs such as MBSR to heighten awareness of the body, release tension, and quiet the mind. Body scan practices typically involve having people lie on their back with legs spread out and arms to the side, palms up. A thorough body scan can take anywhere between 30 and 45 minutes of uninterrupted focus and can produce great benefits for participants. For instance, in her mindfulness research with trauma survivors, Trish Magyari found that body scans were the most helpful aspect to some survivors in their trauma recovery.[21]

But as I covered in the last chapter, placing intense, sustained attention on physical sensations can also be dysregulating for survivors. Asking a survivor to lie down and pay close, myopic attention to specific areas of the body for an extended period of time can be distressing. Having an averse reaction to a body scan—a practice that is often assumed to produce only relaxation and ease—can also be shame inducing, leaving survivors alienated for the fact they can't participate in a basic practice. A body scan therefore needs to be used cautiously in trauma-informed practice and offered with particular modifications.

Keeping with Modification 1 of this chapter, survivors need to feel in choice when practicing a body scan. They must be able to implement the practice in ways that work for them and know they are in control throughout. Modifications can include positioning oneself in different postures (e.g., sitting up), keeping one's eyes open, or lying on one's side. Survivors who opt out or take a break from the practice can be encouraged to rejoin at any time.

Offering preparatory suggestions for the body scan is another key way to instill agency in others.[22] If we let people know what to expect in the practice—and furnishing survivors with modifications they can use during the practice to support their window of tolerance—they are better equipped to have a successful experience (e.g., that they can open their eyes or shift posture). Predictability builds safety and trust. We also want to normalize numbness during a body scan or affirm someone's choice not to linger on a particular area of the body. In my experience working with survivors, I've often found that people assume they *should* be able to feel different areas of their body and are flawed if they can't. But this isn't true. Many survivors can't feel different body parts when first asked, and we want to normalize this experience. Noticing that one cannot feel is actually a great step forward.

Finally, facilitating some kind of debrief with an individual or a group following a body scan can help support survivors. Asking people about their experience elicits useful, relevant information for you, the practitioner. If you learn that someone struggled during a group practice and is feeling dissociated, for instance, you can approach them afterward to offer support. Interacting with people also enlists the social engagement system, which promotes emotional regulation and supports the window of tolerance. Having people share their takeaway also invites and deepens new learning and can normalize any difficult or abnormal experiences they may have had.

(6) BE FLEXIBLE WITH POSTURE

In any posture in which one is practicing meditation, the general aim is to balance being alert while also being relaxed. Traditional postures include sitting, standing, and lying down. In trauma-sensitive mindfulness, we want to be flexible with posture, encouraging people to practice in ways that support their window of tolerance. When we're offering mindfulness instruction, it's useful to state these different options around practice, reminding people that it's okay to move between postures while practicing. In collective spaces, we also want to make sure we have a sufficient number of chairs available for sitting meditation.

Lying meditation can present the added challenge of falling asleep during meditation—something that can become distracting if someone is snoring in a meditation hall. Students who engage in lying meditation can raise their hand in the air with their elbow still on the floor. If the meditator falls asleep, their arm falls, ideally causing them to wake up. It's one suggested way we can guide people to maintain alertness even when lying down.

(7) RESPECT PHYSICAL BOUNDARIES

Respecting the physical boundaries of all clients and students is a funda-mental part of trauma-sensitive practice. While being aware of other peo-ple's boundaries is a generally good practice, it's critical that we work to ensure survivors feel safe, respected, and at choice in our presence and the environment we create. From asking people's permission before touching them to making sure people feel in choice around their personal space, we want to continually attend to people's physical and emotional safety.

As I covered, trauma survivors can often feel out of control in their bodies. They commonly experience intrusive thoughts and emotions, or find themselves coping with chronic dysregulated arousal. Their bodies can be difficult, triggering terrain. Survivors of interpersonal trauma, especially, may have had their personal boundaries violated: their con-sent was not sought, or their sense of choice and agency was breached. For this reason, we must constantly attend to the ways our physical presence impacts another person. It is a good practice not to walk or linger behind a survivor, for instance. Doing so can evoke a sense of being "crept up on" or may kindle a historical trigger. It's best to stay in view of someone and let them continually assess safety.

This holds true with physical contact. If we are in close proximity while talking to someone—kneeling down while they are sitting on a meditation cushion, for instance—we don't want to touch the person's leg or shoulder, even if our intention is to express care. Or, if someone is crying and we have the impulse to put a hand on their shoulder or back, we always want to ask permission first. A simple question—"can I put my hand on your shoulder?"—communicates that we're actively seeking consent and will respect one's physical boundaries. This is especially true if we hold more social power in the interaction. By virtue of being a mindfulness teacher or mental-health professional, we'll hold more power over someone we're teaching or working with. This will be amplified if our social identity is more privileged than theirs (e.g., a man talking to a woman). Sometimes our identity will enable us to empathize with the experience of someone we're working with; other times a power differential will be present, and our presence alone can be triggering. What's important is that we attune to this dynamic in an ongoing manner.

(8) CREATE SAFER SPACES

Creating safer physical spaces involves tending to different aspects of one's environment to support survivors in their practice. By doing so, we actively engage in the process of making an environment as safe and secure as possible. Below are a few suggestions to create a safe, trauma-sensitive environment. Needs will differ based on your location and the specific needs of the people you're working with:

- **Lighting**: A trauma-sensitive space should be relatively well lit. Dim or dark settings can be triggering by diminishing one's ability to actively track for safety. If for any reason you decide to change the lighting in the space, announce this to the person or group and/or ask permission.
- **Protect Privacy**: In the event that you're practicing in a space where there are windows viewable by the general public, these windows can be covered to protect privacy.
- **Exits**: Make sure that exits are identifiable and easily accessible. While this suggestion keeps with basic safety, it is important that survivors have a clear exit path to the door, are not blockaded in, and sense they can leave at any time.
- **Offer a Predictable Class Schedule**: To promote a feeling of agency and self-control, those of you teaching mindfulness to groups can offer a predictable structure for classes.[23] Given

that trauma survivors are often coping with a lot of uncertainty (e.g., when they might have a flashback), offering up a schedule of a class beforehand—and keeping these structures consistent—is a valuable way to promote safety and trust through predictability and transparency. These structures can be changed as a course progresses and you track the emerging needs of the group.

(9) OFFER A SCENT-FREE ENVIRONMENT

All people, and particularly people who have experienced trauma, require access to safe spaces that facilitate transformation and healing. With this in mind, trauma-informed mindfulness practice involves creating a fragrance-free space. This means refraining from wearing perfumes and clothes washed in scented detergents and asking students or clients to do the same. It is a practice that prioritizes safety, accessibility, and health and well-being.

Creating a scent-free space is particularly relevant for survivors. Smell is a powerful sense that can quickly arouse traumatic triggers: a specific cologne or perfume may produce a painful memory. Additionally, a scent-free space supports access for people who experience *multiple chemical sensitivity*—a physical condition resulting from overexposure to chemicals.[24] Those who are targeted by oppression—people of color, those who are impoverished—more often work in environments where they are overexposed to chemicals, resulting in health conditions that can prevent them from accessing spaces that aren't scent free. Whether someone is experiencing traumatic symptoms, multiple chemical sensitivity, or both, we want them to participate fully in the mindfulness practices we're offering. Adopting scent-free spaces is one way to accomplish this.

The East Bay Meditation Center (EBMC) in Oakland, California, is a powerful example of a group adopting scent-free practice. Offering meditation training and teachings from Buddhist and other wisdom traditions, the EBMC was founded on a mission to "foster liberation, personal and interpersonal healing, social action, and inclusive community building" (East Bay Meditation Center, 2017). The EBMC offers a comprehensive resource page to prepare participants in their programs to be scent free and a detailed list of fragrance-free products that one can use.* Some specific guidelines include:

- Using scent-free laundry detergent for the week leading up to a course (or simply adopting scent-free practices on an ongoing basis)
- Avoiding fabric softeners that have strong scents
- Using fragrance-free soap, shampoo, lotions, and hair products
- Reading the ingredient labels on all products used on your body or clothing

Offering a scent-free space also means refraining from burning incense and ensuring that there are scent-free soaps available in bathrooms. It's a modification that requires commitment and practice, and increases accessibility for survivors looking to access safe, transformative, and trauma-sensitive practice.

(10) OFFER GENDER-NEUTRAL BATHROOMS

Offering gender-neutral bathrooms is another practice that enhances safety and accessibility within trauma-sensitive practice. A gender-neutral bathroom means that people of any gender can use them. The goal here is not necessarily to turn every bathroom available into a gender-neutral facility, but to ensure there is at least one gender-neutral bathroom accessible to students and clients. This practice and initiative ensures that all people have a place where they feel as safe as possible using the bathroom.

Why gender-neutral bathrooms? Transgender and gender noncon-

---

* The EBMC took a lot of time and energy compiling this list, and it's a powerful resource for anyone interested in educating themselves about scent-free practices. If you decide to share this list with students and clients, please consider contributing financially to the EBMC (who do not charge registration fees for their programs). See eastbaymeditation.org.

forming people are subject to oppression*—they face harassment, intimidation, and violence on an everyday basis.[25] This is inseparable from trauma. In addition to the direct violence transgender people face, the stress of being continually confronted or questioned about one's choice of restroom is an additional violence, or microaggression, that can lead to overwhelm and dysregulation. As I've raised at different moments throughout the book—and I'll explore more in Chapter 9—adopting trauma-informed practice involves an ongoing commitment to increasing one's consciousness about the ways people are impacted by systems of oppression, including how this relates to trauma. This is especially true if we've been more sheltered from oppression and experience more privilege. Offering gender-neutral bathrooms is one way to make sure that people feel safe, acknowledged, and at choice.

Here are some different ways you can adopt gender-neutral bathroom facilities in the spaces you work within:

- Place gender-neutral bathroom signs on single-occupancy bathrooms.
- If you have access to more than two multi-stall bathrooms, designate one of these bathrooms as gender-neutral.
- Have signs that direct people toward gender-neutral and gender-specific bathrooms.
- If you're not in a position to offer gender-neutral bathrooms, take steps to address this. This may entail asking a neighboring business to share or rent space, or having conversations with a landlord.
- Educate yourself about the importance of gender-neutral bathrooms if you haven't already (e.g., Heartland Trans Wellness Group, 2017).

---

* The term *transgender* is "an umbrella term for people whose gender identity and/or gender expression differs from what is typically associated with the sex they were assigned at birth" (GLAAD, 2017). The term *gender-nonconforming* is used to describe a person whose gender expression differs from traditional views of what is masculine and feminine. Note here that not everyone who is transgender will identify as gender nonconforming and vice versa.

CHAPTER 8

Practice in Relationship:
Supporting Safety and Stability in Survivors

[Trauma] recovery can take place only within the
context of relationships; it cannot occur in isolation.
—Judith Herman

When I first pulled into the dirt parking lot of the Birken Forest Buddhist Monastery in 2005, I was amazed it existed at all. Located in the back-country of British Columbia's interior region, the secluded monastery is completely off the electrical grid and feels in the middle of nowhere. Aligned with the Thai Forest Tradition of Theravada Buddhism, Birken welcomes lay practitioners such as myself interested in practicing along-side the monks and nuns who live there. I'd signed up for a two-week stay, hoping to deepen my practice and discover what living at a monastery was like. Judging by the swarm of black flies waiting for me outside the car, the idealism I carried with me was going to be challenged right away.

In keeping with monastic tradition, monks and nuns at Birken adopted a strict code of precepts, or ethical guidelines: they refrained from handling money, growing and cooking their own food, and making physical contact with others. Monastics also lived in individual cabins, known as *kutis*, which were scattered along a small, beautiful riverbank on the property. These cabins had no electricity, water, or toilet facilities, and were minimalist in design. Each night at dusk I'd watch the monks and nuns walk back to their kutis for continued solitary practice and was inspired by the strict commitments they'd undertaken.

About a week after my arrival, I met a woman named Rachel who'd just arrived at the monastery. She was a university engineering student who'd never practiced meditation and figured she might as well dive in head first. She seemed to enjoy herself, asking questions where appropriate and following the meditation schedule rigorously. But four days in, her mood noticeably shifted. She began walking through public spaces with her head down, and that night I heard her crying in the adjacent room. At breakfast the next morning, I could see she was still in a great deal of emotional pain.

During a question and answer period with one of the monks the next day, Rachel shared more of her story. She'd been on vacation in Thailand four months earlier, during the 2004 Indian Ocean earthquake and tsunami—one of the most devastating natural disasters in history. The death and destruction she'd borne witness to had haunted her ever since. She'd come to the monastery in part because of its connection to Thailand and was struggling with images and memories of the tsunami in meditation practice. She found the hardest part, however, to be the quiet and solitude: "I thought coming here and being in silence would help me heal," she said as she started to cry, "but it's just bringing it back up. I'm trying to be mindful of the memories, but all I feel is sad and alone."

We sat quietly and waited to see how the monk would respond. He stayed present with Rachel as she continued to cry. "Being mindful of this pain can be helpful," he eventually said, "but it alone won't always help. You can stay here, but it also may be best for you to go home and be with family and friends. Sometimes, people—not silence and solitude— are the best medicine for such wounds." Rachel looked up and nodded, seemingly in agreement with what he'd said. I, on the other hand, was surprised: I'd mistakenly assumed the monk would encourage her back into silence and practice, but he could see she might have needed something different from what the monastery could offer.

Since visiting the Birken monastery, I've learned that what the monk said was right and true: we can't heal trauma in solitude. Recovery requires relationship. Whether it's the safe and reassuring smile of a loved one or the trained guidance of a trauma professional, other people are a wellspring of self-regulation. They help us feel safe, modulate our arousal, and support us in staying in our window of tolerance. While solitary mindfulness meditation can be a powerful practice for survivors, it is most effective for survivors when paired with practices that involve interpersonal connection.

This brings us to the fourth principle of trauma-sensitive mindfulness: *practice in relationship*. While mindfulness is a relational practice at its core, this principle refers specifically to interpersonal relationships— as in those between two or more people. Practicing in relationship means we leverage the potential benefits of interpersonal relationship for survivors, buoying their safety, stability, and the window of tolerance. Sometimes this will mean offering longer—or more frequent—interviews to students on meditation retreats or connecting survivors with a trauma professional. Other times it will involve creating specific agreements that support the communities you're offering mindfulness to. Like what the monk did with Rachel, our work is to try to track the individual needs of survivors and offer counsel that best serves their recovery.

SAM

"If I was stronger," Sam said to me, "I'd be able to stick with my practice. But I can't. I feel like a failure."

I nodded into the camera on my computer. Sam had reached out to me from Italy, where he was living in his friend's attic. He'd been a devout meditation practitioner for years, attending 10-day meditation retreats twice a year and maintaining a diligent meditation practice at home. But his last retreat had left him dismayed. Halfway through, he'd started feeling overtaken by rage and panic. He felt waves of intense energy moving up and down his spine, and he broke a sweat trying to hold back a scream he wanted to release into the meditation space. Because of this, Sam began meditating alone in his room, but he was too distracted by an underlying fear of losing control to immerse himself in his practice. Recognizing this only seemed to exacerbate his dread: that night he started having panic attacks, hyperventilating in his solitary room. He eventually met with a teacher, which helped, but the moment the interview ended, he found himself back in the same place: anxious, angry, and uncertain.

Sam was now six weeks out from the retreat and feeling highly dysregulated. He was having trouble sleeping, was spacey and disoriented, and was struggling with panic attacks every other day. Even making simple decisions about what to eat left him overwhelmed. He also felt ashamed for what had taken place on retreat and felt misunderstood when he explained what had happened to others. He was meditating twice a day at his friend's house—trying in vain to gain control back over his body—but he didn't know whether the practice was helping or hindering his progress.

Sitting across from me on the video call, Sam looked frustrated, fragile, and scared. He didn't know what was happening. When I asked if the emotions he'd felt on retreat held relevance for him, he nodded. He'd been raised by a single father who left him alone at home, sometimes for days at a time. He'd learned to make his own meals by the time he was six and read books as a way to cope with the loneliness. Sam had grown up with the deep, pervasive sense that something was wrong with him. Why else would his father have neglected him? Panic attacks had been a regular occurrence in his life—though they'd never been this severe—and the insecurity he often felt inside was unbearable.

Mindfulness mediation had been a refuge for Sam. He'd discovered the practice as a teenager and found that it helped him manage the potent mix of emotions that lay dormant inside—primarily anger, hurt, and shame. Mindfulness proved to be a kind of buffer, supplying Sam some perspective on his inner world. Sometimes on retreats he'd momentarily been able to imagine forgiving his father, extending him compassion during guided loving-kindness practices. But on his most recent retreat, this feeling had disappeared, leaving terror and indignation in its wake.

When I asked if these feelings held relevance for him, Sam opened up further about his past. "When I grew up I spent a lot of time alone in my room," he said, "even when my dad wasn't home. I liked pretending that he was in the kitchen cooking me dinner. When I was on retreat, I looked around my room and it suddenly felt the same way. Like no one was coming for me." Sam's jaw tightened and tears came to his eyes. "It makes me want to cry and punch through a wall at the same time."

This was an entryway into deeper work with Sam. The neglect Sam had experienced was traumatizing—an isolation too much for his young mind and body to bear. The impact of the trauma was showing up in the form of panic attacks, devastating self-blame, and disintegrated memories. Mindfulness meditation had brought this trauma to the surface, but it was unlikely that solitary practice was going to help him through. He needed a particular quality of connection with others to begin working with the extreme anger, self-contempt, and grief that lay dormant inside. Mindfulness would help him on the path to integrating trauma, but at this stage, he needed relationship to heal—the care and safety that he'd been denied as a child.

SAFETY AND NEUROCEPTION

Safety is a key component of trauma-sensitive practice. Unless someone we're working with feels safe, their practice will go nowhere fast. As practitioners, our work is to keep people's safety at the forefront of our mind.

A basic definition of safety is being protected from loss, danger, and harm. One's safety can be material—such as having access to food, water, and shelter—and it can also be relational, such as when we're not fearful for our well-being around other people. When we feel safe, we trust that our personhood will be cared for and our survival is not in peril.

One of the ways we assess safety is through something called *neuroception*, a term coined by Stephen Porges to describe how our "neural circuits distinguish whether situations or people are safe, dangerous, or life threatening" (2004, p. 19). As opposed to *perception*, which depends on cognitive awareness of sensory input, neuroception takes place unconsciously, in the most primitive parts of our brain. We are built to weigh environmental and behavioral cues that help us figure out whether or not we're safe. If we "neurocept safety," our nervous system inhibits our animal defenses (fight, flight, and freeze) and grants us access to our social engagement system. This means we'll be in our window of tolerance. If we don't neurocept safety, we fall back on defensive, sympathetic responses such as fight or flight.

Some trauma survivors experience something called "faulty" neuroception. When this happens, safety cannot be recognized even in an environment that would normally be nonthreatening to them.* This aligns with what we know about trauma, where intrusive thoughts, memories, and sensations prevent us from correctly judging threat in the present moment. Ogden explained it this way:

> Continuing to neurocept danger, [trauma survivors] often experience intrusive fears and phobias, waves of shame and despair, impulses to desperately seek help, fight, flight, freeze, or shut down, that sabotage their efforts to function. . . . [They] experience an ongoing failure of integration. (2015, p. 37)

This, as I covered, is one of the paralyzing costs of trauma: a horrific, overwhelming event comes to play out indefinitely in our bodies and minds. The emotional brain continues to sound the alarm, thwarting survivors from being able to accurately assess when they're safe. For many, this danger is not simply an issue of faulty neuroception. Oppressive conditions mean that safety is not granted to all people. But faulty neuroception does happen, and it can amplify this dynamic. It becomes exceedingly difficult to ascertain when one is safe and one is not.

Relationship is a powerful domain to work with neuroception. Survivors are often hurt in relationship—sometimes directly, and other times

---

* Each of us lives in a world in which, for people in certain social contexts, safety is frequently compromised. In such cases, a person's feeling threatened can't simply be dismissed as an issue of faulty neuroception. As we covered in Chapter 1, people who are systemically marginalized—for example, people of color and poor people in the United States—are more likely to experience forms of state violence tied to systems of oppression. For many people, the world simply isn't safe.

because people weren't present for them in a moment of intense distress. In the container of relationship—especially with a trauma professional—another person can help us generate safety. In my work with Sam, for instance, helping him develop a sense of safety—both in his life and in our relationship—was a vital and immediate focus: I was able to track and attune to his emotions and empathize with any specific fears that were triggered by our work together. I could also help control the pace of his work through questions and interventions, all of which were designed to establish safety in the present. Survivors often need this kind of anchor to work effectively with trauma symptoms.

This is where mindfulness meditation can present issues for survivors. For some people, the setup of a meditation environment can keep them from neurocepting safety. Other times it can directly trigger safety concerns. In meditation, people lose the benefit of obtaining social cues that relate to safety: they close their eyes to meditate or open them to see the backs of the people in front of them. On silent retreats, people tend to not make much eye contact or speak to each other—save a short interview with a teacher every few days. This solitude can support mindfulness, but the lack of social engagement can be triggering for some. The key here is that we remain attuned to the relational needs of survivors in a dynamic way. We resist the temptation to think solitary practice will necessarily be the best fit for someone and stay open to offering modifications that support their relational needs.

RELATIONSHIP AND SELF-REGULATION

In my initial sessions with Sam, my focus was on helping him self-regulate. This involved introducing him to the window of tolerance, finding points of attention that were stabilizing for him, and helping him track signs that he was approaching his thresholds. Sam was having difficulty feeling in control, and I wanted him to feel the opposite: stable, safe, and fundamentally in choice.

Like safety, self-regulation is an important component of trauma recovery. When we are in the throes of dysregulated arousal, it can be tremendously hard to function—akin to being caught in a devastating internal storm and being asked to navigate an external world. By enlisting the support of a trained professional, however, we can learn how to regulate—almost like borrowing a power from them that we desperately need. This is actually a birthright we carry: we're born with a limited capacity to self-regulate and as babies rely on the people closest to us to keep our arousal within our window of tolerance; as infants we learn how to regulate our arousal largely through our caregivers. "Born with limited capacities for self-regulation," Ogden and colleagues put it, "human infants are dependent on the externally mediated interactive regulation of their primary attachment figures to maintain their arousal within the window of tolerance" (2006, p. 41).

This dynamic doesn't necessarily change with time. Even as adults, we depend on people to help us regulate our arousal. The soothing voice of someone we care about—even on the phone—can settle us in an instant after a rough day. Seeing someone's face can be even more regulatory, activating our social engagement system that lies within the window of tolerance. Relationships with trauma professionals, specifically, can help survivors regulate their arousal and learn to do so effectively on their own over time. The point here is that other people—who they feel are safe and trustworthy—can help survivors regulate arousal, whether through settling eye contact, physical touch, or overall presence. If our arousal level is too high, another person can help calm us down through words or by encouraging us to take deep breaths; if our arousal levels are too low, a person can stimulate our attention to urge us back into balance. Like an infant with a caregiver, these adjustments are often nonverbal, taking place largely through cues such as breath, gesture, and vocalization.

When Sam had a session with me, I tracked his physiological signs as much as the content he was sharing through words. While video calls make it slightly more difficult to accomplish this, I'm often surprised how noticeable the slight shifts are that I need to watch—one's inflection, for instance, or facial expressions. The reason I'm tracking for this is that trauma isn't just about a person's words—it's ever present in their physical, lived experience. When I saw Sam starting to become distressed and disorganized in his thoughts, I'd ask him to notice what was happening inside. Depending on his answer, I would offer an intervention designed to take care of his window of tolerance—a few deep breaths, for instance, or concentrating on an area of resource and reassurance. As if I were guiding Sam through a dance, I wanted to help his body remember the rhythm of self-regulation.

It turned out that Sam had always had difficulty modulating his arousal. As I mentioned, he'd been having panic attacks as long as he could remember. He also felt exceptionally anxious when he was physically close to another person—understandable based on his early experiences with his father. To work with this, Sam and I started experimenting by having him evaluate his level of arousal in relationship to me. Over the video call, I'd take my attention away from him, swiveling my chair about 45 degrees from the computer. After he noticed how this affected his body, I then swiveled my chair fully around so he only saw the back of my head. I wanted Sam to keep noticing whether this altered his state.

"Wow," he said, "it's so weird. When you were turned just a bit sideways, I felt much more relaxed. My chest opened up and I could feel my feet on the floor. But then when you turned fully around I had a familiar feeling of anxiety in my throat. It just didn't feel good." With practice, Sam began to notice how external factors influenced his arousal and shifts he could make to stay in his window of tolerance—for instance, breathing more deeply or breaking eye contact. The lesson for him was that he was being influenced by others all the time, in ways that were both regulating and not. In our sessions, we talked about ways I could be with him that would support his sense of stability and window of tolerance.

A technical term for this is *inter-relational psychobiological regulation*—the way our relationships with other people can help us regulate our arousal. When we're in safe, attuned contact with other people, we can more easily access our social engagement system and thereby coregulate each other's arousal. This takes place though nonverbal cues such as making or breaking eye contact, finding an optimal distance between our bodies, and listening to the tone in one another's voices. Larger groups can also provide this kind of support, where practices such as dancing, singing, yoga, drumming, or martial arts bring our bodies together into connection. Whereas trauma disrupts connection within ourselves and other people, community can bring us back into rhythm with one another—a state, known as synchrony, that helps us regulate our arousal.

THE POWER OF COMMUNITY

Community is also a valuable protective factor with trauma. The bonds that we have with others help us live through overwhelming experiences—and, ultimately, help us recover from them. In the wake of a traumatic event, other people can help us feel safe, regulate our arousal, and help us make meaning of our experience. They offer us perspective and remind us we are a part of something bigger. While trauma professionals are often an important part of the recovery process, they are ideally one part of a larger network of support.

In her book A Paradise Built in Hell: The Extraordinary Communities That Arise in Disaster, essayist and social critic Rebecca Solnit explored the power of community through the lens of collective trauma. Solnit investigated the impact of a series of natural disasters on the communities who experienced them—the 1985 Mexico City earthquake, for instance, and Hurricane Katrina in New Orleans. What Solnit documented in her research is that communities don't collapse into violence after events of this nature—as we're often led to believe—but come together into relationship, often with a sense of purpose and resilience. Without romanticizing the impact of natural disasters, which have devastating effects—particularly on oppressed people—Solnit's book reminds us that it is people who help us through arduous experiences. In a moment when social systems that can keep us apart collapse, we come together in creative, resilient, life-affirming ways that remind each of us of our shared humanity.

The point here is that trauma recovery happens in community—whether it is in the aftermath of a natural disaster or a community coming together to build powerful, collective spaces for healing. A considerable body of research tells us that interpersonal relationships are central to our well-being and to lowering the probability of physical illness.[1] As van der Kolk wrote:

> Traumatized human beings recover in the context of relation-ships: with families, with loved ones, AA meetings, veterans' organizations, religious communities, or professional therapists. The role of those relationships is to provide physical and emo-tional safety, including safety from feeling shamed, admonished, or judged, and to bolster the courage to tolerate, face, and process the reality of what's happened. (2014, p. 210)

It's important for trauma-sensitive practitioners to keep the power of community close at hand in our work. As a psychotherapist, I've been conditioned to think of trauma recovery as something that happens behind closed doors, in the presence of a trauma professional. But the integration of trauma also happens in the presence of family and community members who care about our well-being. We want to empower others to lean into this kind of support where possible—whether it's the person sitting beside us in the meditation hall, coming to us to have a conversation, or connecting with our larger community.

Around the time I began working with Sam, I introduced him to Cheetah House, a nonprofit organization in Providence, Rhode Island, focuses on people's adverse responses to mindfulness. Started by Brown professor Willoughby Britton, who I introduced in Chapter 3, Cheetah House supports people who've had challenging experiences in meditation and need support. Sam discovered that Cheetah House had a social media page, and he was able to access useful articles, watch videos and interviews, and engage in conversations about troublesome experiences others also had in meditation.

This community turned out to be one of the most powerful parts of

Sam's healing journey. While our work together was helpful—allowing Sam to begin to feel safe and regulate his arousal—it was ultimately his connections with people in this emerging community that made him feel confident that he'd be able to move through his trauma. He met people who could relate to his experience, who empathized with the way he'd felt misunderstood by others, and who could offer practical suggestions of a path forward. "I just don't feel like as much of a freak show," he said. "I feel understood—and a lot less lonely." Sam had a long way to go in terms of working with his trauma, but connecting with the Cheetah House community was a significant step along his journey.

Having described some of the ways relationship can help survivors find safety and stability—and the way mindfulness meditation can sometimes hinder this process—I want to turn to seven modifications to basic mindfulness practice. These modifications are less focused on therapeutic skills you can employ when you're working with people such as Sam, but are structural practices you can put in place to leverage interpersonal relationships.

PRACTICE IN RELATIONSHIP: TRAUMA-SENSITIVE MODIFICATIONS

(1) SCREEN FOR TRAUMA

A screening is a preliminary assessment of a person to identify potential needs and to support their overall experience. Many mindfulness centers commonly engage in screening procedures, sending out a questionnaire to help gather information about the participant. In trauma-sensitive practice, screens are an opportunity to identify survivors who may end up struggling with mindfulness practice, opening the possibility of connecting prior to a course.

The following are some standard questions you can include in a screen if the practice is a possibility. You can emphasize that these questions are a way to make sure everyone is for everyone's safety on retreat, and they are meant to support the person's experience in practice:

- Have you practiced mindfulness before? Please list dates and length of any prior experiences.
- What do you hope to get out of this course?
- What current stressors are you facing?
- Are there experiences you've had in the past that are still causing you stress?
- Do you have a history of trauma, and if so, are you actively experiencing symptoms that feel connected to this trauma? Examples include flashbacks, nightmares, and having difficulty with attention.
- Are you currently seeing a therapist or counselor, and if so, do they know that you'll be on this mindfulness course?
- Have you ever attempted to take your life, and if so, would you be willing to tell us more about this?
- Are you currently taking medications for physical or psychological conditions? If yes, please share them.
- Are there any other health considerations that you think we should be aware of?
- Is there anything else you would like us to know at this time?

Once returned, these questionnaires provide the opportunity to identify anyone who might benefit from more contact before a course—an e-mail, or possibly a conversation. This kind of outreach establishes trust early on and supports a mindfulness group overall.

For potential students and clients who are actively experiencing traumatic symptoms, feel mentally unstable, or are suicidal, group mindfulness practice is not recommended. While mindfulness-based interventions may be useful for these individuals, it's likely that they would benefit from direct individual attention with a trauma professional first before entering into a mindfulness environment.

(2) UTILIZE TRAUMA PROFESSIONALS

Trauma-sensitive mindfulness involves cultivating relationships with trained trauma professionals. This means that any students you're working with have access to a trauma practitioner (either by referral or on-site), and that you can consult with a trauma professional for guidance and feedback, and to strengthen your own competence around trauma. Having a wide network of people you can seek counsel from fortifies your trauma-informed work.

An ideal professional to consult with for trauma-sensitive mindfulness:

- Has trained specifically in trauma, whether through a psychology or social-work program, or a specialized methodology (e.g., somatic experiencing).
- Can make professional assessments regarding suicidality, self-harm, and other potentially threatening mental-health conditions.
- Has some direct experience with mindfulness and meditation or is reasonably well versed in the practice.
- Has an understanding of how their own social location (race or class) could impact others. This includes the ability to assess the social context of any moment, and an ability to gauge power, privilege, and dynamics around oppression with respect to trauma.

The above characteristics set a high bar. Finding a licensed practitioner who is familiar with trauma and mindfulness—and is available for a short- or long-term retreat—can be challenging, and figuring out how best to compensate adds an extra layer of complication. But the above guidelines provide a suggested benchmark and reference point that you can consider when trying to create a trauma-sensitive environment.

You can utilize trauma professionals by:

- Paying for weekly, monthly, or "by request" consultation sessions with a trauma professional. Entering into a clear agreement—including expectations around availability and how quickly you can expect to hear back in case of an emergency—is recommended.
- Being in direct contact with a student or client's trauma therapist if they have one and grant permission. The therapist you're in connection with will likely guide you through release of information procedures, if you don't already know them in your area.
- Hiring a trauma therapist to be on-site during meditation retreats of one day or longer.
- Inviting trauma therapists with an interest in mindfulness to be a part of your teaching team.

When we act in consultation with someone trained in an area we're focused upon, it allows us to be learners and not shoulder everything ourselves. Developing hubris or self-reliance with trauma can be a setup for problems—either for you or the people you're offering mindfulness practice to.

Can a meditation retreat be trauma sensitive if a professional therapist is unavailable? Ultimately, this depends on a number of factors, including the stage of healing a person or group is at and their experience with mindfulness. Questions you might ask include:

- Do any of the mindfulness teachers have trauma or professional training that enables them to be a resource to participants?
- Does the meditation center have protocols in place in the case that a person runs into emotional difficulty on retreat and asks to leave?
- What steps are being taken to make certain that leadership has a foundation of competence around trauma, and how is this being extended toward the participants?

As with all trauma-sensitive modifications, discretion ultimately rests with you. By checking in with the students and clients and making an assessment in consultation with others, you can make decisions based on what will serve the safety, stability, and overall well-being of the people that you're working with.

(3) DEVELOP A RELATIONSHIP PRE-COURSE

This modification comes from Trish Magyari, a certified MBSR teacher who has conducted research into the applications of mindfulness-based programs and interventions with traumatized individuals.[2] Magyari suggests that mindfulness practitioners establish a collaborative relationship with potential candidates before entering into a mindfulness program. Forming a connection early on leverages the power of relationship toward safety, stability, and success. The following paraphrases some of Magyari's suggestions about establishing this rapport:

- Ensure that the participant has completed the written questionnaire (above).
- Connect with all people in your course or program who reported having a trauma history or active symptoms. Ensure that they are provided the option to have a one-on-one conversation with you, either in person or over the phone. Orient to this call as a chance to solicit more information and begin orienting the person to the course.
- In conversation, invite participants to let you know of any particular requests or needs they may have that would support their practice. "A special request," Magyari wrote, "might be anything from wanting to sit in a certain place in the circle (near you, facing the door, near the door) to wanting to know in advance what is happening, to simply needing more reassurance that you know what to do if they get upset in class" (2016, p. 346). It is also important to be honest

with the participant about what requests you can and can't accommodate and offer as much information as possible to ensure they are in clear expectation and choice.

- Assure the participant that they are in choice about their participation and encourage them to let you know if they are feeling distress during a practice that is prompting them to want to leave. If the person is concerned they won't be able to stay in the class, you can ask what kind of symptoms would compel them to discontinue their practice. Wherever possible, normalize these.

By establishing a relationship early on, you'll empower them to feel in control and in choice during the course. It's also a chance to begin equipping them with tools and suggestions that will help ensure they have a successful experience with mindfulness.

(4) ESTABLISH COMMUNITY AGREEMENTS

Setting a container for collective mindfulness practice helps with safety. Creating a set of community agreements, including expectations about confidentiality, is one important way we can do this. We want survivors to know what they can expect, that they're in choice about participating, and that they're in control of what's being shared inside and outside the room.

Community agreements are less about creating strict rules than about clarifying agreements and expectations for a collective body. We can offer suggestions for these rules, but ultimately it is up to the specific group you're working with to come up with ones that are meaningful to them. Having said that, there are a few community agreements that benefit all groups when laid out from the start:

- **Confidentiality**: A basic agreement that what is shared within the group space will not be shared outside of the group. While we can encourage people to share their individual experiences with mindfulness with people in their lives, we ask that they don't offer any details that would identify others.

- **Set Expectations of Confidentiality Among Mindfulness Teachers**: If you're teaching mindfulness with a team, it's important that students know information may be shared among teaching team members for the benefit of individuals. This means the teaching group can act as a cohesive body, not withholding secrets from one another and staying current about the progress of different students.
- **Dignity**: We ask that each participant respect the dignity of others, refraining from humiliating, abusing, or intentionally harming someone in any way. Violence or intimidation will not be tolerated.

The following is a proposed list of community agreements that you can offer and discuss in any group:

- **One Speaker**: A basic request that one person speak at a time instead of interrupting one another.
- **Move Up, Move Back**: During a period of group sharing, it's encouraged that those who tend to speak a lot in a group listen more and that those who tend to speak less "move up" and take the risk of sharing more.
- **Speak from Your Own Experience**: Rather than intellectualizing or storytelling, it can be useful to encourage people to use "I" statements wherever possible, sharing what is true for them and not generalizing. A community can also agree that people don't simply offer each other unsolicited advice.
- **Ask Permission**: Sharing a personal story about trauma can be a powerful experience, but we want to have people ask for permission first. Sometimes people will launch into triggering details of a traumatic event without first asking the group's

permission, which can feel violating. Between people and in the group, participants can ask each other for permission to ask questions or share stories (e.g., "I appreciated what I heard you say in the debrief and have a story from my past that relates to yours. Would you like to hear it?").

- **Choice**: Participants know they are always in choice during any practices and can pass during any group sharing periods.

Once established, one of your primary responsibilities as a trauma-sensitive practitioner is to make sure that these community agreements are upheld. Survivors will be looking to us to ensure that the safety and container of the group is maintained and that failing to hold to predetermined agreements can break trust in the group.

(5) LEVERAGE INTERPERSONAL CONTACT

Trauma-sensitive mindfulness involves balancing the benefits of solitary mindfulness meditation practice with the potentially beneficial effects of interpersonal relationship. Acknowledging that clients and students will each have different needs, this modification has two components: increasing contact with mindfulness teachers where appropriate and helping facilitate more interpersonal connection between participants in group settings.

On a typical meditation retreat in the insight meditation tradition, students usually have face-to-face interviews with teachers every two days for 15 to 20 minutes. Sometimes these sessions are group interviews, and other times one on one. Depending on the capacity of the retreat staff, this frequency can be increased to once a day and for longer periods of time—at least as an option for participants. This modification is meant to increase interpersonal contact and ensure that no students are drifting too far into overwhelming traumatic stimuli. Interviews also stimulate participants' social engagement system, which helps support attunement, safety, and, by extension, one's window of tolerance.

A second recommendation is that participants have optional increased interpersonal contact with each other while in group settings.

This can be achieved in a variety of creative ways and left to your discretion. Options include:

- Taking 5 to 10 minutes with a group to debrief a meditation period, asking people for a brief check-in about their emotional state and what they learned. This helps us track people more closely and stimulate connection between others. These short check-ins also help normalize challenges and provide a space to share encouragement and success.
- Offering an optional "buddy system" whereby participants have brief, scheduled interactions with self-selected partners. These check-ins can include a basic structure of sharing one's mood, and both successes and challenges from their most recent periods of practice. While not all practitioners may want to participate in this process, it adds an additional layer of interpersonal contact and helps make sure that people don't become lost and overwhelmed in practice.
- Encouraging the formation of support or peer groups outside of the class or program that you're offering. Any such group would be optional.

In interviews or check-ins, we also want to dissuade survivors from sharing their full "trauma story"—whether a singular event or ongoing experience. As much as possible, we want to encourage people to stay present in the here and now. Sometimes the present moment will become filled with thoughts, sensations, memories, and emotions that relate to a trauma, and it is those we want to focus on. In no way do we want to repress people's stories, but rather encourage them to continually bring themselves back to the present and stay in their window of tolerance. There's a continual balance to strike here between not making trauma taboo, while also not retelling—which can lead to reexperiencing—a traumatic experience.

The frequency of interpersonal contact can be left up to your judgment. Teachers and staff can respond to the particular needs of the group based on factors such as the length of the retreat, the size and social context of the group, and information they receive from individual interviews. The point here is to turn up the amount of interpersonal contact people receive to account for the potentially negative effects of solitary practice.

(6) LEARN THE FLASHBACK-HALTING PROTOCOL

If a student or client is experiencing a flashback, we can leverage interpersonal relationship to help a survivor manage them. One helpful strategy is the *flashback-halting protocol* developed by Rothschild (2000, p. 133). Using verbal prompts, the protocol is designed to help people ground themselves in the present moment when they're experiencing a flashback, increasing the likelihood of gaining some control over traumatic symptoms. While the protocol is not a replacement for working with a trauma professional, it can help someone find temporary stability and come back into their window of tolerance.

Recall that during a flashback, survivors are inundated by sensations, images, and emotions related to a traumatic event. Drawn back into the traumatic experience, they effectively lose their capacity for dual awareness in the present moment. When this happens, the *observing self*—which enables us to witness what is happening and gain perspective—becomes fused with the *experiencing self*. During a flashback, it can be hard to know whether we're having a memory of an event as opposed to experiencing the event itself. The flashback-halting protocol attempts to support one's dual awareness, engaging the observing self and helping survivors become aware that they are reexperiencing a trauma in the present moment.

The protocol includes a number of sentences that you can have students or clients say aloud while filling in the blanks:

- Right now I am feeling _____,
- (*insert name of the current emotion, usually fear*)
- and I am sensing in my body _____,
- (*describe your current bodily sensations—name at least three*)

- because I am remembering _____.
- (*name the trauma by title* only—*no details*).
- At the same time, I am looking around where I am now in

    _____,
- (*the actual current year*)
- and I can see _____,
- (*describe some of the things that you see right* now, *in* this *place*)
- and so I know _____ is not happening now/anymore.
- (*name the trauma, by title only, again*; Rothschild, 2000, p. 133)

A few points about using this protocol:

- Remember that for some people, the kind of trauma they are experiencing may not have ended—they could still be in direct danger (in which case you should immediately consult a trained clinician), or they are facing the relentless, unchanging conditions of systemic oppression. The protocol is not a static recipe, in this respect, but a guideline to be tailored to meet the needs of people we're working with.
- Exteroceptive sensations—or exteroceptors—are an essential part of the flashback-halting protocol. Recall that exteroceptors are nerves related to the five senses that help us relate to what is happening outside of our body—touch, taste, smell, sight, and hearing. Rather than relate explicitly to what is happening inside the body—interoceptors—we want to help survivors ground their attention in their surrounding environment as a way to come back to the present.

(7) BE A RESOURCE: CONTINUE TO EDUCATE YOURSELF ABOUT TRAUMA

Trauma-sensitive mindfulness practice is more a path than a destination. We'll never know everything there is to know about trauma.

While I believe there's a base level of aptitude we want to achieve to refer to ourselves as trauma informed—being able to recognize trauma symptoms, for instance—being a trauma-sensitive practitioner asks us to be ongoing learners. We might follow developments in trauma research and stay abreast of contemporary approaches to treatment. Or we can commit to studying the history of trauma and continually examine the connection between trauma, oppression, and modern-day social justice movements. There's no shortage of ways to continue gaining competency around trauma and serve as a resource for our students and clients.

Some of you may also wish to register for a trauma training yourself. You can train in a specific modality, see clients, and explore the complex relationship between mindfulness and trauma in your work. Spirit Rock Meditation Center in Woodacre, California—which holds one of the largest mindfulness teacher training programs in the United States—requests that its students attend a trauma training program (typically somatic experiencing).

(8) INTERNAL FAMILY SYSTEMS

In this chapter, I've focused exclusively on the regulating role of interpersonal relationship when it comes to mindfulness and trauma. But I want to end with a focus on the *intrapersonal* dimension of trauma and a particular psychotherapeutic approach I've found particularly helpful for survivors: Internal Family Systems (IFS). IFS is a practical model that can help people come into skillful relationship with traumatized parts of themselves.

We all have parts of ourselves—parts that want different things and experience the world in different ways. In the same moment, a part of us may want to exercise while another part wants to rest. In relationship with a romantic partner, part of us may want to open up and be vulnerable, while another part wants to pull back in fear. For us to move through the world, each of us has to learn how to navigate these different parts. Like a teacher in front of a room of diverse students with different personalities and concerns, we take different parts into account and learn to chart a course from there.

Traumatic stress leaves us with unintegrated parts of the self. Split off from our consciousness, these parts can remain compartmentalized and out of view, carrying an intense burden of pain. Each of these parts will carry thought patterns, be expressed through our bodies, and come with specific memories and emotions that remain unintegrated. These are the parts of ourselves that carry what was too much to bear.

To heal trauma, as I've explored throughout the book, we must work to integrate these different parts of ourselves. Mindfulness is one incredibly helpful way to do this, helping shine a light on these parts and bring them into view. But simply being mindful of traumatized parts of ourselves does not necessarily lead to their integration. When it comes to trauma, we need to find a way to engage with these parts in a relational way, building connection and trust as opposed to just observing them. When we can do this, we can fully leverage the power of mindfulness for the sake of trauma healing.

IFS offers a way to do this. Developed by Richard Schwartz,[3] IFS integrates concepts from well-established therapeutic models such as narrative, structural, and family therapy. IFS forwards the notion that the mind is composed of a constellation of subpersonalities referred to as "parts"—not dissimilar from a family with different members who all have different temperaments. In IFS work, people learn how to engage with their parts relationally, through inner dialogue, visualization, or sensations in the body.

Each of our parts has valuable and inimitable qualities that make us who we are. We may have a part of ourselves that can be very productive in the face of a deadline or a part that knows how to connect well with others. IFS thinks of these unique, discrete parts as playing useful roles within us—parts within the larger whole. In the case of trauma, parts of us can end up taking on roles that can seem destructive or extreme. When a life experience overwhelms us, parts absorb and respond to the trauma in different ways. Some freeze in fear, others blame themselves, and yet others get angry. IFS helps people learn how to connect with parts that respond in these varying ways and brings calmness and compassion and understanding to them.

One of the most important insights IFS offers is that parts are often attempting to keep us from becoming overwhelmed. Whether by hiding the pain away, managing it, or trying to de-escalate our experience, parts all are trying their best and looking out for us. They have a positive intention. Often, however, it may not feel like this inside. There will be parts that we can't seem to access and that keep us trapped in pain. But if we can start orienting to parts with curiosity about the role they're playing, this can be a pivot point: instead of our minds or bodies being a problem, or pathologized in some manner, we learn to be inquisitive about parts—even those that seem problematic. The work here, van der Kolk wrote, "is to assure the internal system that all parts are welcome and that all of them—even those that are suicidal or destructive—were formed in an attempt to protect the self-system, no matter how much they seem to threaten it" (2014, p. 283). IFS thus has us orient to ourselves in a way that is deeply compassionate—something that aligns with mindfulness, but takes an extra step in a direction of self-leadership.

IFS relies upon the belief of a core universal "Self" that plays an essential role in our healing—placing it at odds with Buddhist teaching. In IFS, it's proposed that we are all born with a Self that carries universal qualities: courage, calmness, compassion, and clarity, for instance. You could think of the Self as the sun, in this respect, with the parts being clouds that get in the way of the sun. The sun is always there, in the background, but sometimes parts dominate the horizon and our view. The work is to connect with the Self that is always there and have the Self come into relationship with parts—bringing the qualities of Self to our parts.

The Self, in this respect, does not need to be cultivated with IFS. It is an ever-present essence that lies beneath protective parts and cannot be damaged with trauma—only covered over. When a part is running the show instead of the Self, IFS refers to this as being "blended" with a part. In these instances, the Self cannot see that a part is running the show, engaging in its signature behaviors. Rather than a part of us being scared, or protective, we *are* these things, and acting from the beliefs of this part.

In IFS, it is the development and nurturing of *mindful self-leadership* that is the key to trauma healing. Mindfulness itself enables us to come into a deeper relationship with ourselves—we purposefully, compassionately attend to our present-moment experience and come to know ourselves in deeper and more intimate ways. Self-leadership, meanwhile, is a way of engaging with parts of ourselves in active ways. IFS gives us a practical method to bring more Self energy into our system, which relaxes protective parts and soothes parts that are hurting. When this is combined with mindful awareness, it is a powerful tool on the way to healing trauma.

At first, this cultivation of Self-leadership isn't something we can do on our own. IFS is an intricate, well-developed system that relies on more than a few simple techniques. To cultivate mindful Self-leadership, we need to work with a therapist who has trained in IFS. This is because it's difficult to know when we're in a part and when we're in Self, especially when it comes to healing trauma. Trauma sets up an entire system of parts that will work hard to ensure we don't experience trauma again— protective parts that will have us dissociate from our experience or distract us with thoughts about the future. To heal, we need help sorting through the multifaceted system of parts inside of us. Often we'll ask parts to "step back" so we can bring more Self into connection with parts, which is ultimately healing. Unless we've had practice doing this with someone who knows the IFS system, we can end up lost in the matrix of parts inside of us.

The notion of asking parts to step back highlights one of the most powerful aspects of IFS when it comes to healing trauma: making requests of parts in order to help them heal. When we come into relationship with a part of us that holds trauma, it is not uncommon for us to feel overwhelmed: we may feel terrified, nauseated, or inundated with thoughts and memoires about the trauma. The part floods our consciousness, showing us what it experienced and what it is holding on to. In

IFS, it becomes possible to make requests of these parts, asking them to tone down their intensity in order to more easily come into connection. Traumatized parts of us are often desperate for contact and often overwhelm us from inside this desperation. If a part knows that by reducing the intensity of its expression it will receive connection, love, and support, it is often willing to do so.

CHAPTER 9

Understand Social Context:
Working Effectively Across Difference

Allyship and solidarity offers a space for healing
and transformation for those who are targeted
by oppression and experiences of trauma.
—Chris Lymbertos
Community Organizer, Arab Resource
and Organizing Center

"My father passed away in December of racism. He was only fifty-three years old, and he passed of racism."

I looked around and saw heads nodding left and right. The standing room-only crowd of 300 not only understood what was being said by the speaker, but was in full agreement. I paused and took it in, realizing I'd never heard something so personally and pointedly shared before.

I was in Detroit for the 2010 U.S. Social Forum—a gathering of thousands of activists and organizers interested in building a broader social justice movement. The speaker was Patrisse Cullors, a self-identified working-class, queer Black woman and community organizer. Three years later, Cullors would go on to cofound Black Lives Matter with Alicia Garza and Opal Tometi, both African American activists who've organized around rights for domestic workers, immigrant rights, and ending police brutality and violence against queer and transgender people of color. I was increasingly working with social justice organizers who were healing their own trauma, and I had come to the forum wanting to deepen my understanding of how I'd been shaped by systems of privilege and oppression. That day, Cullors had shown me that I had a long way to go in my work.

In the months following the social forum, I began paying attention to the way I talked about death. I noticed that I often spoke of death in personal, physical terms—saying that someone died of a heart attack, for instance. But rarely did I name the social, political, and economic factors that played a role. I talked about this with a friend, who suggested I explore the work of Paul Kivel, a White, anti-racist educator who'd been down a similar road. "It took me a long time," Kivel once wrote, "to see that the great majority of individual deaths that don't involve someone dying in peace in old age are probably related to some form of exploitation and inequality, despair and lack of hope" (2004, p. 6).

During this time, I learned more than ever that I'd been taught to see the world through an explicitly individualist lens. The personal had never been political. I'd grown up convinced that anyone could pull themselves up by their bootstraps—that people could do what they wanted with their lives if they just worked hard enough. But this wasn't the case. As a White, straight, healthy man from an upper-middle-class background, I had larger social systems in place that were helping me—and creating barriers for others. I just hadn't noticed them. My family members hadn't died of racism, and the reality is we didn't have to worry about this as a possibility in our daily lives.

As I covered in Chapter 1, many of us will be conditioned to think of trauma as an individual experience. The orientation of trauma recovery work often follows suit, focusing exclusively on systems that live *inside* the body—the relationship between the SNS and PNS, for instance, or disparate parts of ourselves that split off in the aftermath of trauma. Trauma-sensitive practice, however, requires a holistic approach and must also factor in systems that live outside the body. This includes the relationship between an individual and the larger social systems (e.g., a family, community, institutions, and social norms) that surround them.* Integration—which, again, is at the crux of recovery—asks us to connect the internal and external systems that are involved in traumatic stress.

This brings us to the fifth principle of trauma-sensitive mindfulness: *understand social context.* Understanding social context means that we can see and acknowledge difference—knowing that each of us has a unique history and is being shaped in a particular way by the systems around us. It also means that we can skillfully navigate difference and help someone to feel safe in the context of working with mindfulness and trauma. If we fail to actively engage with social context, we become a liability in our mindfulness-based work.

Absent an understanding of how individual and social systems interact, we can potentially cause harm, break people's trust, and perpetuate systems of domination. This isn't a matter of political correctness or saying the "right thing," but offering a truly liberatory framework for those we work with. As Cullors pointed out at the social forum, systems of inequality aren't just theoretical—they have profound material consequences that relate to people's health and safety, and ultimately connect to trauma. Understanding how these systems function and relate to trauma is imperative in trauma-sensitive work.

NARI

I first heard from Nari over e-mail. She'd had a frustrating experience in a mindfulness community and wanted to share her story. She also wanted to see if I had suggestions on whom she could speak with.

A few weeks earlier, as I'd later learn, Nari had attended her first ever meditation retreat. She was there with one of her closest friends and was delighted to have finally arrived. She'd practiced meditation for half a

---

* As I mentioned in the Introduction and Chapter 1, my exposure to this framework came through *generative somatics* (see generationFIVE, 2017; generative somatics, 2017; Shenker et al., 2014).

year already, and she felt excited at the prospect of deepening her practice at a residential retreat.

Underlying the excitement, however, lay a concern: while her friend had talked lovingly about her meditation community, she'd also shared that most of the group members were White and older than her. This wasn't a problem, per se, but Nari imagined the dynamic could cause some unwanted stress, given that she was a person of color.

Arriving at the retreat, Nari discovered she had just cause for concern: she appeared to be the only person of color there. Stepping outside after registering, she'd let out a long exhale. She knew how to compartmentalize these feelings of alienation, and she was here for her own growth. Besides, she reasoned, the retreat was in silence, so how bad could it be?

After a day of practice, Nari had her first interview with one of the teachers—a chance to check in about how everything was going. She smiled entering the office and exchanged pleasantries with the teacher, an older White man whose instruction she'd been enjoying.

"Where are you from?" he said, making casual conversation.

"I'm local," Nari responded, "just a few hours south."

"No," the teacher said, "I mean, where is your family from?"

Nari sighed. Her parents had both immigrated from Korea before she was born, yet this was a question she faced all the time. She reminded herself that the teacher was simply trying to make conversation—albeit a bit clumsily.

"My parents are from Korea."

"Did you grow up meditating with your family, then?" the teacher asked. Nari cast her eyes to the floor and felt her frustration grow.

"Because I'm Asian?" she replied when she finally looked up.

"Yes, well, I mean . . ." The teacher hesitated and then changed the topic. Nari went on with the interview but at that moment felt herself shut down inside. Meditation was hard enough without having to navigate these kinds of dynamics, and here they were again, front and center.

When she'd returned to the practice hall, Nari couldn't stop thinking about the interview. It wasn't that such a comment was new—she'd experienced racism her entire life—but she now found herself at what was supposed to be a nourishing retreat, bracing for another such comment that might be directed her way. Despite her attempts to shift her internal narrative, she'd lost trust in the instructor. That night, she pulled her friend aside and let her know she'd decided to leave the retreat early the next day.

I felt sad as I finished reading the e-mail. Questions about origin and assumptions about cultural practices—while not intended as invasive, and seemingly innocuous—are constant reminders of the imbalance of agency that exists between groups who have power and groups who don't. People with less power are constantly contending with the reduction of their experiences as exotic or consumable. The more aware of racism I'd become in my life, the more I'd heard how common Nari's experience was—everyday interactions where biases that lay beneath the surface came into full view. I didn't know what it was like to be on the receiving end of an assumption that had its root in racial oppression. How could I best support Nari? What would be useful to hear from me?

SOCIAL CONTEXT

All of us belong to groups. Some of these groups are ones we choose, such as a group of friends or people who share an interest. Other groups are those that are assigned to us, such as the generation we were born into—baby boomers or millennials, for instance. Whether we identify with these groups or not, they inform our identities and influence our lives.

The interconnected web of identities we carry can be thought of as our *social context*—a particular set of factors that influence our lives in any given situation. Social context includes one's social identity (age, gender, race, ethnicity, class background, sexual identity, dis/ability, or religion), locale (a city, a town, a suburb), peers, community, and country of residence. To understand our social context, we need to consider how social groups function, why they matter, and how they relate to trauma. Our experiences of the world—including our interactions with each other—

are informed by social groups and factor into how we can be effective in our work as trauma-sensitive practitioners.

In the current social context in North America, certain social groups have more power, access, and privilege than others. In the United States, women are paid 78% of what men make for doing the same job—a percentage that hasn't changed in over a decade.[1] This pay gap also varies significantly by race: African American women make 63% of White men's wages, and Hispanic and Latina women make 54%.[2] This means that it takes women of color seven to eight extra months to be paid what the average White man makes per calendar year.

It goes without saying that trauma can affect anyone, regardless of what groups they belong to. But as I covered in Chapter 1, research tells us that people in marginalized social groups face conditions that make them more vulnerable to experiencing traumatic events. American families living in urban poverty have been shown to experience higher levels of exposure to trauma,[3] and people who identify as transgender were found to be 28% more likely to experience physical violence than those who considered themselves gender normative.[4] Again, while traumatic events can happen to anyone, anywhere, at any time, social context will always be a component.

Understanding social context enables us to attune more accurately and skillfully to our clients and students—something that helps establish safety. As I've covered throughout the book, safety is key to trauma-sensitive practice. Unless we feel some degree of safety, it becomes extremely difficult to self-regulate and stay in our window of tolerance. If a client or student is spending their time and energy concerned with self-protection instead of self-awareness, practicing mindfulness becomes next to impossible. To establish safety, people need to feel trust in those guiding them—a visceral sense that they'll be seen, cared for, and understood for the complex people they are.

One way we can generate this kind of trust is to preemptively establish a basic understanding of another person's world—including the social conditions they are shaped and impacted by. This involves developing an awareness of social context, and how privilege, oppression, and power get played out. By ensuring we're attuned to the social identities someone carries—and considering how these identities might interact with ours—we can adjust our interventions to try to effectively meet the needs of the person we're working with. This isn't a static process but a dynamic one, asking us to listen to others and be in continual self-reflection about how social context is shaping interactions we're having. If we're not doing this, it becomes easy to unintentionally reinforce racist, sexist, and otherwise oppressive dynamics that are connected to the proliferation of trauma—not just for our students or clients, but in our communities, cities, countries, and world.

In my first interaction with Nari, one of the first things I did was validate her experience. We'd set up a phone call, and I let her know I had appreciated that she'd reached out to me. The second thing I did was ask her a series of questions to gather more information about her experience—how was she feeling about the experience today and what would be useful in the conversation with me? I resisted the temptation—especially as a man—to rationalize what the meditation teacher had said or begin explaining anything to her. Recognizing that we were communicating across difference—me as a psychotherapist, and as a White man—I wanted to empower her in the interaction versus dominating the conversation. My underlying assumption was that she knew what was best for her and had reached out to me specifically for a reason. My job was to find out what that was while not making any assumptions about her—which had happened to her on retreat. Again, this wasn't a matter of political correctness but a responsiveness to social context. I wanted to acknowledge the oppression she'd faced and interact skillfully with her inside of that.

OPPRESSION

Oppression can be defined as an unjust exercise of power and authority.[5] It involves cruel and unjust treatment, subjecting people to a stifling pressure that can lead to intense distress. "Being oppressed," bell hooks succinctly wrote, "means the absence of choices" (1984, p. 5).

Like trauma, oppression is interconnected to structures big and small. As I covered in Chapter 1, interpersonal trauma is inseparable from systems of oppression that have exploitation at their root. At the level of an individual, oppression can be internalized, as in the case when a person comes to believe stereotypes associated with a group they are a part of. Interpersonally, oppression occurs in a number of ways, from overtly aggressive acts, such as when a Muslim woman is verbally attacked on a bus because she is wearing a hijab, to less visible, covert interactions, such as when a Black family moves into an otherwise friendly White neighborhood and no one welcomes them. Large-scale systemic oppression is expressed in institutions like schools, banks, the media, and historical and contemporary forces such as slavery and acts of genocide, colonization, and religious persecution. It also works to perpetuate and uphold interpersonal and internalized oppression. From interpersonal racism to mass violence, oppression takes place when power derived from systems of privilege is used to cause harm to those without privilege, reinforcing patterns of exploitation and dominance.

For some, particularly those in positions of advantage, systems of oppression are meant to be hard to see. Feminist scholar Marilyn Frye used the analogy of a birdcage to explain why systems of oppression can be difficult to see.[6] Focusing on one wire of a cage (i.e., an individual act of discrimination) erases the view of all the other wires that make up the cage (i.e., the social forces of oppression), making it seem impossible that the bird is actually trapped. In the same way, if we consider *only* a sideways comment or an untoward look that another person gets, we may fail to be responsive to his or her experience within a broader context (think back to Yvonne in Chapter 3). Why was that comment such a big deal? Why can't that person just get over it?

When viewing a caged bird, it is only by stepping back and seeing the structural arrangement of wires that comprise the entire cage that clarifies why the bird doesn't fly away. For people experiencing oppression, sometimes the comment was a big deal because it was a minor eruption within major systems of "isms," such as sexism, racism, classism, ableism, heterosexism, and so on, that erode at the value of certain individuals based on their social groups. These "isms" are tied to laws, policies, basic economic resources, and social norms that function as a backdrop to our daily lives.

SOCIAL IDENTITY

Systems of oppression divide groups into two categories: those that are privileged and everyone else. This division creates binaries that divide different identities into those that are desirable and those that are undesirable. Many of us have identities that position us on both sides of the binary: White and poor, Black and able-bodied, and so forth. "This is the nature of supremacy," anti-oppression educator Leticia Nieto wrote. "One group is consistently overvalued, and to foster the benefit of that smaller group, everyone else is devalued" (Nieto et al., 2010, p. 38).

Social identities are rich, elaborate, and problematic. They connect us with others, creating a sense of belonging and contributing meaning to our lives. At the same time, social identities, or categories, are artificially constructed and often based on outdated notions that restrict freedom and choice. Although categories of identity vary according to culture, they are profoundly entrenched expressions of the ongoing ways society grapples with expressions of difference. It is important for us to know the dividing lines that occur within categories of social identity—the binaries that sort out who is privileged by a system and who is not. Knowing such increases our awareness of the social context of a given moment and can inform our interventions when it comes to trauma-sensitive practice.

Below I'm going to cover nine social classifications we can track when assessing social context in trauma work. These classifications can be found in Nieto's book *Beyond Inclusion, Beyond Empowerment*, a powerful guide to social change practice in the context of oppression. Nieto utilizes the "Addressing" Model,[7] so named for its acronym, ADDRESSING, which covers the social classifications each of us belongs to: age, disability, religious culture, ethnicity, social class culture, sexual orientation, Indigenous heritage, national origin, and gender. While each of these has its contradictions and stirs different feelings in people depending on life history, their use is in clarifying how certain elements of social identity affect individuals in the matrix of interconnection.

Age corresponds to the experience of marginalization felt by those younger than 18 and older than 64. Connected to a system of oppression called ageism, the category encompasses the systemic overvaluing of middle-aged adults in most domains of society, as well as the vulnerability and suffering of children and elders. Examples of ageism include losing or being denied a job, being refused travel or health insurance, and receiving a different or lower quality of service due to one's age.

Disability refers to the experience of those with visible physical impairments such as muscular dystrophy or partial paralysis, as well as less visible impairments such as cognitive challenges and chronic illnesses. Discrimination toward disabled people is known as ableism; as disability activists Patti Berne, Stacey Milbern, and Lisa Weiner-Mahfuz (2015) remind us, people with impairments are not oppressed by their physical or intellectual limitations as much as by this interlocking system of beliefs about their capabilities. Examples of ableism include inaccessible public spaces, violence perpetrated on disabled people, inaccessibility to consistent employment, language that intentionally or inadvertently targets people (e.g., "that's lame" or "that's retarded"), and objectification in medical and mental institutions.

Religious culture refers to the religion in which one was raised or participates. In the United States, Christians are privileged over non-Christians: Christian holidays, such as Christmas and Easter, come with state-sanctioned time off from work and school, while other religions' holy times are not similarly recognized; and many classrooms—historically, at least—include mandatory Christian prayer. In the evaluation of social context, recognizing Christian hegemony does not entail criticizing the religion itself, but rather acknowledging the pervasiveness of its institutions and values in civic life in North America—and examining how that may act on people who don't share Christian heritage or traditions. Muslim people are also particularly targeted by oppression, experiencing exacerbated levels of state-sanctioned violence both within and outside the United States.[8] Women's reproductive rights—the rights relating to reproduction and reproductive health—are also challenged by Christian hegemony, particularly for poor women and women of color.[9]

Ethnicity denotes membership in ethnic or racial groups, with privilege allocated to those perceived as White. This system of privilege, and the corresponding oppression of people of color, is known as racism, examples of which include being profiled by police, being passed over for a job, and facing innumerable acts of interpersonal racism throughout one's day by virtue of one's perceived racial identity. Through colonialism, the social construct of race dehumanizes people of color as less deserving of basic human dignity, and also privileges the extraction of resources from less valued peoples.[10]

Social class culture describes the access to institutions afforded based on class background, with privilege conferred upon people from middle- and upper-class backgrounds while excluding those from poor and working-class backgrounds. Examples of classism include assumptions about someone's intelligence founded on his or her class and denial of educational opportunities to poor or working-class children. The United States is a country largely made up of working people who produce for the wealth of a few, while often not having access to the goods of their labor. Notably, this category is called social class "culture" to indicate that this kind of privilege is not simply a matter dictated by wealth. Being middle- to upper-class opens doors to higher education, owning property, and influence within institutions of control, notwithstanding an individual's high income or lack thereof.

Sexual orientation relates to romantic or sexual attractions, preferences, and choices. In terms of social capital, sexual orientation comprises two groups: (1) heterosexual people and (2) everyone else. This latter and more marginalized group includes lesbian, gay, bisexual, transgender, questioning, intersex, and asexual people. The oppression associated with this category is heterosexism, homophobia, or transphobia that manifests, for example, in institutions failing to recognize relationships as valid if they are not heterosexual and in the denial of housing, employment, and access to public services to people who don't identify as straight. While recent legal gains in marriage push back against systems of oppression, heterosexuality is still considered the default, a more natural and normal state of being.

Indigenous heritage, in the context of the United States, refers to the experiences of people whose ancestors are native to the Americas. In this category, Native (Native American, First Nations) people are systemically targeted by anti-Indigenous oppression; this stems from the historic, systemic genocide of European colonization of North America and extends today to such examples as the ongoing misuse of traditional Native land for waste storage and nuclear testing, the destruction of cultural artifacts resources such as burial grounds, and the ongoing occupation of Native lands, which forces ongoing displacement. The inclusion of this category in an analysis of modern-day oppression recognizes that the colonization of Native people is both historic and ongoing, and that Indigenous peoples and lands all over the world have been subject to the constant extraction of resources—while having their traditions romanticized and commodified in the process.

National origin alludes to birth nationality. Within this category, those who are born in the United States are privileged while those who are not face discrimination. This dynamic is often referred to as anti-immigrant oppression,[11] or crimmigration,[12] and manifests in the barriers faced by undocumented immigrants as well as the threat of legal entanglement and sudden deportation. While humans have migrated since time immemorial, capitalist nationhood restricts, punishes, and maligns the migration of people seeking a better life, while encouraging the migration of corporations seeking cheaper costs and greater profits. Nationhood defines who belongs and is privileged (e.g., the right to be safe), and who does not belong (e.g., is criminalized).

Gender describes the range of characteristics pertaining to—and differentiating between—masculinity and femininity, including nonbinary gender identities (e.g., people may identify as a man, women, both, neither, or something entirely different). Whereas our sex includes physical attributes such as external genitalia and internal reproductive structures used to provide us with a sex assignment at birth, gender is associated with an expression and understanding of our identity. Sexism is the oppression that divides biological males from females, transgender, and intersex people. For example, in professional contexts, men usually enjoy higher pay, more authority, and opportunities for advancement while institutions often uphold the myth of meritocracy—the notion that progress is based exclusively on ability and talent versus one's social status. Inside of this category, those who are cisgender (meaning one's gender identity corresponds with the sex they were assigned at birth) are more privileged than those who are transgender. Examples of cisgender privilege can include using a public restroom without fear of verbal abuse, and using public facilities (e.g., gym locker rooms) without being harassed because of your gender expression.

The above offers an introduction to each of the nine categories, a very small slice of what they each signify. As you can see in each one, identity is reduced to a very simple binary—either you're privileged in the category or you're not. Inside of this, there is a complex range of privilege and oppression within each category that is mitigated by other identities we hold. They are intersectional. As Audre Lorde wrote, "There is no such thing as single-issue struggle because we do not live single-issue lives" (1984, p. 138). What's important is that oppression tangibly and materially affects people's lives. If we're willing to look closely at this fact, incorporating understanding of how oppression works and where we fit into the equation, we're more likely to accurately read social context and its influence on cases of trauma.

TRUTH AND REALITY

"But this person's race shouldn't matter," the person across from me said, looking flustered. We were in a trauma supervision group, and I was talking about my work with Nari. After our conversation over the phone, Nari had decided to book a session with me, and I was consulting about the racial dynamic between us. It was a multiracial consultation group, and there was disagreement about whether I should be the one to raise the issue of race or leave it to Nari. The person who'd spoken up was

White and believed that it would be offensive for me to say anything. "I was raised to believe all people are equal," he said, "so I actually don't notice whether someone is White or not. I think that's racist."

Social identity presents us with a contradiction. While the categories I covered above are all social constructions, they all have a substantial impact on all of us—especially those who are targeted by oppression. This presents us with a tension between what Nieto referred to as *truth* and *reality*.[13] The truth is that our identities are much more complex than the options provided to us in the Addressing Model. In *reality*, however, our lives are tremendously impacted by these categories in a multitude of ways.

Let's take race as an example. Research shows that the DNA of any two human beings is 99.9% identical—we all share the same set of genes, and on a biological level, there is little to no genetic difference between us.[14] But racism undeniably exists and negatively impacts oppressed people's health.[15] "Racial categorization is problematic to begin with," Nieto wrote. "Yet simply knowing that this category is absurd doesn't neutralize the effects of racism" (Nieto et al., 2010, p. 41).

Holding both of these truths is a challenge. But it's something we must grapple with inside of trauma-sensitive practice. If a therapist or teacher overemphasizes truth, like my colleague in the supervision group, they may be limiting their ability to work effectively with clients by dismissing their lived experiences. As White, anti-racist activist Tim Wise shared in an interview:

> It's a sign of privilege for Whites to say they are going to view people of color only as people. If I don't see their race, I'm not going to see their lives as they really are. I'm seeing them as abstract "human beings," not as people who've had certain experiences. I'm going to miss or misunderstand how their experiences have shaped them. (Nieto et al., 2010, p. 42)

But if we fall too far on the side of reality, we might assume social constructs are real and believe stereotypes we've internalized. We might assume there is a singular experience of disability, for instance, and offer sweeping advice based on implicit assumptions. The work here is to find an optimal balance between truth and reality by listening intently to the experiences of others and staying attuned to the stereotypes at work in our own consciousness.

Research suggests that we notice social differences whether we like it or not. We do this by making snap judgments about others through *implicit bias*—the unconscious attitudes or stereotypes we hold toward all kinds of social groups. In neurology and social and cognitive psychology, research has continually revealed that all of us hold implicit biases that often don't align with our internalized values and declared beliefs.[16] We believe our decisions to be congruent with our conscious beliefs, but in fact it's often unconscious processes that are in control. Research also shows us that our implicit biases will favor the social groups that we belong to,[17] and that implicit biases will often be *against* members of socially stigmatized groups—LGBT people, for instance, or those who are overweight.[18] This is the impact of larger systems of oppression: we internalize stereotypes about others and then unconsciously play them out in our daily lives.

If we're to gain competence with social context, we must unpack and interrogate some of the biases we hold toward others. Being honest with ourselves about our internalized beliefs and self-correcting these opens the possibility of skillfully helping an individual heal from trauma—and of reshaping, even at a micro level, the larger systems in which these attitudes developed. Acknowledging our biases helps inform our interventions, increases our capacity for empathy, and helps us find a middle path between the truth and reality.

In my initial consultation call with Nari, I found myself holding the tension between truth and reality. The truth was that our differences didn't feel like a barrier to me—I could hold the fact that they were social constructions. At the same time, I knew our differences held tangible, material consequences for us, in the way we were treated in the world, and the way any therapeutic relationship would materialize. I was open to working with her, but of course, that decision wasn't up to me. My job was to hold this complexity, remain empathic, and ensure that Nari was left fully in choice.

After some conversation, Nari and I decided not to work together. It became clear to her that she needed to be supported by someone who knew what it was like to be a person of color—who could empathize, deeply, with both her lived experience of racism and how this had intersected with her experience on retreat. It was a positive interaction that left both of us with dignity. And while this interaction was relatively short, it reflected work and study I'd done on my end to navigate such a conversation with some competence and skill. With that said, I now want to shift to four specific modifications that address the principle of the chapter and provide practical steps for incorporating an awareness of social context into your trauma-sensitive work.

UNDERSTAND SOCIAL CONTEXT: TRAUMA-SENSITIVE MODIFICATIONS

(1) WORK SKILLFULLY WITH SOCIAL CONTEXT

The primary proposed modification of trauma-sensitive mindfulness is to more competently work with social context. This means having an awareness of your own social memberships and the dynamics of power in a given moment, and how this might impact any given interaction. If we don't have a lot of awareness about privilege and oppression, we can start by asking the following questions:

- How is social context influencing this situation or dynamic right now?
- How might I be acting on beliefs, values, or assumptions that are unrelated to this moment?
- Where do I need to increase my competence around social context (e.g., racism, gender oppression)?

Depending on our social identity, we are more likely to be aware of experiences that restrict our choices and freedom versus those experiences that lend us advantage. The work here is to ensure that we're not perpetuating dynamics of oppression in our work and are attempting to create safety for our students and clients.

Why is tracking these dynamics especially important for those who experience more privilege? Nieto here used the example of the relationship between soldiers and their superiors to discuss how oppression functions, and why we need to learn about it in light of our social identity.[19] When an officer walks into a military setting, Nieto explained, soldiers stop what they're doing and stand up to salute. It is much more likely that a soldier will notice an officer than the other way around—the soldier is carefully trained to respond to power dynamics and behave in certain ways with his superiors. In the social systems of which we're all a part, those with more power are less likely to pay attention to the power dynamics of a given situation. People who carry privilege are taught to think of themselves as the norm and are able to spend their energy pursuing their personal goals and interests, rather than attuning to power and consequence. If someone is targeted by oppression, they constantly face barriers and circumstances that impact them in big and small ways. Structures and institutions restrict their choice and movement, and they receive devaluing messages about their worth. This is the larger social context in which trauma-sensitive practice will be taking place.

One potential pitfall in attempting to promote competence with social context is the shaming and self-censoring that can result. While becoming more "culturally aware" or competent is a good thing, it's important that those with more privilege aren't simply forcing their internalized prejudices underground—only to have them pop up elsewhere. As Liz Goodwin wrote:

> If we focus on creating politically correct environments that control or punish biased expressions, we can sometimes achieve nothing more than the temporary suppression of behaviors intrinsic to systems of oppression. We all tend to conceal our

prejudices, yet underlying supremacist beliefs and attitudes in us continue, and can even become stronger. (Nieto et al., 2010)

Again, the work here is to be honest and compassionate with ourselves about what our work is. Those who have been more sheltered from oppression have the task of staying awake to dynamics that label some people normal and others not. Understanding social context requires diligent study and practice, depending on our own history.

This is where the window of tolerance fits in. Recall that on the upper zone of the window, we have chaos: the world is too much, and we can't take in the information that's coming at us. We feel stressed out to the point where anxiety undermines our efforts. In the bottom zone, we have stagnancy and boredom. We're not learning anything, and we rest in a motionless status quo. Between these poles, we have the window of tolerance—an optimal zone of learning that helps us develop in a sustainable way. On this middle path, it is more likely we can remain centered and connected to what we care about. We know what we know, but more importantly what we don't. All of this supports trauma-sensitive practice.

(2) BE WILLING TO DISCUSS LINEAGE AND CULTURAL APPROPRIATION

The second modification of this chapter builds on the first—the significance of developing a rigorous analysis of the ways social context connects to trauma healing. This modification asks that we talk to students and clients about where the specific form of mindfulness we are engaging comes from and the lineage that brought each of us to these healing techniques. By doing so, we build trust, disrupt potentially oppressive dynamics, honor history, and give people a sense of choice and agency when it comes to their healing. I'll begin with a story to illustrate this modification.

A colleague of mine once described an exchange she witnessed in her undergraduate psychology class. Each class, her instructor opened and closed by striking a singing bowl. Used as a meditation aid in a number of traditions, the singing bowl would create a beautiful, melodic sound that resonated throughout the room. The instructor felt this gave students the chance to focus at the beginning of class and pause before transitioning back into their hectic lives.

One evening at the end of class, a student stopped to ask the teacher how he'd acquired the bowl and if he knew where it was from. He told her he didn't know where it was from, that he had acquired it from a local bookstore. He said he loved the sound and handed the student the bowl.

"I like the sound too," she said, examining the bottom of the bowl. Then the smile on her face faded. "You know, judging by this character, the bowl is from Japan, not too far from where my family is from. Mostly, we use this kind of bell in traditional funeral rites and worship of our ancestors."

The instructor asked her if she thought it was okay if he used it.

"That's up to you," the student said. She placed the bowl down and walked away, shaking her head.

As I described above, to help students and clients feel safe, we need an awareness of social context. This includes the ability to be humble in the face of what we do not know. Rather than try to be perfect and know everything, we can practice building a genuine curiosity about other people, other cultures, and social conditions. By developing some competence in this realm, we can also learn to make links we might otherwise miss at first glance. When working with trauma, we're especially looking for dynamics that relate to privilege, oppression, and harm. In doing so, we let this information inform our interventions, adding depth to our work.

In the example above, when the instructor couldn't offer any substantial context about his singing bowl, he broke trust with the student. Without considering social context, he was using a tool sacred to another person's culture. While this might not have been an intentionally malicious act, his insufficient knowledge about the singing bowl's origin had a negative impact.

In the systems of oppression described in this chapter, domination plays out in many ways: from wide-scale violence to subtler acts of discrimination. Another manifestation of oppression is *cultural appropria-tion*—exploiting aspects of a culture that's not one's own. While mutual acts of cultural sharing take place all the time, cultural appropriation refers to a power dynamic in which members of a dominant group take objects or rituals from a group of people who have been systematically oppressed—using them to their own advantage, and exploiting the people the practice came from. As such, marginalized groups lose the power to choose how their customs and practices are used. For instance, non-Indigenous companies market and sell traditional Indigenous head-dresses, or war bonnets, at Halloween for non-Indigenous people to wear. This is an act of cultural appropriation.

What does this have to do with trauma and mindfulness? Let's start with trauma: acts of cultural appropriation often end up trivializing vio-lent historical oppressions that are linked to intergenerational trauma. Sporting mascots in the United States frequently adopt Native war figures that are linked to colonialism and genocide, and non-Native people have been known to wear symbols such as a war bonnet. The core dynamic here is that one powerful group takes what it wants from a cultural tradi-tion, without regard for the people or circumstances that fashioned it—or its possible role in their oppression.

Western Buddhists have been accused of appropriating mindfulness teachings to turn a profit by selling magazines or courses. Of course, this is highly complex: Buddhism has evolved tremendously over millennia, spreading from India, to China, to several other countries, assuming dif-ferent cultural aspects from the people and places it touches. The first Western teachers practiced mindfulness in countries such as Burma and Thailand in the 1960s and 1970s and, with the blessings of their teachers, brought Buddhism to the United States and offered it with reverence for historical tradition. Practices also change with time and are adapted to fit the needs of the people practicing. So is mindfulness as it is being practiced in certain places a form of cultural appropriation, cultural sharing, or both?

One thing here is certain: whether we're offering mindfulness teachings as a secular intervention or as part of a Buddhist path, we're doing so inside of a social context where cultural appropriation happens. The integrity of our work suffers if we're not aware that appropriation is rooted in systems of domination that perpetuate harm and can cause or exacerbate trauma.

How, then, can we build safety and trust with the people we work with and ensure that we're drawing on basic mindfulness instruction skillfully? The key is to learn about the lineage you are practicing in, and be transparent with students and clients about where teachings came from and let people choose the degree to which they want to participate. Letting people know about the lineage of one's work, including potential contradictions, grants them the agency to opt in or out of the process. Acknowledging the complexity and variance of mindfulness as it is being taught—rather than obscuring its potential appropriation—opens the door to choice. We take a moment to let people know where we're coming from, answer any questions, and be as honest and transparent about mindfulness as we can.

(3) TAKE ACTION

In Chapter 3, I discussed the choice that we as practitioners face when confronted with interpersonal forms of trauma rooted in social and economic oppression. In these moments, we find ourselves in a conflict between perpetrator and victim and become forced to choose a side.

For those of us who choose to side with those who are targeted by oppression, there are a number of ways we can take action. Here are five:

- **Self-examine and take action**. Look critically in your organization, community, private practice, to personal life to examine biases and areas where you might try to stay neutral or inadvertently side with oppression. From here, take steps to address injustice. How, for example, can we create and encourage an environment that raises consciousness and awareness of both oppression and the many movements taking action to bring equity?
- **Speak out against injustice**. Whether we're witnessing an act of oppression in our mindfulness community or engaging with

some form of institutionalized oppression, we can find ways to interrupt oppression by using our voices, starting conversations, and getting support.

- **Join a grassroots community organization and mobilize to fight systemic injustice.** Seek out movements that are waging campaigns working to transform oppressive systems that perpetuate trauma, and get involved.
- **Lift up the voices of those who are fighting against injustice.** Through social media and our personal networks, we can share the writing and voices of people who have been committed to exposing oppression.
- **Radically increase awareness.** As with mindfulness training, learning takes place when we engage with people who have more experience than we do. It is the same with building social consciousness. To increase our awareness about oppression, we can engage with organizations that align with our values, and teachers and mentors willing to help us become more effective in our work.

(4) RESOURCE SOCIAL AND ENVIRONMENTAL JUSTICE MOVEMENTS

This final modification asks trauma-sensitive practitioners to take active steps toward committing resources to movements that are advancing social justice—and by extension challenge conditions that create and perpetuate systemic trauma. Whether we're a monthly donor to a grassroots organization, or part of an institution that's making a larger contribution, trauma-sensitive practice is supported by resourcing movements fighting for justice.

A core principle of this book is that we become more powerful and accountable trauma-informed practitioners when we think about trauma in a systemic way. Conceptualizing interpersonal trauma as simply an individual tragedy leaves out the systemic conditions that so often lie at the root of trauma—racism, transphobia, poverty, and state violence, for example. As I covered in this chapter, understanding the systemic aspects of trauma helps us be more responsive to people's lived experience of trauma and understand the social context we're operating within.

Throughout history, communities have organized together to resist and confront systems that create and perpetuate collective trauma. Social and environmental justice movements have won concrete improvements in people's lives, and envisioned a world that is racially and economically just, in which wealth, land, and power are shared. These movements have taken leadership from poor and working-class communities and communities of color, whose bodies and labor make our society run and have the most at stake in ending oppressive systems. Transformative movements have also included healing practitioners of different kinds, who support communities to heal from trauma and access resilience, well-being, and freedom.

Trauma-informed practice, I believe, asks us to be responsive to the needs of these movements—in particular through the practice of sharing resources and making financial contributions. Within the current conditions of capitalism, social movements need direct financial support: nonprofit organizations—including social change organizations as well as religious institutions—in the United States currently receive 72% of their funding from individuals, and only 15% from philanthropic foundations.[20] Research also tells us that the most money given away in the Unites States also comes from middle-income, working class, and poor families.[21] Social and environmental justice organizations depend on a wide range of donations from a variety of people, and as trauma-informed practitioners we can support movements of our choice—whether through a major annual donation or monthly contribution, depending on our access to financial resources.

We can also resource movements in different ways. For trauma-sensitive practitioners who come from communities that are directly impacted by oppressive systems, we can find and join community-based organizations that are organizing for change. For those of us who live with more class and race privilege, we can support those organizations and join those that organize our communities as allies and in other ways. We can be responsive to the economic realities of the majority of people, and consider making our fee structures accessible to people with less financial access (in particular members of organizations working for social change), who are often the most impacted by traumatic systems.

Transforming Trauma

At the turn of the millennium in Montgomery, Alabama, public markers memorializing the slave trade didn't exist. In a city dotted with signs commemorating events related to the civil rights movement and the Confederacy, public acknowledgement of Montgomery's prominent role in the domestic slave trade in the United States was notably absent.

But this changed in 2013. Activist and law professor Brian Stevenson, founder and executive director of the Equal Justice Initiative (EJI)—a nonprofit organization challenging mass incarceration and racial and economic injustice—began advocating for a series of historical markers that would document Montgomery's participation in the slave trade.[1] EJI argued that people would benefit from a physical space in which residents and visitors to the city would, in the light of day, consider the traumatic history of racism and slavery in the country—a call to confront history rather than deny, repress, and repeat it.[2] "You can't understand civil rights or the Civil War without an appreciation of slavery and what the slave trade did to places like Montgomery," Stevenson said. "Talking about this is a challenge, but it's a necessity" (Kachmar, 2013).

I learned about Stevenson and EJI's work in the summer of 2015. A few weeks earlier, 21-year-old white supremacist Dylann Roof had opened fire in Emanuel African Methodist Episcopal Church in Charleston, South Carolina, murdering nine people. I came across an interview with Stevenson about the shooting in which he drew grounded connections between the hate-fueled murders and the historical trauma of slavery. "Very few people in this country have any awareness of just how expansive and how debilitating and destructive America's history of slavery is," he said. "I don't believe slavery ended in 1865, I believe it just evolved."

Trauma often refuses to be buried, tamped down, or pushed aside. Despite our best efforts to distract or numb ourselves, shards of trauma eventually make their way to the surface. Sometimes this can happen on an individual scale, while other times there are more collective awakenings, with the reality of trauma breaking through into public awareness. A woman speaks out about an assault she experienced at the hands of a public figure, for example, and public dialogue about sexism and the violence associated with it erupts.[3] Or a small protest led by Indigenous people against environmental racism sparks people from across the country to join the action, evoking a long history of trauma due to settler colonialism.[4]

To heal trauma, it must first be addressed. This was part of the argument Stevenson and EJI made in Montgomery: to confront the ongoing impacts of racism and slavery, the public needed a forum to do so. Otherwise historic amnesia would rule the day. Of course, facing such trauma is no small task. It requires resolve, commitment, courage, and the right kind of support. For those of us with more privilege, facing historical traumas in which we may be implicated asks us into accountability—one where we grow our capacity to stay present and resist the pattern to dissociate, blame others, or become underaccountable in the face of suffering.

How can we best do this? How can we remain stimulated to address trauma as opposed to sinking into immobility, desensitization, and helplessness? Under the weight of so much traumatic violence endlessly replayed on the news, what is the best way to respond? How can we show up for this pain in a way that's meaningful and transformational?*

---

* For practitioners who have grown up being treated as "White" (which we know to be a social rather than biological category, and therefore fluid), we have a lot to gain from engaging these questions. Not only can we better serve clients, work with peers, and love our families and friends. Not only can we come to know ourselves better. These alone are vitally important and life-affirming gains. But there is a layer below. It may take courage to interrogate what we've taken for granted our whole lives, including the subtle and not-so-subtle lies that racism tells us about who we are and who other people are. It may take determination and support to change

As I've argued in this book, mindfulness is a tool that can help increase our capacity to be with a range of experiences—be it joy, love, or traumatic stress. Practicing mindfulness is about learning to see clearly and having a willingness to look without filters at present-moment experience. In the realm of our consciousness—the thoughts, memories, and experiences that comprise who we are—mindfulness promotes a brave, unflinching appraisal of the minute places and of the overall state of affairs. It is a skill and practice that can help galvanize our courage and act as a supportive hand at our back in the hardest of moments—like a friend standing beside you offering quiet reassurance that you've got what it takes. Mindfulness can help us expand our window of tolerance so that we have more room to experience life in the fullest sense. As we strengthen our ability to be with pain, we can also welcome more pleasure and peace.

Yet mindfulness also isn't a quick fix, of course. There is no easy cure for healing trauma. The case I've made in this book is that mindfulness can increase the chances of our successfully integrating trauma by enhancing self-regulation. As an adjunct to trauma treatments, mindfulness can assist in our turning toward trauma with greater mental stability, an improved facility for self-regulation, and the ability to cultivate courage and compassion in the face of dysregulating symptoms.

By extension, adopting a trauma-sensitive mindfulness framework is also not as easy as simply making the decision to introduce mindfulness as a tool in treatment. Trauma-sensitive mindfulness is not something we can pick up at a weekend workshop and then add to the list of our offerings. Just as mindfulness is learned through the dedicated application of it—with increasing skill, depth, and sensitivity over time—trauma-sensitive practice is an ongoing orientation to practice and a commitment to be a continual learner. This is what I've advocated for in this

---

the behaviors we've been conditioned into for years. The reward that lies on the other side? We can stop participating in the massive divide-and-rule scheme that constitutes racism's historical origins and current purpose on this continent. We can align ourselves with equality and justice, and in this way, step toward the possibility for true healing on the collective as well as individual levels.

book—asking those of us offering mindfulness teachings to the public to ensure we're trained in a trauma-sensitive practice that includes individual trauma as well as systemic trauma or the impacts of oppression.

In the years since beginning this project, awareness about the potentially adverse effects of mindfulness practices has come to the foreground. There's a growing realization among those offering mindfulness to the public that mindfulness alone can't solve everything. As some researchers have uncovered, it can even cause difficulties for students and clients on the path. The basic argument of this book is not that mindfulness causes trauma, but that it can uncover it. At times, it can also amplify traumatic symptoms. What students and clients need are skilled mindfulness teachers who understand that a nuanced approach to mindfulness is necessary to meet the needs of survivors grappling with trauma.

At an even broader scale, I believe we're at a crucial crossroad with trauma-informed practice. Going down one fork of that road, it shrinks into a checklist. This is akin to "diversity training" in institutions, where the focus is largely on interpersonal actions and an insistence on ignoring our collective conditions. At its most reductionist, the focus here becomes "tell me what not to say," or being "politically correct." Along the other road, there's work toward racial justice, which involves looking at how larger structures pertain to one another and locating ourselves in that bigger picture. Walking this path offers greater recognition of our own and other people's dignity and worth. It also calls all of us into claiming our own agency for what actions we want to contribute toward transforming the society in which we live. Given that trauma-sensitive practice involves a commitment to both individual and collective well-being, this latter road is the one we must travel.

Transformative, trauma-informed work means orienting to the trauma of individuals, but also attending to the larger social systems that surround us. In this book I have argued that personal change and social change are inseparable. As mindfulness practitioners, we must understand how social systems operate and our own position of privilege or disadvantage within these systems. People in positions of privilege must be especially vigilant. I hope this book's practical suggestions for offering trauma-sensitive mindfulness practice—while keeping an eye on the bigger picture—may help in fulfilling that commitment.

I wrote this book to fully engage the topic of trauma and to advocate for continuing conversations between trauma survivors, mindfulness educators, and trauma professionals. My hope is that with time and collaboration, we can come together to solve the intense problems that we are facing in dynamic and creative ways. At the end of the day, the question for many of us may be: Why is it so important to engage with trauma? What is so important about this collective turning toward trauma, including facing the conditions that underlie it?

Interdependence is fundamental to human survival—no matter how much divide-and-rule systems try to erase that reality. As we seek to bring our own selves into alignment with what we care about, we must remember that everything within and around us—our own bodies' nervous systems, our neighborhoods, our economies, our social services, our national stories and aspirations and challenges—is in continual conversation. When we acknowledge still-open wounds like legacies of slavery,[5] mass incarceration,[6] Islamophobia, and anti-immigrant racism,[7] we can see we need healing and transformation for individuals and also the larger systems we are a part of.

EJI's Bryan Stevenson turned toward the history of slavery in America for people's dignity and for social justice, and undoubtedly he knows the personal reasons that motivate him to work, against odds, so that the trauma of that history can be witnessed in the bright light of day. Each of us, in our own way, will need to find this stake for ourselves and take accountable action toward a more just, compassionate future.

Acknowledgments

Listen
with the night falling we are saying thank you
—W. S. Merwin

It is important that I tell you their names, that you
know that I have never achieved anything alone.
—Ta-Nehisi Coates

I'm indebted to those whose love and labor made this book possible.

Thank you, Deborah Malmud, for believing in this project. Your team at Norton was a pleasure to work with.

To my editors: Mattie Bamman, thank you for your vision and setting me on a steady course. Sophie Hagen, thank you for your wise counsel and offering a foothold to begin the climb. Kendra Ward, thank you for your brilliant editing and 20 years of friendship—working with you was a dream come true. Toni Burbank, thank you for your generosity of spirit and intellect, and teaching me that complex ideas could remain accessible. Robyn Russell, thank you for showing me where to look, but not telling me what to see; you're a force of nature and I'm so grateful we met.

To the group of men I call family: Daniel Rechtschaffen, thank you for opening the door and loving me along the way. David Coates, thank you for lighting a fire beneath me and keeping me on purpose and path.

Steve Seto, thank you for your insightful counsel when I needed you most. David Yadegar, thank you for your laughter and loving encouragement, and Govinda Bader, thank you for your belief in the project and your love and friendship. Adrian Klaphaak, thank you for sharing your bright, beautiful heart.

To my community at *generative somatics*, thank you for your work toward a more just, compassionate world. Staci Haines, thank you for your unwavering support and helping me become the person I hoped I was. Spenta Kandawalla, thank you for your leadership and the ways you've held me as a teacher, healer, and friend. Hilary Moore, thank you for opening my mind to what was possible, and your steady love along the path. Chris Lymbertos, thank you for who you are and all you do. Fayza Bundalli, thank you for your friendship and commitment to disability justice, and Sumi Rajkumar, for sharing your brilliance. Danielle Feris, thank you for helping me think differently about resource, and Adrienne Maree Brown for helping me think differently about love. Jennifer Ianniello, thank you for your friendship, feedback, and the smoked olives. An additional thank you to Alta Starr, Morgan Bassichis, Gesine Wenzel, Liu Hoi-Man, Lara Barth, Nathan Shara, Paola Laird, RJ Maccani, Vassi Johri, Xochitl Bervera, Denise Perry, Raquel Lavina, Prentis Hemphill, and Lisa Thomas-Adeyemo.

I'd be lost without close friends. Ashley Bauman, thank you for your love and partnership as we risked toward our longing. Amy Larimer and Drew Krafcik, thank you for taking me in and teaching me about family and unconditional love. Claire Kimmel, thank you for your magic and grace. Catherine Wilcox, thank you for friendship over lifetimes, and Maegan Willan for making this all possible. Kirby Huminuik, thank you for being a comrade at the intersection of psychology and social justice, and Lisa Woodruffe for reminding me what's most important. Jessica Garfield-Kabbara, thank you for your fierce allyship and always helping me see the bigger picture. Taylor Rechtschaffen, thank you for modeling courage, Nuria Gomez for your steadfast support, and Valerie Chafograck for teaching me how to move and pray at the same time. Savahn

Rosinbum, thank you for teaching me about love and rest, and Danielle Bezaire, for taking my hand and never letting go.

Colleagues and friends with particular expertise offered countless gifts. Willoughby Britton and Jared Lindahl, thank you for your ground-breaking scholarship and huge, loving hearts. Aya Cheaito, thank you for your commitment to healing justice, and Tempel Smith, for sharing your well-earned insights about mindfulness, trauma, and healing. Brett Wheeler, Jon Roth, and Jill Shepherd, thank you for your powerful feedback as Buddhist practitioners, and Richard Strozzi-Heckler for teaching me how to see and what to look for. Clare Bayard, thank you for believing in this project, and your insights about trauma, oppression, and collective liberation—this book is so much stronger because of you. Thank you to Erin Wiegand at North Atlantic Books for your counsel and understanding. Thank you also to Donna Willmott, Dylan Cooke, Isaac Lev Szmonko, Molly McClure, Rahula Janowski, and Will Dominie from the Catalyst Project for holding the 2015 Anne Braden Anti-Racist Organizing Training program—I learned so much from each of you.

To my teachers: Babette Rothschild, thank you for your mentorship and being so "encouragable." Jorge Ferrer, thank you for your love and rigor, and helping me bring this idea to fruition. Don Hanlon Johnson and Robert Masters, thank you for your skillful guidance through the dissertation process, and Bonita Long, Susan Dahinten, Anne Carrier, Tom Blom, and Beth Haverkamp, for teaching me how to write. Tara Brach and Rick Hanson, thank you for believing in me, and Kerry Brady for showing me that trauma healing is possible. Thank you also to my amazing clients, from whom I learn so much.

Thank you to friends who supported me in ways big and small: David Young, Elizabeth Husserl, Zayin Cabot, Brett Sharenow, Lani Yadegar, Kat Conour, Katherine Crichton, Alisha Gard, Kerry Buller, RJ Jennings, Tim Toliver, Alex Portnoy, David Nichol, Pat, Garry, and Jeffrey Lander, Bob, Laura, Christopher, and Katie Clemes, Wesley Rosacker, Kirsten Perkins, Joie Mazor, Thomas Fillingham, Elan Freydenson, Scott Fischer, Laura van der Noot Lipsky, Jayme Stone, Ben Schik, Tyler Mayo, Claire Whitmer, Andrew Rattee, Donald Rothberg, Jacquelyn Richards,

Michael Danzansky, Cate Gaffney, Molly Johnstone, Piya Banerjee, Rick Snyder, Sarwang Parikh, Sefora Ray, Stephen Julich, Will Kabat-Zinn, Dara Silverman, Mahrs Schoppman, Therese Noel Allen, Kisae Petersen, Piya Banerjee, and Paul Kivel. Sarah Abbott, thank you for opening my heart and introducing me to the moon.

To Amy Woodruffe, Tanya Behardien, Briana Herman-Brand, Dylan Bosseau, and Zahra, Zoë, and Soli, thank you for the opportunity to be a part of your lives and opening me to love. To my brother, Ryan Treleaven, and my sister-in-law, Nadine Alby, I'm inspired by your grace. And to my grandmother, Beatrice, thank you for cheering me on and helping me laugh about my gray hair.

Finally, I'd like to dedicate this book to my parents. Thank you for standing by me every step of the way, and reading me *Go Dog Go* every night as a child. To my mother, Lorraine, thank you for believing in me as a teacher and encouraging me as a writer, and to my father, Wesley, for picking me up when I stumbled and offering careful feedback on every chapter. I love you both.

References

AAUW. (2017). The pay gap is even worse for black women, and that's everyone's problem. Retrieved from http://www.aauw.org/2015/07/21/black-women-pay-gap/

Alexander, M. (2010). *The new Jim Crow: Mass incarceration in the age of colorblindness.* New York, NY: The New Press.

Allen, M., Dietz, M., Blair, K. S., van Beek, M., Rees, G., Vestergaard-Poulsen, P., & Roepstorff, A. (2012). Cognitive-affective neural plasticity following active-controlled mindfulness intervention. *The Journal of Neuroscience, 32*(44), 15601–15610.

American Association of University Women. (2017). *The simple truth about the gender pay gap.* Washington, DC: Author. Retrieved from http://www.aauw.org/resource/the-simple-truth-about-the-gender-pay-gap/

American Psychiatric Association. (2013). *Diagnostic and statistical manual of mental disorders* (5th ed.). Washington, DC: Author.

Anda, R. F., Felitti, V. J., Bremner, J. D., Walker, J. D., Whitfield, C. H., Perry, B. D., & Giles, W. H. (2006). The enduring effects of abuse and related adverse experiences in childhood. *European Archives of Psychiatry and Clinical Neuroscience, 256*(3), 174–186.

Anzaldúa, G. (1987). *Borderlands: la frontera.* San Francisco, CA: Aunt Lute.

Anzaldúa, G. (ed.). (1990). *Making faces, making Soul/Haciendo caras: Creative and critical perspectives of feminists of color.* San Francisco, CA: Aunt Lute Books.

Bachman, R., Zaykowski, H., Kallmyer, R., Poteyeva, M., & Lanier, C. (2008). Violence against American Indian and Alaska Native women and the criminal justice response: What is known. Washington, DC: *National Institute of Justice.*

Baer, R. (2003). Mindfulness training as a clinical intervention: A conceptual and empirical review. *Clinical Psychology: Science and Practice, 10*(2), 125–143.

Baer, R. (2016). Assessment of mindfulness and closely related constructs: Introduction to the special issue. *Psychological Assessment, 28*(7), 787–790.

Baer, R. A. (ed.). (2015). *Mindfulness-based treatment approaches: Clinician's guide to evidence base and applications.* New York, NY: Academic Press.

Baker, A., Goodman, J. D., & Mueller, B. (2015). Beyond the chokehold: The path to Eric Garner's death. *The New York Times.* Retrieved from https://www.nytimes.com/2015/06/14/nyregion/eric-garner-police-chokehold-staten-island.html?_r=0

Baker, K. J. M. (2016). Here is the powerful letter the Stanford victim read aloud to her attacker [Web post]. Retrieved from https://www.buzzfeed.com/katiejmbaker/heres-the-powerful-letter-the-stanford-victim-read-to-her-ra?utm_term=.mfZMn5GyY#.rfeOqNJxe

Baldwin, J. (1962). As much truth as one can bear. *New York Times Book Review*, 11, pp. 35–38.

Baldwin, J. (1963). *The fire next time*. New York, NY: Dial Press.

Banitt, S. P. (2012). *The trauma tool kit: Healing PTSD from the inside out*. New York, NY: Quest Books.

Banks, S. J., Eddy, K. T., Angstadt, M., Nathan, P. J., & Phan, K. L. (2007). Amygdala–frontal connectivity during emotion regulation. *Social cognitive and affective neuroscience*, 2(4), 303–312.

Becker, C. B., Zayfert, C., & Anderson, E. (2004). A survey of psychologists' attitudes towards and utilization of exposure therapy for PTSD. *Behaviour Research and Therapy*, 42(3), 277–292.

Benson, H., Beary, J. F., & Carol, M. P. (1974). The relaxation response. *Psychiatry*, 37(1), 3–46.

Berne, P., Milbern, S., & Weiner-Mahfuz, L. (2015). *Disability justice: New intersections between race, justice, and disability*. Retrieved from http://www.sinsinvalid.org/PDFs/DJBriefing_Powerpoint.pdf

Biakolo, K. (2016). How to explain cultural appropriation to anyone who just doesn't get it. *Alternet*. Retrieved from http://www.alternet.org/culture/cultural-appropriation-pho-lionel-shriver-jamie-oliver-Tim-jacobs

Black, M. C., Basile, K. C., Breiding, M. J., Smith, S. G., Walters, M. L., Merrick. M. T., . . . Stevens, M. R. (2011). *The National Intimate Partner and Sexual Violence Survey (NISVS): 2010 summary report*. Atlanta, GA: National Center for Injury Prevention and Control, Centers for Disease Control and Prevention.

Boon, S., Steele, K., & van der Hart, O. (2011). *Coping with trauma-related dissociation*. New York, NY: Norton.

Boorstein, S. (1995). *It's easier than you think: The Buddhist way to happiness*. New York, NY: Harper.

Bradley, R., Greene, J., Russ, E., Dutra, L., & Westen, D. (2005). A multidimensional meta-analysis of psychotherapy for PTSD. *American Journal of Psychiatry*, 162(2), 214–227.

Briere, J., & Scott, C. (2014). *Principles of trauma-therapy: A guide to symptoms, evaluation, and treatment* (2nd ed., DSM-5 update). Thousand Oaks, CA: Sage.

Brown, K. W., & Ryan, R. M. (2003). The benefits of being present: mindfulness and its role in psychological well-being. *Journal of personality and social psychology*, 84(4), 822.

Brown University. (2017). *The varieties of contemplative experience: Project overview*. Accessed at https://www.brown.edu/research/labs/britton/research/varieties-contemplative-experience

Bubar, R. (2010). Cultural competence, justice, and supervision: Sexual assault against Native women. *Women and Therapy*, 33, 55–72.

Camp of the Sacred Stones. (2017). Standing Rock Sioux tribe DAPL resolution. Retrieved from http://sacredstonecamp.org/resolution/

Capelouto, S. (2014). Eric Garner: The haunting last words of a dying man. *CNN*. Retrieved from http://www.cnn.com/2014/12/04/us/garner-last-words/

Carson, C. (1981). *In Struggle: SNCC and the Black Awakening of the 1960s*. Cambridge, MA: Harvard University Press.

Carson, J. W., Carson, K. M., Gil, K. M., & Baucom, D. H. (2006). Mindfulness-based relationship enhancement (MBRE) in couples. In R. A. Baer (ed.) *Mindfulness-based treatment approaches: Clinician's guide to evidence base and applications* (pp. 309–331). New York, NY: Academic Press.

Carter, R. T. (2007). Racism and psychological and emotional injury: Recognizing and assessing race-based traumatic stress. *The Counseling Psychologist, 35*(1), 13–105.

Center for Disease Control and Prevention. (2016). *Injury prevention and control: Data and statistics*. Washington, DC: Author. Retrieved from https://www.cdc.gov/injury/wisqars/facts.html

Chou, T., Asnaani, A., & Hofmann, S. G. (2012). Perception of racial discrimination and psychopathology across three U.S. ethnic minority groups. *Cultural Diversity and Ethnic Minority Psychology, 18*(1), 74–81.

Coates, T. (2014). The case for reparations. *The Atlantic*. Retrieved from https://www.theatlantic.com/magazine/archive/2014/06/the-case-for-reparations/361631/

Collins, K., Connors, K., Davis, S., Donohue, A., Gardner, S., Goldblatt, E., & Thompson, E. (2010). Understanding the impact of trauma and urban poverty on family systems: Risks, resilience, and interventions. *Baltimore, MD: Family Informed Trauma Treatment Center*. Retrieved from www.nctsnet.org/sites/default/files/assets/pdfs/understanding_the_impact_of_trauma.pdf

Cook, J. L. & Cook, G. (2005). *Child development: Principles and perspectives*. Boston, MA: Allyn and Bacon.

Corcoran, K. M., Farb, N. A., Anderson, A., & Segal, Z. V. (2009). Mindfulness and emotion regulation: Outcomes and possible mediating mechanisms. In A. M. Kring & D. M. Sloan (eds.), *Emotion regulation and psychopathology: A transdiagnostic approach to etiology and treatment* (pp. 339–355). New York, NY: Guilford Press.

Creswell, J. D., Way, B. M., Eisenberger, N. I., & Lieberman, M. D. (2007). Neural correlates of dispositional mindfulness during affect labeling. *Psychosomatic Medicine, 69*(6), 560–565.

Cullen, M. (2011). Mindfulness-based interventions: An emerging phenomenon. *Mindfulness, 2*(3), 186–193.

Damasio, A. R. (1994). *Descartes' error*. New York, NY: Random House.

Daniels, A. (2014). As wealthy give smaller share of income to charity, middle class digs deeper. *The Chronicle of Philanthropy*. Retrieved from https://www.philanthropy.com/article/As-Wealthy-Give-Smaller-Share/152481

DeGruy, J. (2005). *Post traumatic slave syndrome: America's legacy of enduring injury and healing*. New York, NY: HarperCollins.

Deitz, M. F., Williams, S. L., Rife, S. C., & Cantrell, P. (2015). Examining cultural, social, and self-related aspects of stigma in relation to sexual assault and trauma symptoms. *Violence Against Women, 21*(5), 598–615.

De Jong, J. T. V. M., Komproe, I. H., Van Ommeren, M., El Masri, M., Araya, M., Khaled, N., van de Put, W. & Somasundaram, D. (2001). Lifetime events and posttraumatic stress disorder in 4 postconflict settings. *Journal of the American Medical Association,* *286,* 555–562.

Desbordes, G., Negi, L. T., Pace, T. W., Wallace, B. A., Raison, C. L., & Schwartz, E. L. (2012). Effects of mindful-attention and compassion meditation training on amygdala response to emotional stimuli in an ordinary, non-meditative state. *Frontiers in Human Neuroscience, 6,* 292–303.

Disha, I., Cavendish, J. C., & King, R. D. (2011). Historical events and spaces of hate: Hate crimes against Arabs and Muslims in post-9/11 America. *Social Problems, 58*(1), 21–46.

Dreier, P. (2016). Caught on camera: Police racism. *Prospect.* Retrieved at http://prospect.org/article/caught-camera-police-racism

Dube, S. R., Anda, R. F., Felitti, V. J., Chapman, D. P., Williamson, D. F., & Giles, W. H. (2001). Childhood abuse, household dysfunction, and the risk of attempted suicide throughout the life span: Findings from the Adverse Childhood Experiences Study. *Journal of the American Medical Association, 286*(24), 3089–3096.

East Bay Meditation Center. (2017). Mission and history [Web post]. Retrieved from https://eastbaymeditation.org/about/mission-history/

Eisen, A. (2014). *Operation ghetto storm: 2012 Annual Report on the extrajudicial killings of 313 Black people by police, security guards, and vigilantes.* Retrieved from http://www.operationghettostorm.org/uploads/1/9/1/1/19110795/new_all_14_11_04.pdf

Elliott, D. M. (1997). Traumatic events: Prevalence and delayed recall in the general population. *Journal of Consulting and Clinical Psychology, 65,* 811–820.

Emerson, D., Hopper, E., & Levine, P. A. (2011). *Overcoming trauma through yoga: Reclaiming your body.* Berkeley, CA: North Atlantic Books.

Epstein, M. (2013). *The trauma of everyday life.* New York, NY: Penguin.

Equal Justice Initiative (EJI). (2013). Slavery in America: The Montgomery slave trade (Report). Retrieved at http://eji.org/sites/default/files/slavery-in-america-summary.pdf

Feagin, J., & Bennefield, Z. (2014). Systemic racism and US health care. *Social Science & Medicine, 103,* 7–14.

Fine-Dare, K. S. (2002). *Grave injustice: the American Indian repatriation movement and NAGPRA.* Lincoln, NE: Univerity of Nebraska Press.

Foa, E. B., Chrestman, K. R., & Gilboa-Schechtman, E. (2008). *Prolonged exposure therapy for adolescents with PTSD: Emotional processing of traumatic experiences: Therapist guide.* London: Oxford University Press.

Foa, E. B., & Kozak, M. J. (1986). Emotional processing of fear: exposure to corrective information. *Psychological bulletin, 99*(1), 20.

Frans, Ö., Rimmö, P. A., Åberg, L., & Fredrikson, M. (2005). Trauma exposure and post-traumatic stress disorder in the general population. *Acta Psychiatrica Scandinavica, 111*(4), 291–290.

Freud, S. (1896). The aetiology of hysteria. In *The standard edition of the complete psychological works of Sigmund Freud,* trans. J. Strachey (pp. 187–221). London: Hogarth Press.

Frye, M. (1983). *The politics of reality: Essays in feminist theory.* New York, NY: Crossing Press.

Gallup, G. G. (1977). Tonic immobility: The role of fear and predation. *Psychological Record, 27,* 41–61.

Gardner-Nix, J., & Costin-Hall, L. (2009). *The mindfulness solution to pain: Step-by-step techniques for chronic pain management.* Oakland, CA: New Harbinger.

Garfield, J. L. (1995). *The fundamental wisdom of the middle way: Nâgârjuna's Mûlamadhyamakakârikâ.* London: Oxford University Press.

generationFIVE. (2017). Ending child sexual abuse: A transformative justice handbook. Retrieved from http://www.generationfive.org/wp-content/uploads/2017/06/Transformative-Justice-Handbook.pdf

generative somatics. (2017). What is somatics? Retrieved from http://www.generativesomatics.org/content/what-somatics

GLAAD (2017). Retrieved from https://www.glaad.org/reference/transgender

Goldin, P. R., & Gross, J. J. (2010). Effects of mindfulness-based stress reduction (MBSR) on emotion regulation in social anxiety disorder. *Emotion, 10*(1), 83–91.

Gray, E. (2016). This letter from the Stanford sex offender's dad epitomizes rape culture. *Huffington Post.* Retrieved from http://www.huffingtonpost.com/entry/brock-turner-dad-letter-is-rape-culture-in-a-nutshell_us_57555bace4b0ed593f14cb30

Green, A. R., Carney, D. R., Pallin, D. J., Ngo, L. H., Raymond, K. L., Iezzoni, L. I., & Banaji, M. R. (2007). Implicit bias among physicians and its prediction of thrombolysis decisions for Black and White patients. *Journal of General Internal Medicine, 22*(9), 1231–1238.

Greenwald, A. G., & Krieger, L. H. (2006). Implicit bias: Scientific foundations. *California Law Review, 94*(4), 945–967.

Gunaratana, B. (2011). *Mindfulness in plain English.* London: Simon and Schuster.

Haines, S. (2007). *Healing sex: A mind-body approach to healing sexual trauma.* San Francisco: Cleis Press.

Hanson, R. (2009). *Buddha's brain: The practical neuroscience of happiness, love, and wisdom.* Oakland, CA: New Harbinger.

Hays, P. A. (1996). Addressing the complexities of culture and gender in counseling. *Journal of Counseling & Development, 74,* 332–338.

Healing Collective Trauma. (2013). Kindred collective: Cara Page. Retrieved from http://www.healingcollectivetrauma.com/cara-page.html

Heartland Trans Wellness Group. (2017). *Gender neutral bathrooms.* Retrieved from http://transwellness.org/resources/educational-materials/gender-neutral-bathrooms/

Hemphill, P. (2017). Healing justice is how we can sustain Black lives. *Huffpost.* Retrieved from http://www.huffingtonpost.com/entry/healing-justice_us_5899e8ade4b0c1284f282ffe

Herbermann, C. G. (Ed.). (1922). *The Catholic encyclopedia: Supplement I.* New York, NY: Encyclopedia Press.

Herman, J. L. (1997). *Trauma and recovery.* New York, NY: Basic Books.

Hernández, C. C. G. (2014). Creating crimmigration. *Brigham Young University Law Review.* Retrieved from https://ssrn.com/abstract=2393662 or http://dx.doi.org/10.2139/ssrn.2393662

Hochman, D. (2013). Mindfulness: Getting its share of attention. *The New York Times.* Retrieved from http://www.nytimes.com/2013/11/03/fashion/mindfulness-and-meditation-are-capturing-attention.html

Hollis-Walker, L., & Colosimo, K. (2011). Mindfulness, self-compassion, and happiness in non-meditators: A theoretical and empirical examination. Personality and Individual differences, 50(2), 222–227.

Hölzel, B. K., Carmody, J., Evans, K. C., Hoge, E. A., Dusek, J. A., Morgan, L., . . . & Lazar, S. W. (2009). Stress reduction correlates with structural changes in the amygdala. *Social Cognitive and Affective Neuroscience, 5*(1), 11–17.

Hölzel, B. K., Lazar, S. W., Gard, T., Schuman-Olivier, Z., Vago, D. R., & Ott, U. (2011). How does mindfulness meditation work? Proposing mechanisms of action from a conceptual and neural perspective. *Perspectives on psychological science, 6*(6), 537–559.

hooks, b. (1984). Feminist theory: From margin to center (2nd ed.). Cambridge, MA: South End Press.

Hughes, D. (2013). Intersubjective mindfulness. In D. J. Siegel & M. Solomon (eds.), *Healing moments in psychotherapy* (pp. 17–33). New York, NY: Norton.

Hülsheger, U. R., Alberts, H. J., Feinholdt, A., & Lang, J. W. (2013). Benefits of mindfulness at work: The role of mindfulness in emotion regulation, emotional exhaustion, and job satisfaction. *Journal of Applied Psychology, 98*(2), 310–325.

Jackson-Dwyer, D. (2013). *Interpersonal relationships* (Vol. 10). New York, NY: Routledge.

Janet, P. (1911). *L'Etat mental des hystériques* (2nd ed.). Paris: Felix Alcan.

Johnson, C. G. (2015). Bryan Stevenson on Charleston and our real problem with race. *The Marshall Project.* Retrieved from https://www.themarshallproject.org/2015/06/24/bryan-stevenson-on-charleston-and-our-real-problem-with-race#.oYAIK9UUp

Kabat-Zinn, J. (1994). *Wherever you go, there you are: Mindfulness meditation in everyday life.* London: Hachette.

Kabat-Zinn, J. (2011). Some reflections on the origins of MBSR, skillful means, and the trouble with maps. *Contemporary Buddhism, 12*(01), 281–306.

Kachmar, K. (2013). New Markers document Ala. city's role in slave trade. *USA Today: The Montgomery (Ala.) Advertiser.* Retrieved from https://www.usatoday.com/story/news/nation/2013/12/11/slave-trade-historic-markers-alabama/3989611/

Kearney, D. J., McDermott, K., Malte, C., Martinez, M., & Simpson, T. L. (2012). Association of participation in a mindfulness program with measures of PTSD, depression and quality of life in a veteran sample. *Journal of clinical psychology, 68*(1), 101–116.

Kelley, R. D. G. (2017). What did Cedric Robinson mean by racial capitalism? *Boston Review.* Retrieved from http://bostonreview.net/race/robin-d-g-kelley-what-did-cedric-robinson-mean-racial-capitalism

Kilpatrick, D. G., Resnick, H. S., Milanak, M. E., Miller, M. W., Keyes, K. M., & Friedman, M. J. (2013). National estimates of exposure to traumatic events and PTSD prevalence using DSM-IV and DSM-5 criteria. *Journal of Traumatic Stress, 26*(5), 537–547.

King, A. P., Erickson, T. M., Giardino, N. D., Favorite, T., Rauch, S. A., Robinson, E., Kulkarni, M., & Liberzon, I. (2013). A pilot study of group mindfulness-based cognitive therapy (MBCT) for combat veterans with posttraumatic stress disorder (PTSD). *Depression and anxiety, 30*(7), 638–645.

Kivel, P. (2004). *You call this a democracy? Who benefits, who pays, and who really decides?* New York, NY: Apex Press.

Kraus, D. (1993). *Concepts of modern biology.* Englewood Cliffs, NJ: Globe Book Company.

Lazar, S. W., Kerr, C. E., Wasserman, R. H., Gray, J. R., Greve, D. N., Treadway, M. T., McGarvey, M. Quinn, B., Dusek, J. A., Benson, H., Rauch, S. L., Moore, C. I., &

Fischl, B. (2005). Meditation experience is associated with increased cortical thickness. *Neuroreport, 16*(17), 1893–1897.

Lebron, D., Morrison, L., Ferris, D., Alcantara, A., Cummings, D., Parker, G., & McKay, M. (2015). *Facts matter! Black lives matter! The trauma of racism.* New York, NY: New York University Silver School of Social Work. Retrieved at http://www.mcsilver.org/wp-content/uploads/2015/04/Trauma-of-Racism-Report.pdf

LeDoux, J. (1998). *The emotional brain: The mysterious underpinnings of emotional life.* New York, NY: Simon and Schuster.

Levine, P. A. (1997). *Waking the tiger: Healing trauma.* Berkeley, CA: North Atlantic Books.

Levine, P. A. (2010). *In an unspoken voice: How the body releases trauma and restores goodness.* Berkeley, CA: North Atlantic Books.

Lichtblau, E. & Fausset, R. (2016). U.S. warns North Carolina that transgender bill violates civil rights laws. *The New York Times.* Retrieved from https://www.nytimes.com/2016/05/05/us/north-carolina-transgender-bathroom-bill.html

Lindahl, J. R., Fisher, N. E., Cooper, D. J., Rosen, R. K., & Britton, W. B. (2017). The varieties of contemplative experience: A mixed-methods study of meditation-related challenges in Western Buddhists. *PLoS ONE, 12*(5): e0176239.

Lodhi, H. (2015). Does systemic oppression really exist? *Huffpost.* Retrieved from http://www.huffingtonpost.com/humera-lodhi/a-muslim-at-mizzou-does-s_b_8539080.html

Lorde, A. (1984). *Sister outsider: Essays and speeches.* Berkeley, CA: Crossing Press.

MacLean, P. D. (1990). *The triune brain in evolution: Role in paleocerebral functions.* New York, NY: Springer Science.

Magyari, T. (2016). Teaching individuals with traumatic stress. In D. McCown, D. K. Reibel, & M. S. Micozzi (eds.), *Resources for teaching mindfulness: An international handbook* (pp. 339–358). New York, NY: Springer.

Mahler, J. (2016). For many women, Trump's 'locker-room talk' brings memories of abuse. *The New York Times.* Retrieved from https://www.nytimes.com/2016/10/11/us/politics/sexual-assault-survivor-reaction.html?action=click&contentCollection=Politics&module=RelatedCoverage&region=Marginalia&pgtype=article

Manna, A., Raffone, A., Perrucci, M. G., Nardo, D., Ferretti, A., Tartaro, A., & Romani, G. L. (2010). Neural correlates of focused attention and cognitive monitoring in meditation. *Brain Research Bulletin, 82*(1), 46–56.

Massachusetts Institute of Technology. (2015). Kids corner-brain gear, the Gabrrieli Lab [web post]. Retrieved from http://gablab.mit.edu/index.php/14-sample-data-articles/149-kids-corner-brain-gear

McCown, Reibel, & Micozzi (eds.) (2016). *Resources for teaching mindfulness: An international handbook.* New York, NY: Springer.

Merckelbach, H., & Muris, P. (2001). The causal link between self-reported trauma and dissociation: A critical review. *Behavior Research and Therapy, 39*(3), 245–254.

Mitchell, K. S., Dick, A. M., DiMartino, D. M., Smith, B. N., Niles, B., Koenen, K. C., & Street, A. (2014). A pilot study of a randomized controlled trial of yoga as an intervention for PTSD symptoms in women. *Journal of Traumatic Stress, 27*(2), 121–128.

Movement for Black Lives. (2016). *A vision for Black lives: Policy demands for Black power, freedom, & justice.* Retrieved from https://policy.m4bl.org/wp-content/uploads/2016/07/20160726-m4bl-Vision-Booklet-V3.pdf

Movement Generation Justice and Ecology Project. (2012). *From banks and tanks to cooperation and caring: A strategic framework for a just transition.* Retrieved from http://movementgen.electricembers.net/wp-content/uploads/2016/11/JT_booklet_English_SPREADs_web.pdf

National Center for Charitable Statistics. (2015). Charitable giving in america: Some facts and figures. Retrieved from http://nccs.urban.org/data-statistics/charitable-giving-america-some-facts-and-figures

National Coalition of Anti-Violence Programs. (2014). *Lesbian, gay, transgender, queer, and HIV-affected intimate partner violence in 2013.* New York, NY: Author. Retrieved from http://www.avp.org/storage/documents/ncavp2013ipvreport_webfinal.pdf

National Network to End Domestic Violence. (2015). *'14 domestic violence counts national summary.* Washington, DC: Author. Retrieved from http://nnedv.org/downloads/Census/DV-Counts2014/DVCounts14_NatlSummary_Color-2.pdf

Nieto, L., Boyer, M. F., Goodwin, L., Johnson, G. R., Smith, L. C. & Hopkins, J. P. (2010). *Beyond inclusion, beyond empowerment: A developmental strategy to liberate everyone.* Olympia, WA: Cuetzpalin.

Nsiah-Jefferson, L. (1989). Reproductive laws, women of color, and low-income women. In *Reproductive Laws for the 1990s* (pp. 23–67). New York, NY: Humana Press.

Nyanamoli, B. (1972). *The life of the Buddha, as it appears in the Pali canon, the oldest authentic record.* Kandi, Sri Lanka: Buddhist Publication Society.

O'Connell, B., & Dowling, M. (2014). Dialectical behavior therapy (DBT) in the treatment of borderline personality disorder. *Journal of Psychiatric and Mental Health Nursing, 21*(6), 518–525.

Ogden, P. (2015). *Sensorimotor psychotherapy: Interventions for trauma and attachment.* New York, NY: Norton.

Ogden, P. & Fisher, J. (2015). *Sensorimotor psychotherapy: Interventions for trauma and attachment.* New York, NY: Norton.

Ogden, P., Minton, K., & Pain, C. (2006). *Trauma and the body: A sensorimotor approach to psychotherapy.* New York, NY: Norton.

Olive, V. C. (2012). Sexual assault against women of color. *Journal of Student Research, 1,* 1–9.

Oppression. (2017). In Merriam-Webster.com. Retrieved from https://www.merriam-webster.com/dictionary/oppression?utm_campaign=sd&utm_medium=serp&utm_source=jsonld

Orenstein, D. (2017). Study documents range of challenging meditation experiences. Retrieved from https://news.brown.edu/articles/2017/05/experiences

Ortner, C. N., Kilner, S. J., & Zelazo, P. D. (2007). Mindfulness meditation and reduced emotional interference on a cognitive task. *Motivation and Emotion, 31*(4), 271–283.

Ostafin, B. D., Robinson, M. D., & Meier, B. P. (eds.). (2015). *Handbook of Mindfulness and Self-regulation.* New York, NY: Springer.

Ozer, E. J., & Weiss, D. S. (2004). Who develops posttraumatic stress disorder? *Current Directions in Psychological Science, 13*(4), 169–172.

Pickert, K. (2014, February 3). The mindful revolution. *TIME Magazine,* pp. 34–48.

Pierce, C., Carew, J., Pierce-Gonzalez, D., & Willis, D. (1978). An experiment in racism:

TV commercials. In C. Pierce (ed.), *Television and education* (pp. 62–88). Beverly Hills, CA: Sage.

Pole, N., Best, S. R., Metzler, T., & Marmar, C. R. (2005). Why are Hispanics at greater risk for PTSD? *Cultural Diversity and Ethnic Minority Psychology, 11*(2), 144–161.

Porges, S. W. (2004). Neuroception: A subconscious system for detecting threats and safety. *Zero to Three, 24*(5), 19–24.

Porges, S. W. (2011). *The polyvagal theory: Neurophysiological foundations of emotions, attachment, communication, and self-regulation.* New York, NY: Norton.

Poynting, S., & Mason, V. (2007). The resistible rise of Islamophobia: Anti-Muslim racism in the UK and Australia before 11 September 2001. *Journal of Sociology, 43*(1), 61–86.

Quigley, W. P. (2003). *Ending poverty as we know it: Guaranteeing a right to a job at a living wage.* Philadelphia, PA: Temple University Press.

Raffo, S. (2011). Resourcing: Fundraising as part of supporting and building community. *Grassroots Fundraising Journal.* Retrieved at http://www.amyvarga.com/wp-content/uploads/2017/02/Resourcing-Fundraising-as-Part-of-Supporting-and-Building-Community.pdf

RAINN. (2017). Effects of sexual violence. Retrieved from https://www.rainn.org/effects-sexual-violence

Ray, R. A. (2008). *Touching enlightenment: Finding realization in the body.* Boulder, CO: Sounds True.

Rinfrette, E. S. (2015). From trauma to healing: A social worker's guide to working with survivors. *Health & Social Work, 40*(1), 65–66.

Roberts, A. L., Gilman, S. E., Breslau, J., Breslau, N., & Koenen, K. C. (2011). Race/ethnic differences in exposure to traumatic events, development of post-traumatic stress disorder, and treatment-seeking for post-traumatic stress disorder in the United States. *Psychological Medicine, 41*(01), 71–83.

Rocha, T. (2014). The dark knight of the soul. *The Atlantic.* Retrieved from https://www.theatlantic.com/health/archive/2014/06/the-dark-knight-of-the-souls/372766/

Rogers, K. L. (1994). Trauma redeemed: the narrative construction of social violence. In McMahan, E. M. & Rogers, K. L. (eds.) *Interactive Oral History Interviewing* (pp. 31–46). New York, NY: Routledge.

Rothbaum, B. O., Hodges, L., Alarcon, R., Ready, D., Shahar, F., Graap, K., & Baltzell, D. (1999). Virtualreality exposure therapy for PTSD Vietnam veterans: A case study. *Journal of Traumatic Stress, 12*(2), 263–271.

Rothman, E., Hathaway, J., Stidsen, A. & de Vries, H. (2007). How employment helps female victims of intimate partner abuse: A qualitative study. *Journal of Occupational Health Psychology, 12*(2), 136–143.

Rothschild, B. (2000). *The body remembers: The psychophysiology of trauma and trauma treatment.* New York, NY: Norton.

Rothschild, B. (2010). *8 keys to safe trauma recovery: Take charge strategies to empower your healing.* New York, NY: Norton.

Rothschild, B. (2011). *Trauma essentials: The go-to guide.* New York, NY: Norton.

Rothschild, R. (2017). *The body remembers, volume 2: Revolutionizing trauma treatment.* New York, NY: Norton.

Russell, D. E. (1984). *Sexual exploitation: Rape, child sexual abuse, and workplace harassment*. Thousand Oaks, CA: Sage.

Samuelson, M., Carmody, J., Kabat-Zinn, J., & Bratt, M. A. (2007). Mindfulness-based stress reduction in Massachusetts correctional facilities. *The Prison Journal, 87*(2), 254–268.

Sapolsky, R. M. (1994). *Why zebras don't get ulcers*. New York, NY: W. H. Freeman.

Scaer, R. (2001). *The body bears the burden*. New York, NY: Routledge.

Scalora, S. (2015). Mindfulness-Based Stress Reduction: An interview with Jon Kabat-Zinn. *Huffington Post*. Retrieved from http://www.huffingtonpost.com/suza-scalora/mindfulnessbased-stress-r_b_6909426.html

Schnurr, P. P., Friedman, M. J., Engel, C. C., Foa, E. B., Shea, M. T., Chow, B. K., & Turner, C. (2007). Cognitive behavioral therapy for posttraumatic stress disorder in women: A randomized controlled trial. *Journal of the American Medical Association, 297*(8), 820–830.

Schwartz, R. (1994). *The internal family systems model*. New York, NY: Guilford Press.

Schwartz, R. C. (2013). Moving from acceptance toward transformation with internal family systems therapy (IFS). *Journal of clinical psychology, 69*(8), 805–816.

Selye, H. (1973). The evolution of the stress concept: The originator of the concept traces its development from the discovery in 1936 of the alarm reaction to modern therapeutic applications of syntoxic and catatoxic hormones. *American Scientist, 61*(6), 692–699.

Shapiro, S. L., Schwartz, G. E., & Bonner, G. (1998). Effects of mindfulness-based stress reduction on medical and premedical students. *Journal of behavioral medicine, 21*(6), 581–599.

Shaver, P. (2011). *Cosmic heritage: Evolution from the big bang to conscious life*. New York, NY: Springer Science.

Shenker, J., Viturro, M., Haines, S., Kandawalla, S., & Lavina, R. (2014). *Transforming lives, transforming movement building: Lessons from the National Domestic Workers Alliance strategy – organizing – leadership (SOL) initiative*. Retrieved from http://www.soltransforminglives.org/pdf/sol-transforming-lives-executive-summary-4.pdf

Sheppard, B. (2016). New battles at standing Rock for water and life. *Green Left Weekly*, 14.

Shilony, E., & Grossman, F. K. (1993). Depersonalization as a defense mechanism in survivors of trauma. *Journal of Traumatic Stress, 6*(1), 119–128.

Siegel, D. J. (1999). *The developing mind* (Vol. 296). New York, NY: Guilford Press.

Siegel, D. J. (2007). *The mindful brain: Reflection and attunement in the cultivation of well-being*. New York, NY: Norton.

Siegel, D. J. (2010). *Mindsight: The new science of personal transformation*. New York, NY: Bantam.

Silliman, J., Fried, M. G., Ross, L., & Gutiérrez, E. (2016). *Undivided rights: Women of color organizing for reproductive justice*. Chicago, IL: Haymarket Books.

Sobsey, D., & Doe, T. (1991). Patterns of sexual abuse and assault. *Sexuality and Disability, 9*(3), 243–259.

Solomon, M. F. & Siegel, D. J. (eds.). (2003). *Healing trauma: Attachment, mind, body, and brain*. New York, NY: Norton.

Staas, C. (2014). *State of the science: Implicit bias review 2014*. Columbus, OH: Kirwan Institute.

Stand With Standing Rock. (2017). For Native 'water protectors,' Standing Rock protest has become fight for religious freedom, human rights. Retrieved from http://standwithstandingrock.net/native-water-protectors-standing-rock-protest-become-fight-religious-freedom-human-rights/

Stolberg, S. G. & Bidgood, J. (2016). Freddie Gray died from 'rough ride,' prosecutors assert. *New York Times.* Retrieved from https://www.nytimes.com/2016/06/10/us/caesar-goodson-trial-freddie-gray-baltimore.html?r=0

Stotzer, R. L. (2009). Violence against transgender people: A review of United States data. *Aggression and Violent Behavior, 14*(3), 170–179.

Strozzi-Heckler, R. (2014). *The art of somatic coaching: Embodying skillful action, wisdom, and compassion.* Berkeley, CA: North Atlantic Books.

Sue, D. W., Capodilupo, C. M., Torino, G. C., Bucceri, J. M., Holder, A., Nadal, K. L., & Esquilin, M. (2007). Racial microaggressions in everyday life: Implications for clinical practice. *American Psychologist, 62*(4), 271–286.

Tang, Y., Hölzel, B., & Posner, M. I. (2015). The neuroscience of mindfulness meditation. *Nature Reviews Neuroscience, 16,* 213–225.

Taren, A. A., Creswell, J. D., & Gianaros, P. J. (2013). Dispositional mindfulness covaries with smaller amygdala and caudate volumes in community adults. *PLoS One, 8*(5), e64574.

Tartakovsky, M. (2016). Using mindfulness to approach chronic pain. *Psych Central.* Retrieved from http://psychcentral.com/lib/using-mindfulness-to-approach-chronic-pain/

Taylor, V. A., Grant, J., Daneault, V., Scavone, G., Breton, E., Roffe-Vidal, S., . . . Beauregard, M. (2011). Impact of mindfulness on the neural responses to emotional pictures in experienced and beginner meditators. *Neuroimage, 57*(4), 1524–1533.

Teasdale, J. D., Segal, Z. V., Williams, J. M. G., Ridgeway, V. A., Soulsby, J. M., & Lau, M. A. (2000). Prevention of relapse/recurrence in major depression by mindfulness-based cognitive therapy. *Journal of Consulting and Clinical Psychology, 68*(4), 615.

Terr, A. I. (1993). Multiple chemical sensitivities. *Annals of Internal Medicine, 119*(2), 163–164.

Thompson, R. W., Arnkoff, D. B., & Glass, C. R. (2011). Conceptualizing mindfulness and acceptance as components of psychological resilience to trauma. *Trauma, Violence, & Abuse, 12*(4), 220–235.

Timm, J. C. (2013). PTSD is not a disorder, says medal of honor winner. *MSNBC.* Retrieved from http://www.msnbc.com/morning-joe/ptsd-not-disorder-says-medal-honor

Tirman, J. (2012). Why do we ignore civilians killed in American wars? *The Washington Post.* Retrieved from https://www.washingtonpost.com/opinions/why-do-we-ignore-the-civilians-killed-in-american-wars/2011/12/05/gIQALCO4eP_story.html?utm_term=.bcdcc990bf66

Treleaven, D. (2010). Meditation, trauma, and contemplative dissociation. *Somatics, 16*(2), 20–24.

Turow, R. G. (2017). *Mindfulness skills for trauma and PTSD: Practices for recovery and resilience.* New York, NY: Norton.

U.S. Department of Justice. (2015). *Bureau of Justice Statistics: National Crime Victimization Survey, 2010–2014.* Washington, DC: Author.

U.S. Department of Veterans Affairs. (2016). *How common is PTSD?* Washington, DC: Author. Retrieved from http://www.ptsd.va.gov/public/PTSD-overview/basics/how-common-is-ptsd.asp

U.S. National Center for Trauma-Informed Care. (2016). *Trauma-informed approach and trauma-specific interventions.* Washington, DC: Author. Retrieved from https://www.samhsa.gov/nctic/trauma-interventions

Vago, D. (2012, October). Understanding the neurobiological mechanisms of mindfulness [Video file]. Retrieved from https://www.youtube.com/watch?v=WPHgxYkgDbk

van der Kolk, B. (2014). *The body keeps the score: Brain, mind, and body in the healing of trauma.* New York, NY: Viking.

Vygotsky, L. S. (1980). *Mind in society: The development of higher psychological processes.* Cambridge, MA: Harvard University Press.

Wagner, H. L. (2007). *Elie Wiesel, messenger for peace.* New York, NY: Infobase Publishing.

Waller, N. G, Putnam, F. W., & Carlson, E. B. (1996). Types of dissociation and dissociative types: A taxometric analysis of dissociative experiences. *Psychological Methods, 1,* 300–321.

Watts, M. J. (2000). Contested communities, malignant markets, and gilded governance: justice, resource extraction, and conservation in the tropics. In C. Zerner (ed.) *People, plants, and justice: The politics of nature conservation* (pp. 21–51). New York, NY: Columbia University Press.

Welwood, J. (2002). *Toward a psychology of awakening: Buddhism, psychotherapy, and the path of personal and spiritual transformation.* Boulder, CO: Shambhala Publications.

Williams, M. (2013). Can racism cause PTSD? Implications for DSM-5. *Psychology Today.* Retrieved at https://www.psychologytoday.com/blog/culturally-speaking/201305/can-racism-cause-ptsd-implications-dsm-5

Wilson, J. (2013). *Mindful America: Meditation and the mutual transformation of Buddhism and American culture.* London: Oxford University Press.

Wineman, S. (2003). Power-under: *Trauma and nonviolent change.* (n.p.): Steve Wineman.

Women's Timh. (2017). Unity Principles. Retrieved from www.womensTimh.com/principles

Woods, B. (2016). "I hear the screams every night": Freddie Gray's death haunts man who shot video. *The Guardian.* Retrieved from https://www.theguardian.com/us-news/2016/jul/20/freddie-gray-death-haunts-man-filmed-video-baltimore

World Health Organization. (2014). *Injuries and violence: The facts 2014.* Geneva, Switzerland: Author. Retrieved from http://apps.who.int/iris/bitstream/10665/149798/1/9789241508018_eng.pdf?ua=1&ua=1&ua=1

Wylie, M. S. (2015). The mindfulness explosion: The perils of mainstream acceptance. *Psychotherapy Networker, 39,* 19–25.

Young, E. (2012). Gut instincts: The secrets of your second brain. Retrieved from https://www.newscientist.com/article/mg21628951.900-gut-instincts-the-secrets-of-your-second-brain/

Zeidan, F., Johnson, S. K., Gordon, N. S., & Goolkasian, P. (2010). Effects of brief and sham mindfulness meditation on mood and cardiovascular variables. *The Journal of Alternative and Complementary Medicine, 16*(8), 867–873.

Zweifach, B. W. (1959). The microcirculation of the blood. *Scientific American, 200*(1), 54–60.

Endnotes

INTRODUCTION

1. Treleaven, 2010
2. Elliott, 1997; Kilpatrick et al., 2013
3. As Steve Wineman (2003) wrote in his book *Power-Under: Trauma and Nonviolent Social Change*, "Oppression, which is the systemic abuse of power, renders people powerless. In turn, powerlessness is the hallmark of traumatic experience. It is therefore inevitable that trauma will be pervasive in a society organized around domination, both because oppression creates countless discrete acts of domination and because institutionalized oppression in itself creates powerlessness and trauma."
4. Levine, 2010
5. Haines, 1999
6. "Transformative Justice," Generation Five writes, "is an approach for how we—as individuals, families, communities, and society—can prevent, respond to, and transform the harms that we see happening in our world" (2017, p. 37)
7. Shenker, Viturro, Haines, Kandawalla, & Lavina, 2014
8. Brown & Ryan, 2003
9. https://vimeo.com/37880309
10. Magyari, 2016

CHAPTER 1:

The Ubiquity of Trauma: Visible and Invisible Forms

1. Baker, 2016
2. Baker, 2016
3. Gray, 2016
4. Freddie Gray died on April 19, 2015, seven days after he was detained by the Baltimore police for possessing what officers alleged was an illegal switchblade knife that was later found to be legal. While being transported in a police van, Gray fell into a coma, and his eventual death was ascribed to severe spinal cord injuries. After the medical examiner's report ruled Gray's death a homicide, criminal charges were filed against six police officers (Stolberg & Bidgood, 2016).

5. Black et al., 2011
6. Eisen, 2014
7. My friend's reaction to the senior Turner's characterization of rape as "20 minutes of action" was shaped by her lifetime of living in a world shaped by patriarchy, where gendered violence is portrayed as normal male behavior—even affirming of manhood. Likewise, we might wish that police murders of people of color were infrequent accidents or simply due to a few "bad apple" officers, but the issue is inseparable from systemic and historical factors.
8. Kearney, McDermott, Malte, Martinez, & Simpson, 2012; King et al., 2013; Thompson, Arnkoff, & Glass, 2011; Turow, 2017
9. Hollis-Walker & Colosimo, 2011; Turow, 2017
10. Lindahl, Fisher, Cooper, Rosen, & Britton, 2017; Rocha, 2014
11. U.S. National Center for Trauma-Informed Care, 2016
12. Hochman, 2013
13. Cullen, 2011
14. Wylie, 2015
15. Those who are targeted by systems of oppression experience trauma at the hands of these particular systems (e.g., white supremacy). As journalist Humera Lodhi (2015) wrote about the experience of being Indian Muslim in America, "Systemic oppression is very real and very scary. . . It isn't the racial slurs hurled out as I walk down the street that bother me. It isn't that people have a harder time empathizing with my tragedies. It isn't even people in authority making ignorant judgments based on appearances. It's feeling unsafe, alienated, and powerless within my own city, my own community."
16. Stotzer, 2009
17. When we're experiencing traumatic stress, as I'll explore in Chapter 4, parts of our brain and body designed to help us "rest and digest" are drowned out by our body's alarm system, which is being constantly activated. As a result, survivors can often experience a decrease in appetite.
18. Selye, 1973
19. Woods, 2016
20. The description of PTS as a "disorder" is controversial in some circles. A number of veterans have argued that calling PTSD a disorder stigmatizes the experience, and hurts and ostracizes those who may be struggling with it. As United States military veteran Ty Carter said in an interview with MSNBC, "If you just call it stress, which it really is, it explains the fact that it's a natural reaction to a traumatic experience. It's our bodies and minds natural reaction to try and remember and avoid those situations" (Timm, 2013)
21. Kilpatrick et al., 2013; Ozer & Weiss, 2004
22. Rothschild, 2011
23. Our social location can often be a factor in answering these questions. Hate speech may have a different impact on Black, Jewish, or disabled people whose communities' experience of hate speech has been historically accompanied by acts of organized mass violence and attempted genocide, for instance.
24. Siegel, 2010. For a more in-depth conversation about integration—including its relationship to trauma and mindfulness—see The Mindful Brain (Siegel, 2007), Mind-

sight: The New Science of Personal Transformation (Siegel, 2010), and especially his opening chapter in *Healing Trauma: Attachment, Mind, Body, and Brain* (Solomon & Siegel, 2003).

25. One liability with integration is beginning to label everything as traumatic. We can end up saying things like, "That line at the grocery store was traumatic." Here, we need to apply common sense. Trauma is reserved for events that fundamentally threaten our safety.

26. Carter, 2007

27. Frans, Rimmö, Åberg, & Fredrikson, 2005

28. Anda et al., 2006

29. World Health Organization, 2014

30. Center for Disease Control and Prevention, 2016

31. Black et al., 2011

32. U.S. Department of Justice, 2015

33. National Network to End Domestic Violence, 2015

34. Rothman, Hathaway, Stidsen, & de Vries, 2007

35. War, of course, does produce trauma. The U.S. Department of Veterans Affairs (2016) estimates that 11–20% of war veterans return home with devastating traumatic symptoms, and the department found that an average of 20 veterans take their lives every day. Some veterans believe these statistics are artificially lowered in order to minimize the real costs of war. War also brutalizes civilian populations through the traumatic impacts of political violence, death and injury, famine, occupations, and forced displacements. A study published in the *Journal of the American Medical Association* found rates of trauma in countries that experienced war were three to five times higher compared with countries that did not (De Jong et al., 2001). The shocking images that emerge from besieged cities and refugee camps continually remind us of the costs of wide-scale conflict. In addition, civilian war survivors do not always have the option to leave the site where they experienced trauma, let alone to escape continued threat. Home becomes fundamentally dangerous. Traumatic events may not cease when wars are officially declared over.

36. Capelouto, 2014

37. As I stated in the introduction, my systemic understanding of trauma comes primarily from *generative somatics*, an organization working at the intersection of personal and social change. Partnering with leaders and organizations committed to social and environmental justice (e.g., the National Domestic Workers Alliance, the Asian Pacific Environmental Network) and what they call "politicized" healers, Generative Somatics makes a compelling argument for the necessity of addressing both personal and systemic forms of trauma. See www.generativesomatics.org.

38. Dreier, 2016

39. Baker, Goodman, & Mueller, 2015

40. Children, for instance, are especially vulnerable to trauma. Between 1995 and 1997, the Centers for Disease Control and Prevention and Kaiser Permanente partnered to conduct the Adverse Childhood Experiences (ACE) Study, one of the largest investigations into the impact of childhood trauma on lifelong physical health. In a retrospective study of over 17,000 participants—most who were White and financially stable enough to afford medical insurance—the Adverse Childhood Experi-

ences Study found that childhood trauma was much more common than expected: one in ten children was in a home where a parent was being treated violently, and one in four had been physically abused (Anda et al., 2006). Tracking these children over time, the study also revealed that early traumatic experiences take a toll on one later in life: children with multiple traumatic experiences had a far greater likelihood of suffering from chronic depression and experiencing significant health problems. They were also three to five times more likely to attempt suicide (Dube et al., 2001). Trauma, as van der Kolk (2014) argued, is an issue of public health.

41. Black et al., 2011
42. Black et al., 2011
43. Bubar, 2010; Olive, 2012
44. Stotzer, 2009
45. Sobsey & Doe, 1991
46. Bachman, Zaykowski, Kallmyer, Poteyeva, & Lanier, 2008
47. Roberts, Gilman, Breslau, Breslau, & Koenen, 2011
48. Pole, Best, Metzler, & Marmar, 2005
49. World Health Organization, 2014

CHAPTER 2:

Meeting the Moment: Mindfulness and Traumatic Stress

1. Deitz, Williams, Rife, & Cantrell, 2015
2. Baer, 2016
3. Zeidan, Johnson, Gordon, & Goolkasian, 2010
4. Ostafin, Robinson, & Meier, 2015
5. These components—as well as the notion of enhanced self-regulation—come from two papers that explore mechanisms of mindfulness: Britta Hölzel and colleagues' (2011) article "How Does Mindfulness Meditation Work? Proposing Mechanisms of Action from a Conceptual and Neural Perspective," and Yi-Yuan Tang, Britta Hölzel, and Michael Posner's (2015) review titled "The Neuroscience of Mindfulness Meditation."
6. Hülsheger, Alberts, Feinholdt, & Lang, 2013
7. Goldin & Gross, 2010
8. Some survivors also experience such visceral signs without recalling a specific event—sometimes referred to as affect without recollection. The experiencing of the visceral signs of trauma can also translate into "no experiencing," nothingness and emptiness, a debilitating dissociation that includes feeling nothing at all (blunting of affect), or "no self," a sense of depersonalization and derealization in which the survivor feels fragmented, un-whole, having no "self" at all and dissolving into annihilation.
9. Baer, 2003; Tang, Hölzel, & Posner, 2015
10. Foa, Chrestman & Gilboa-Schechtman, 2008; Foa & Kozak, 1986
11. Bradley, Greene, Russ, Dutra, & Westen, 2005; Schnurr et al., 2007
12. For a more thorough discussion of the relationship between exposure therapy and trauma, see van der Kolk, 2014, pp. 220–223; Becker, Zayfert, & Anderson, 2004; Rothbaum et al., 1999; and Foa, Chrestman, & Gilboa-Schechtman, 2008.

13. My colleague Tempel Smith, a Buddhist teacher and trained trauma professional, pointed out to me that this is an example of the third foundation of mindfulness, sometimes known as mindfulness of mind or consciousness (*citta* in Pali and Sanskrit).

CHAPTER 3:

Shaped by the Past: A Brief History of Mindfulness and Trauma

1. Inside of this conversation about war and soldiers, it's essential to name the devastating and traumatic effects war has on civilians who are often left unnamed. United States wars in Iraq, Korea, Vietnam, and Cambodia were extremely deadly, and casualities beyond United States troops are rarely mentioned. As John Tirman (2012) wrote in an op-ed for the *Washington Post* titled "Why do we ignore the civilians killed in American wars?": "The major wars the United States has fought since the surrender of Japan in 1945—in Korea, Indochina, Iraq and Afghanistan—have produced colossal carnage. For most of them, we do not have an accurate sense of how many people died, but a conservative estimate is at least 6 million civilians and soldiers. Our lack of acknowledgment is less oversight than habit, a self-reflective reaction to the horrors of war and an American tradition that goes back decades."
2. Fine-Dare, 2002
3. Carson, 1981; Rogers, 1994
4. Hemphill, 2016
5. Russell, 1984
6. Lorde, 1984
7. Anzaldúa, 1990
8. Here, for example, is a section of the "Unity Principles" from the Women's March (2017)—a protest following the inauguration of Donald Trump: "We believe that Women's Rights are Human Rights and Human Rights are Women's Rights. We must create a society in which women—including Black women, Native women, poor women, immigrant women, disabled women, Muslim women, lesbian, queer, and trans women—are free and able to care for and nurture their families, however they are formed, in safe and healthy environments free from structural impediments."
9. Lebron et al., 2015
10. DeGruy, 2005
11. Williams, 2013
12. Chou, Asnaani, & Hofmann, 2012
13. Movement Generation Justice and Ecology Project defines White Supremacy as "the idea that white people are inherently superior to all other people of the planet. White Supremacy rests on the pseudo-science of race and eugenics and was created by a small group of elite Europeans as a way to justify unprecedented violence and destruction of entire ecosystems and peoples, most acutely those of African descent. The racial hierarchy that places African peoples and peoples of African descent as the 'inferior,' results in an Anti-Blackness that can and does infect the culture and consciousness, along with white supremacy, of peoples across the planet—even the

colonized. White supremacy elevates 'white mindedness' and European culture over all the other diverse ways of knowing on the planet" (2012, p. 11).

14. Quigley, 2003, p. 8
15. Vago, 2012
16. Nyanamoli, B.
17. Vedanā is not "emotion" or "feelings" but the very pleasantness, unpleasantness, or neutrality of an experience.
18. Rothschild, 2010
19. Kabat-Zinn, 2011
20. Benson, Beary, & Carol, 1974
21. Wylie, 2015
22. Baer, 2015
23. Therapies that utilize mindfulness include Mindfulness-Based Cognitive Therapy (MBCT) and Dialectical Behavioral Therapy (DBT), which have been shown to be effective in preventing relapses of depression (Teasdale et al., 2000) and working with borderline personality disorder (O'Connell & Dowling, 2014), respectively. Mindfulness is also used by therapists to support relationship, whether that's with couples (e.g., Mindfulness-Based Relationship Enhancement; Carson, Carson, Gil, & Baucom, 2004), or between medical practitioners and their patients (Shapiro, Schwartz, & Bonner, 1998).
24. Samuelson, Carmody, Kabat-Zinn, & Bratt, 2007
25. This is occurring against the backdrop of a history of cultural appropriation by and within the West. The theft of cultural ideas and practices is baked into the history of colonization, where practices are decontextualized, stripped of meaning, and often turned for a profit. Of course, this also wades into issues such as the difference between cultural theft and appropriation versus cultural sharing, appreciation, and exchange. As Kovie Biakolo (2016) writes about in her article on the topic, what distinguishes cultural sharing from appropriation has to do with power and privilege. In Chapter 9, I'll speak more to this issue and its relation to trauma-sensitive practice.
26. Pickert, 2014; Wilson, 2013
27. Writers have also noted that a deep engagement with Buddhism can reveal the kinds of complex, difficult, and contested ideas common to diverse cultural traditions. MBSR is a distinctly contemporary practice that expresses tensions between psychological science, cultural appropriation, and capitalism, for instance, yet still seems to provide something helpful that is drawn from our long human healing tradition.
28. Brown University, 2017
29. Lindahl, Fisher, Cooper, Rosen, & Britton, 2017
30. As reported in a press release by Brown University (Orenstein, 2017), "The study purposely sought out 'challenging' experiences because they are underrepresented in the scientific literature, the authors said. With that goal, the study therefore was not designed to estimate how common those experiences are among all meditators. Instead the purpose of the Varieties of Contemplative Experience study was to provide detailed descriptions of experiences and to start to understand the multiple ways they are interpreted, why they might happen and what meditators and teachers do to deal with them."

31. Briere & Scott, 2014
32. Gardner-Nix & Costin-Hall, 2009
33. Tartakovsky, 2016
34. Scalora, 2015

CHAPTER 4:

The Brain and Body in Trauma and Mindfulness

1. Gallup, 1977
2. Levine, 2010
3. LeDoux, 1998
4. Allen et al., 2012
5. Hölzel et al., 2009; Taren, Creswell, & Gianaros, 2013
6. Banks, Eddy, Angstadt, Nathan, & Phan, 2007; van der Kolk, 2014
7. Creswell, Way, Eisenberger, & Lieberman, 2007; Ortner, Kilner, & Zelazo, 2007
8. Taylor et al., 2011
9. Desbordes et al., 2012
10. Desbordes et al., 2012

CHAPTER 5:

Stay Within the Window of Tolerance: The Role of Arousal

1. Garfield, 1995
2. Siegel, 1999
3. Vygotsky, 1980
4. Ogden et al., 2006
5. Rothschild, 2011
6. Rothschild, 2010
7. Damasio, 1994
8. Rothschild, 2011

CHAPTER 6:

Shift Attention to Support Stability: Avoiding the Fear/Immobility Cycle

1. Levine, 2010
2. In a version of this myth told by the Roman poet Ovid, Medusa was originally a beautiful maiden who was raped by Poseidon, a Greek deity. Upon discovering this violation had taken place in her temple, Athena became so enraged that she transformed Medusa into a monster. It's a version of the myth that illustrates the way victims can end up blamed for the actions of perpetrators.
3. Lichtblau & Fausset, 2016
4. Stotzer, 2009
5. For a more thorough discussion of this, see Chapter 7, where I cover the difference between exteroceptive (external) and interoceptive (internal) sensations—specifically the way that survivors tend to place a disproportionate emphasis on interoceptive sensations, and the consequences this has in the context of mindfulness.

6. Levine, 1997
7. You can find this video at https://vimeo.com/90741652. Accessed March 15, 2016
8. Levine, 2010
9. Manna et al., 2010
10. Turow, 2017
11. Healing Collective Trauma, 2013

CHAPTER 7:

Keep the Body in Mind: Working with Dissociation

1. Ray, 2008
2. van der Kolk, 2014
3. Rothschild, 2017
4. Scaer, 2001
5. Kraus, 1993
6. Massachusetts Institute of Technology, 2015
7. Zweifach, 1959
8. Strozzi-Heckler, 2014
9. Rothschid, 2000
10. Young, 2012
11. Rothschild, 2000
12. Boon, Steele, & van der Hart, 2011
13. Waller, Putnam, & Carlson, 1996
14. Boon, Steele, & van der Hart, 2011
15. Shilony & Grossman, 1993
16. Merckelbach & Muris, 2001
17. Magyari, 2016
18. Mitchell et al., 2014
19. Welwood, 2002
20. Boon et al., 2011
21. Magyari, 2016
22. Magyari, 2016
23. This proposed modification comes from Trish Magyari's (2016) chapter on teaching mindfulness to traumatized individuals in the book *Resources for Teaching Mindfulness: An International Handbook* (McCown, Reibel, & Micozzi, 2016).
24. Terr, 1993
25. Stotzer, 2009

CHAPTER 8:

Practice in Relationship: Supporting Safety and Stability in Survivors

1. Jackson-Dwyer, 2013
2. Magyari, 2016
3. Schwartz, 1994; Schwartz, 2013

CHAPTER 9:

Understand Social Context: Working Effectively Across Difference

1. American Association of University Women, 2017
2. AAUW, 2017
3. Collins et al., 2010
4. National Coalition of Anti-Violence Programs, 2014
5. Oppression, 2017
6. Frye, 1983
7. Hays, 1996; Nieto et al., 2010
8. Disha, Cavendish, & King, 2011
9. Nsiah-Jefferson, 1989; Silliman, Fried, Ross, & Gutiérrez, 2016
10. Watts, 2000
11. Rinfrette, 2015
12. Hernandez, 2014
13. Nieto et al., 2010
14. Shaver, 2011
15. Feagin & Bennefield, 2014
16. Staas, 2014
17. Greenwald & Krieger, 2006
18. Green et al., 2007
19. Nieto et al., 2010
20. National Center for Charitable Statistics, 2015
21. Daniels, 2014

CONCLUSION

1. Equal Justice Initiative, 2013
2. EJI also took on the project of documenting the sites of lynchings in the United States: 3,959 in 12 southern states. For more information, see http://eji.org/reports/lynching-in-america and Johnson, 2015
3. Mahler, 2016 (for resources, also see RAINN, 2017)
4. Camp of the Sacred Stones, 2017; Stand With Standing Rock, 2017
5. DeGruy, 2005
6. Alexander, 2010
7. Poynting, & Mason, 2007

Index

In this index, f denotes figure and n denotes note.